MW00895334

US NAVY

HISTORY OF THE US NAVY

JAMES M MORRIS

LONGMEADOW PRESS

This 1993 edition published by
Longmeadow Press
201 High Ridge Road
Stamford CT 06904

Produced by
Brompton Books Corporation
15 Sherwood Place
Greenwich, CT 06830

ISBN 0-681-41813-3

Printed in Hong Kong

0 9 8 7 6 5 4 3 2

Page 1: The 5-inch 54 caliber guns installed aboard the guided-missile ship, the USS *Norton.*
Page 2-3: The USS *Constitution* rakes the crippled *Guerriere* off Nova Scotia, 19 August 1812.
This page: The USS *Raleigh*, with pontoons lashed to her sides, lists to port after Japan's devastating raid on Pearl Harbor.

CONTENTS

INTRODUCTION

To understand the role of the US Navy in the nation's history, it is essential to review briefly the crucial role that sea power has played in the destiny of other leading nations throughout history. Sea power—the ability to control the nation's sea lanes with sufficient strength to ensure its vital interests—has been and remains a key ingredient in the fate of nations whether in ancient, medieval or modern times. The historical record amply demonstrates that nations seldom rise to major status and are never able to maintain a position of preeminence if they disregard their naval and maritime potential. Mastery of the sea has always been a dynamic power factor, and nations that neglect their navies do so at the peril of their present and future well-being.

Sea Power in Early Times

Man's destiny has always been tied to the sea. Iron-Age men fashioned boats of planks and added oars for paddling and rudders for steering. Egyptian *kepen* 207 feet in length, with keels and double masts, carried goods up and down the Nile by about 1400 BC. Indeed, all ancient peoples located on rivers and seas recognized the need to trade and colonize on near and distant waters. Trade and colonies, moreover, demanded protection, so navies were born. Ramses III, for example, had a well-organized naval force and turned back the Libyans, Syrians and Philistines from Asia Minor in the Battle of Pelusian in the late twelfth century BC. The Cretans (or Minoans), however, were probably the leading sea power in those times. Their powerful fleet patrolled the sea lanes from the Dardanelles in the east to the Strait of Bonifacio, between Corsica and Sardinia, in the west. The Cretans were succeeded as sea lords by the Phoenicians, who controlled the North African coast and circumnavigated the African subcontinent from the Red Sea all the way to the Gates of Hercules (Gibraltar). They were effectively challenged by the Greek states, with their mighty war vessels of two, three, and more banks of oars and triple-pronged rams at their bows. The Romans, too, built a powerful navy that they used to good effect in their Punic Wars against the Carthaginians, wars finally lost by the North African power when Hannibal's ineffective navy lost control of the coast of Spain and thereby endangered his lines of supply.

As the Middle Ages dawned in the Mediterranean and Western world, and economic and political stagnation settled over the land, some commerce still continued to flow to and from the Baltic and North Seas and the Levant to the east. Wheat, wines, timber, tin and wool moved by sea from northern to southern European ports, there to be exchanged for

Below: British forces, joined by men from the New England colonies, land to capture Louisburg, Cape Breton Island, from the French in 1745.

sugar, cheeses, oil, oranges, spices and fine cloth from India, Egypt and the Barbary Coast. The oar-powered galley gradually lost its position of dominance in commerce and defense to the wind-powered 'round ship' with up to four masts, a forecastle at the bow and an after-castle at the stern. Trade was further facilitated by the development of such navigational instruments as the 'log' to measure a ship's speed by the time required to pass knots spaced 49 feet apart on a thrown line, and the astrolabe, which gave a relatively accurate measure of latitude. The sextant was also developed—the compass was known from China—and seamen could now venture farther and farther from protective shorelines in search of trade and conquest. Although full-time navies disappeared in this period of political and economic confusion, tradesmen-warriors like the fierce Vikings still plied the seas. Often naval forces were decisive, as in William of Normandy's conquest of England with over 1000 vessels in 1066, or in the case of the Third and Fourth Crusades in the late twelfth and early thirteenth centuries, as ships carried warriors and supplies to the Middle Eastern battlefields.

The effects of naval power were also graphically demonstrated during France's long and eventually successful Hundred Years' War against England (1337–1453). The fortunes of the two antagonists rocked back and forth from French victories at LaRochelle and Cherbourg in the late fourteenth century to English victories with a rebuilt navy in the early fifteenth. Final French victory came with command of the seas under the naval rebuilding program of Jacques Coeur. Sea power and national power strode hand in hand through the Middle Ages, as they had through ancient times, although some emerging land-based monarchs were loath to see the connection—until the discovery, claim and colonization of North America made the relationship too obvious to deny.

European Nations Discover the New World

If we discount as highly improbable the story that North America was first discovered in the sixth century by the Irish monk St Brendan and his compatriots in a *curragh* (a ribbed, oak-tanned oxhide vessel with a mast and sail), the first Europeans to touch North American shores were undoubtedly Norsemen from Greenland under the leadership of Leif Ericsson about the year 1000. Having established a tiny settlement at L'Anse aux Meadows on the northern tip of the Newfoundland coast, the Norse made three more voyages to the area, but the tiny colony eventually languished. Only centuries later did other powers rediscover the Western Hemisphere. This time the Europeans came to stay and to build new lands.

Although the search for new sea lanes for Far Eastern trade was the major dynamic in propelling European powers far west of their Atlantic shores—the old trade routes through the Mediterranean Sea and the Levant having been cut by the victorious Ottoman Turks, to whom Constantinople itself fell in 1453—science and technology also played a major role in the opening of the New World. Most of the credit must go to the Portuguese Prince Henry 'the Navigator,' who established what might well be called an oceanographic institute at Sagres early in the fifteenth century. Here this Portuguese monarch quizzed ship captains about the seas and navigation; assembled mathematicians, cartographers and ship designers; collected all the geographic books available, including those of Herodotus, Marco Polo and Ptolemy; amassed *portolani* (sea charts) from seamen; encouraged the development of the triple-masted, lateen-sail caravel; and aided in the development of the cross-staff for better reckoning of latitude than was possible with the primitive astrolabe. As a result of the work at Sagres, Portuguese and other European sailors could now sail farther still, often hundreds of miles into the Atlantic. The door to reaching the fabled East by an all-water route was cracking open. Yet westward from Europe across the uncharted Atlantic, they would find not the fabulous lands described by Marco Polo, but an even more bounteous continent soon to be opened to European development.

The man responsible for opening the Western Hemisphere to colonization and trade was Christopher Columbus, an experienced Italian mariner sailing for Their Most Catholic Majesties of Spain, Ferdinand and Isabella. His first epoch-making voyage of 1492–93, in which he was aided in many ways by Martin and Vincente Pinzon of Palos, his home port, brought him fame and promise of more royal support, even though it was unclear whether 'Hispaniola' was really off the coast of Japan as Columbus believed. Three subsequent follow-up voyages brought only disease and death, hostility from the native peoples, mismanagement and finally disgrace and an obscure death for Columbus.

But the New World had been opened, and those European nations with available maritime and naval power hastened to claim and develop it as they could. In 1497 John Cabot, an Italian sailing under the colors of Henry VII of England, made a voyage of exploration along the North American coast but disappeared on a second voyage the following year. In the decades that followed, other voyages set forth under the flags of Portugal, Spain, England and France; by the middle of the sixteenth century it was clear that, rather than being an archipelago off the eastern coast of China or Japan, a New World, an entire continent, had been discovered, a continent that had no fabled but illusory 'Northwest Passage' to the Orient. The belief in this passage had led many early discoverers up the river and bay systems of the eastern coast on voyages of futility. The names of Giovanni da Verrazzano, Jacques Cartier, Martin Frobisher and others stand as testimony to European determination to explore this new land for gold, glory and national honor.

As it became obvious that the New World was a treasure house of wealth and possibilities for nations to extend themselves outward by colonization, the European monarchs gave their backing to enterprising individuals and groups who would undertake the task. Although the Spanish, Portuguese and French were early in the field, and thus seized the lion's share of territories stretching almost from pole to pole, it was English enterprise that claimed the eastern coast of North America from latter-day Maine to Georgia. This solid and expanding foothold developed into a series of settlements in the most favorable locations along the coast and also in the Caribbean. These colonies eventually developed into the most permanent and wealthy extensions of European control in all of North America.

England's New-World Colonies

Although Sir Walter Raleigh's colony at Roanoke in the Carolinas saw three groups of settlers arrive in the years 1585–87, a relief expedition in 1590 found no survivors; thus England's first sizable attempt at colonization failed. Despite this failure, the growing power of England could not be denied, and, after defeating her long-time rival Spain's Armada in 1588 she moved steadily to create colonies in North America. England had an expanding population, capital available for new ventures and a monarchy interested in colonial development. Above all, she had seized the maritime and naval initiative from her competitors and thereafter would not be denied.

Yet England's position as a maritime power and colonizer was still subject to dispute by other nations, especially France and Spain. France was in a splendid position to challenge England for 'God, gold, and glory,' and Spain still represented a considerable threat. As England began to plant colonies along the Eastern Seaboard, beginning in 1607 at Jamestown and continuing through the seventeenth century, France was doing the same to the north along the St Lawrence River Valley and into the Great Lakes and Mississippi River regions—thus effectively hemming in the English to the north and west. Spain continued its rule in the south and southwest, down through Mexico and Central America and on to the great South American continent. This eventually led to major conflicts as the English, French and Spanish North American colonies became part of the great struggles for empire.

Above: **Christopher Columbus (1451–1506) made his first landfall in the New World on 12 October 1492 at Watling's Island in the Bahamas.**

In the meantime, the English colonists, from the rocky New England coastal colonies, through the broadening and fertile expanse of the middle colonies, into the region as far south as Georgia, found their lives inexorably tied to the seas. The Atlantic Ocean had served them originally only as the pathway to Europe and the source of resupply and reinforcement, but soon these land-oriented agrarian peoples discovered that the rivers and seas represented an indispensable element in their growth and prosperity. The virgin lands could not be exploited without river craft to take the colonists and their goods to and from the interior. Boats of all types skimmed up and down rivers carrying goods and people to farms and plantations. At the mouths of rivers great and small, coursing sometimes hundreds of miles into the rich interior, bays of all sizes served as anchorages for ships to take the colonists' goods to market and bring back from Europe or other colonies the manufactures and supplies they needed.

Furthermore, especially in New England but also down the coast, the colonists found an abundance of fish. They used them first for their own sustenance and later for trade along the coast and even with Caribbean and European ports. Fishing became an important occupation and fish surpluses soon became an important trade commodity.

The rise of colonial trade internally, with the Caribbean colonies and with England and other European countries, led, in turn, to the birth and growth of a shipbuilding industry. In England timber was becoming scarce. In the American colonies, especially New England, timber of all the necessary kinds was plentiful and near the coast where shipbuilders could ply their lucrative trade. So successful was this colonial industry that by the late seventeenth century many English vessels were being built in colonial shipyards, and English shipwrights began an exodus from the mother country to the building yards of the American colonies in search of the higher wages available there.

By the end of the seventeenth century, then, the English colonies hugging the Atlantic shores and stretching inland to the Appalachian Mountains found themselves bound to the sea. This despite the fact that only 10 percent of the colonial population earned its living directly in trade, fishing, shipbuilding and allied industries. Agricultural goods from the Middle Colonies, the 'breadbasket colonies,' and from farms and plantations north and south found their markets via coastal and ocean vessels sailing the Atlantic expanse. Tobacco, rice and indigo from Southern farms and plantations reached their domestic or European markets by a myriad of vessels. In turn, farmers and plantation gentry obtained supplies for farm or table—supplies of incredible variety, for tastes simple or extravagant—via the coastal and ocean sea lanes. Fishermen sold their surplus in the markets of the colonies and the world. Shipbuilders, shipowners and seamen plied their skills to the benefit of all. Without trade upon coastal, Caribbean and Atlantic waters, the emerging English colonial economy would have ground to a halt. Whoever would disturb that trade network or challenge it in any way would endanger the expanding colonies.

To protect these precious trade routes, the North American colonists looked to the mother country. After all, they were English colonies under English law and protection. The Crown and Parliament agreed. The American colonies, an integral part of the Empire, were precious sources of supplies to England and a major market for its manufactured goods. Both the mother country and the colonies recognized their vital interdependence, and considered their political and economic ties sacred and worthy of spirited defense. Challenges came from outside, not from inside, the system at this point.

England, the Colonies and the Wars for Empire

The challenge for North America came primarily from France. Catholic France was the natural enemy of Protestant England. In addition, either the French would dominate Europe and the colonies in trade and power, or England would. The two nations stood as hearty young gladiators in the arena that was Europe, each determined that the other would not dominate, each determined that he would not be overcome. On the sidelines stood Spain and Holland, willing to intervene to regain lost glory and right old wrongs should either major contestant falter. In this posture the great Wars for Empire between France and England, the titanic clashes of major powers in a life-and-death struggle for domination of Europe and the colonies, began in 1689 and continued intermittently until 1763. In these wars the colonists stood by their mother country. Her protection was their protection; her destiny was their destiny.

Both nations were ready for the great conflict that began in 1689. When Louis XIV of France had come to the throne in 1661, the French Navy was in a sad condition. Louis's navy had but a handful of ships, officers and seamen. Thirty years later the Sun King's Navy could challenge both England and Holland, separately or together. This miracle had been achieved by subsidizing shipbuilding, improving naval bases, enhancing the quality of both officers and men and establishing all the auxiliary industries needed for maritime and naval strength. At the same time, Louis had built up the French colonies by various forms of government assistance. By the 1680s France had a true navy and was a power to be reckoned with.

England, on the other hand, had allowed her navy to languish after having rebuilt it in the wake of the three disastrous Anglo-Dutch Wars from the 1650s to 1674. She had embarked on a major naval program in 1677, only to see it falter in the face of domestic difficulties between 1678 and 1684. But from 1678 on, the British Navy began to revive under the capable direction of Charles II, James II and their brilliant aide Sir Samuel Pepys. By the onset of the first of the great wars for empire, the British were rearmed and 'at the ready' for any challenge Louis XIV and France might make.

As Louis made his move into the Netherlands in an attempt to expand his kingdom in 1689, he faced not only neighboring

Holland but also England in the person of William of Orange (now ruling there as the husband of Mary II after the Glorious Revolution had overthrown the Stuart king James II). This offensive set off the War of the League of Augsburg—referred to in the colonies as 'King William's War'—which lasted until 1697 and was fought in both Europe and America.

The British Navy was well occupied at home in the early months of the war with James II's attempt to regain the throne by an invasion of Ireland with French naval help. Although the colonies as a whole were hardly disturbed by the war, the seagoing colonists smarted over raids by privateering vessels out of French Canada, which ranged American waters from the St Lawrence to the West Indies preying on commercial and fishing vessels. As the principal victims, colonists from Massachusetts, Connecticut and New York took matters into their own hands in April 1690 and provided eight small ships and 800 men for an attack on Port Royal, Nova Scotia, the privateers' base of operations. The attack, led by Sir William Phips, was unopposed, and the following month the colonists demonstrated the religious antagonism inherent in the conflict by plundering the local Catholic church and smashing its altar. Their subsequent attack, with 34 ships and 2000 men, upon the great citadel of Quebec turned into a fiasco, and the volunteers returned home to sit out the rest of the war without any major French threat to their lives or fortunes. The European phase of the war dragged on for another seven years.

Even the formal end of the war, however, brought no end to French privateering and attacks on colonial fishermen, so

Below: **The Spanish Armada sails from Ferrol, July 1588.**

the colonists were happy to join with the mother country when the War of the Spanish Succession—'Queen Anne's War' in the colonies—broke out in 1702. This war, which lasted until 1713, originated when King Charles II of Spain willed his throne to the grandson of Louis XIV to protect his country from being partitioned by the various European Powers. This arrangement, vehemently opposed by England and Holland as a move by Louis to expand to the south, set off the war. France and Spain were on one side, England and Holland on the other. The English colonists in America took up the cause again by engaging in three operations involving naval power, the latter two utilizing British naval units directly. In the first, Colonel William Rhett of Charleston, South Carolina, was commissioned a vice-admiral in 1706 to command a home-grown flotilla against five Spanish ships raiding the town. The defense was successful, and the South Carolinians mounted a successful retaliatory expedition the following year against Pensacola in Spanish Florida.

In the second action, the American colonists and British naval and military units joined forces in 1710 to stage an amphibious operation against Port Royal, Nova Scotia (returned to France after the previous war). The expedition consisted of four frigates, 30 transports and 1400 men under the leadership of Colonel Francis Nicholson, a British soldier. The operation was quick and successful, aided by the fact that the French had only 300 men in the town and no naval support. Privateering was effectively thwarted again.

The third operation also involved the Royal Navy. Nine warships plus 12,000 army troops (including five regiments of crack British soldiers) and colonial volunteers, launched a major attack on Quebec to gain control of the St Lawrence. They left Boston in July 1711 and arrived on 22 August, only to find themselves completely lost in the fog and gales of the Gulf of St Lawrence. After losing eight of his 60 transports and 900 men in the fog and confusion, the commanding admiral, Hovenden Walker, gave up and returned with his ships and men to England. Given this misuse of seapower, the British and their colonists could only count as good fortune the fact that French naval power had declined drastically during the course of the war and thus played no part in the defense of Quebec. What had been a fiasco could have been a disaster.

The war ended in 1713, and Louis XIV died two years later. The fundamental conflict was suspended for a quarter of a century as each nation recovered from the strains of war and regirded itself for the inevitable renewal of the fight. Domination of Europe and of the colonies had not been settled.

In 1744 the wars for empire broke out again. Austria and Prussia had joined the old combatants of England (now Great Britain after the Act of Union of 1707), France and Spain. Prussia's desire for Austrian territory had been added to the list of issues involved. The war was known in Europe as the War of the Austrian Succession and in America as 'King George's War.' It lasted for four years, until 1748.

The battles that raged in Europe were large land engagements, but in the American colonies they took the familiar form of Indian attacks on the frontiers and privateering on the coastal waters. The only major engagement in which the colonies were involved was an attack on Louisbourg on Cape Breton Island, a keystone

of French power and a base for privateering, near the mouth of the St Lawrence. In this attack of April 1745, the colonial land and naval forces from New England were aided by the Royal Navy, which blockaded Louisbourg while the fortress was besieged by the colonials. Only one French warship arrived, and it was easily captured. The successful siege ended in June, and the chaplain of the colonial forces personally chopped to pieces the altars and images in the town's Catholic church. When Louisbourg was returned to France by the Treaty of Aix-la-Chapelle which ended the war, the American colonists were outraged—1000 of their compatriots had died in the prolonged siege of the city. Yet no one could deny the important part the Colonial and Royal Navies had played in the successful siege of 1745, nor could they deny the importance of the Royal Navy thereafter in protecting the colonists from depredations and even invasions by French and Spanish forces.

Right: General James Wolfe whose victory at Quebec set the seal on the British success in the French and Indian War.
Below: British warships on the St Lawrence during the siege of Quebec in 1759. The city fell on 13 September.

When war broke out again in 1756 after an uneasy peace of only eight years, naval power again played a major role in the outcome of this fourth and decisive phase. Disgusted with British naval lethargy early in the conflict in the face of a revived French naval effort, the Crown named William Pitt as Minister of War. The new minister surrounded himself with young, tough military men who were anxious to carry the fight to the enemy. A fleet of 40 ships under the command of Vice-Admiral Edward 'Old Dreadnought' Boscawen, accompanied by 14,000 soldiers under Jeffrey Amherst and James Wolfe, easily overran Louisbourg in July 1758 and moved on to take the citadel of Quebec. This was accomplished by September 1759, after a giant British fleet that included 49 men-of-war closed off any chance of French reinforcements reaching their besieged comrades. Quebec fell, then Montreal the next year, then all of French Canada. When a huge French invasion fleet was later scattered by the Royal Navy before reaching England's home shores, the writing was on the wall for the French in this Seven Years' War (the 'French and Indian War' in colonial parlance). Having allowed its navy to be weakened while the British Navy grew ever stronger, the French could not sustain their campaigns for empire. They were forced to sue for peace, and the resulting Peace of Paris of February 1763 stripped from them virtually all their North American possessions, including all of Canada. They were left with only a few islands off Newfoundland and in the Caribbean. The French had suffered a devastating defeat by sacrificing their fleet to the demands of their land armies. Given another chance a decade later, they did not repeat their mistake.

Britain, on the other hand, now lord of all India and North America east of the Mississippi thanks to her naval prowess and control of the sea, allowed her fleet to deteriorate thereafter. She paid the price, as her American continental colonies slipped from her authority and demanded their political freedom.

Above: The most famous of the US Navy's early battles; the action between the *Bonhomme Richard* and the *Serapis*.

PART I

A RELUCTANT NAVAL POWER

COLONISTS AND REVOLUTIONARIES

Troubles broke out in the colonies in 1775, troubles caused largely by the Crown's decision to pay off its heavy war debts and its new costs of garrisoning expanded American territories by having the colonies pay a greater share in taxes, with higher rates and strict enforcement. This was a fundamental change in policy within the mercantile system of colonial trade and manufacturing—from one of demanding minimal taxes to one of imposing heavier taxes and stricter control. As trouble loomed large because of colonists' resistance to this change, the British Navy was in poor shape to help impose the Crown's will upon them. After the Peace of Paris of 1763, the navy had been cut back to the bone in an effort to save money, and naval administration itself became a victim of graft and corruption. John Montagu, the Earl of Sandwich, First Lord of the Admiralty from 1771 to 1778, allowed the navy to languish still further.

When, therefore, the colonists rose in rebellion in 1775 to resist British efforts to control them by force of arms, Vice-Admiral Samuel Graves in Boston had only 29 ships available to blockade and control the 1800-mile coastline of North America. And in subsequent months and years the naval situation continued to be tight, especially when the French joined the fray in 1778; what began as a limited colonial police action became a world war, with the British fighting the Americans, the French, the Spanish and the Dutch.

Below: General Benedict Arnold commanded the American forces in the Battle of Valcour Island in October 1776.

On the other hand, the rebellious colonies had no saltwater navy at all at the beginning of the conflict and were hard pressed to create one thereafter. Their efforts were feeble at best, whether in the form of the Continental Navy or the various independent small navies created after the conflict began by eleven of the colonies. The key to eventual victory for the Americans lay in a freshwater victory on Lake Champlain, and in the French Navy that would match British naval power and finally outduel it in the critical Battle of the Chesapeake (1781) that broke the back of British determination to put down the American rebellion.

American naval efforts were always small and basically ineffective on the Atlantic coastal waters and high seas. It is safe to say that the colonies' saltwater navies had no appreciable effect on the outcome of the Revolution. Although Massachusetts colonists may have thrilled at Jeremiah O'Brien's capture of the schooner *Margaretta* at Machias, Maine, in June 1775, the victory was of limited practical consequence. So were the exploits of the small vessels sent out by General George Washington to seize British supplies early in the war. Congress did not move effectively to remedy the situation until shocked by the bold bombardment of the town of Falmouth, Maine, in October of that year. Following this incident, ships were purchased and others were ordered built on 13 October 1775—marking this date as the birthday of the US Navy. The Naval Committee (which ran the Continental Navy throughout the rebellion independent of Washington's control) finally got around to appointing officers for the American vessels, although many assignments were patently political. The officers were typically relatives of the men in charge of naval affairs.

Esek Hopkins, for example, was a man of limited naval background but a brother of the politician Stephen Hopkins of Rhode Island, a member of the seven-man Naval Committee. Yet Esek Hopkins was given command of the 24-gun frigate *Alfred*. In February 1776 he left the Delaware with seven support vessels under orders to drive Lord Dunmore's fleet out of Chesapeake Bay and then clear the Carolina coast. Bypassing the Virginia Capes to avoid the British forces, Hopkins went to the Bahamas instead and captured the city of Nassau, most of the valued gunpowder there having been removed by the local governor before his attack. Making his way north again, Hopkins and his squadron were attacked off New London in the middle of the night of 6 April 1776 by a lone British ship, the 20-gun frigate *Glasgow*. After a four-hour exchange of fire and chase, the *Glasgow* sailed away to the protection of the British fleet at Newport, and Congress faced the unpleasant duty of court-martialing Hopkins for allowing the vessel to escape. Hopkins and his fleet made for Providence to rebuild and never sailed again as a squadron. Hopkins ultimately resigned his command.

If the American Navy could not stand up to its British counterpart in head-to-head engagements—as indeed it could not, and most vessels soon bobbed quietly in protected harbors under effective British blockade—the same could not be said for American privateers. Privateers were vessels given legal permission (letters of marque) to raid British commerce and supply vessels. They were virtually the only consistent naval offensive the Americans could muster on coastal waters and the high seas, the British Navy having bottled up the regular seaborne fighting forces. Soon sloops, schooners and converted fishing vessels under state congressional authority were busily raiding British commerce along the coast, off the Gulf of St Lawrence, in the warm Caribbean and even in European waters. It was a lucrative business and an effective weapon of war. Soon the British were forced to convoy their supply vessels and arm their merchantmen to beat off the American raiders, who even then found that by clever decoying they could seize an occasional merchant prize. During the war about 2000 American privateers took over 2200 British ships. But these measures could not win the war, and by summer of 1776 the situation on land and sea looked desperate for the infant American nation.

Even David Bushnell's amazing inven-

Above: **The British line bears down during the Battle of Valcour Island.**

tion, the *Turtle*, an innovative one-man submarine of double-shell oak-stave construction, with a ballast tank for descending and ascending, a depth gauge, a snorkel breathing tube, and a screw to bore into an enemy ship's hull to attach a time-fuse bomb, failed in its purpose. Commanded by an army sergeant, Ezra Lee, the *Turtle* was towed down the Hudson River, then cut free to assault Admiral Richard ('Black Dick') Howe's squadron in New York Harbor on the night of 6 September 1776. Although the outgoing tide swept Lee far beyond his target, by turning the manual propeller he was able to make his way back to the British squadron and to a point directly under the hull of Howe's flagship, HMS *Eagle*, of 64 guns. Lee must have been exhausted by his ordeal with the tide, but he went to work operating the screw mechanism on top of the *Turtle* to attach the explosive charge. The screw hit metal strapping on the hull and would not penetrate, and, since dawn was approaching, Lee abandoned the effort and made for shore. The *Turtle* was the first submarine to survive a war mission, but she failed to effect the outcome of the naval war. Neither numbers nor technology could come to the aid of the beleaguered American armies, as the British seized control of American ports almost at will and blockaded the coastal cities.

American and French Naval Victories

At this point, however, one of the most crucial American victories of the Revolution occurred. In June 1776, while the Americans were in full retreat from Canada after a failed invasion attempt, the Continental Congress decided the American forces should make a stand at Lake Champlain. The pursuing British Army under General Guy Carleton wanted to gain control of Lake Champlain and Lake George, plus Fort Ticonderoga and Albany. With these as a base, the British

Below: **The British revenue schooner *Gaspée* is captured and burned by a party of American protesters in June 1772.**

Left: **John Paul Jones indignantly refuses to surrender to the *Serapis*: 'I have not yet begun to fight.'**

could then move at will down the Hudson from Albany and up the river from New York City to cut the colonies in two. Sensing the urgency of the situation, the Continental Congress authorized the building of an American defensive fleet on Lake Champlain. It was to be commanded by one of the most renowned American military leaders, General Benedict Arnold. Carpenters were sent from Philadelphia, and naval stores and arms were shipped from New York and Connecticut. Within six weeks a naval squadron of ten new vessels and five existing vessels was ready.

Arnold maneuvered his fleet into position between Valcour Island and the New York shore of Lake Champlain and waited for the British, descending with their inland fleet. On 11 October 1776, the 30-ship British fleet came on. Arnold allowed them to pass Valcour before attacking, so that the British would have to beat back against the wind. The fight raged from 11:00 o'clock in the morning until dusk. The outnumbered Americans were beaten, and that night Arnold and his remaining vessels slipped away. The British caught them two days later and completed the destruction of the tiny fleet, but in losing, Arnold had won. He and his men had delayed the British by forcing them to build a fleet to match the American flotilla. This postponed the attack on Fort Ticonderoga and Albany until too late in the season to continue campaigning. The British were forced to withdraw. Had Albany been taken in 1776, it could have served as a base from which to continue the northern offensive the following year, and undoubtedly the colonies would have been cut asunder. Arnold and his 'navy' had bought a precious year for the colonial cause.

When the British moved down the Lake Champlain route the next year, they were forced to start far north and eventually met defeat at the Battle of Saratoga in October 1777. Saratoga, in turn, brought the dawdling French into full alliance with the Americans now that it appeared the British could be defeated and the French could exact vengeance for the losses of the Seven Years' War. With the French Navy in the war to counterbalance the overwhelming British naval predominance against the Americans, victory seemed possible. France entered the alliance with the United States in 1778 with a rebuilt navy. By then the French Navy had 80 ships of the line and 67,000 men and was a force to be reckoned with. Early French naval engagements, however, were not promising. Admiral Charles le Comte d'Estaing arrived off New York in April 1778 with the Toulon fleet but refused to enter harbor to take on Admiral Richard Howe's fleet. Moving instead to Newport, Rhode Island, he bottled up the British fleet there and bombarded the city. But when Admiral Howe brought up his fleet to challenge d'Estaing, neither antagonist would attack and both were scattered in a storm. Howe returned to New York and d'Estaing moved to the Caribbean, with no damage done on either side.

Nor did the fortunes of war appear to favor the Americans and their French allies during the remainder of the year. Nicholas Biddle's 32-gun frigate *Randolph* was destroyed by the 64-gun ship of the line HMS *Yarmouth*. An American expedition under Dudley Saltonstall to the mouth of the Penobscot River in Maine to destroy a British base being built there turned into a complete fiasco when a small British squadron's arrival forced the Americans to run upriver and surrender or burn their craft. Then in August 1778 d'Estaing's fleet was finally goaded into attacking the British at Savannah, Georgia, with 20 ships of the line and 5500 troops. Attempting a bombardment from the land and a storming of the British lines, the French were driven into a swamp and lost over 1000 men. Disgusted at the fortunes of war, d'Estaing sailed home.

American fortunes improved but little in 1779, although 23 September of that year

Right: **A feature of the battles on the Great Lakes was the use of small gunboats, as shown in this view of the Battle of Valcour Island.**

Above: **The 10-gun sloop *Sachem* of the Continental Navy *circa* 1776–77. Note the design of the flag.**
Left: **Lieutenant John Paul Jones presides as the Stars and Stripes is hoisted for the first time aboard the *Lexington*, 4 July 1776.**

saw the greatest sea victory of the American cause. The man responsible was John Paul Jones (born John Paul, Jr). Having gone to sea in 1761 at the age of 13 from his native Scotland, Jones sailed in the Atlantic and Caribbean trades for many years and attained a captaincy by the age of 21. When the war with Britain broke out, Jones secured a commission in the Continental Navy. Having served well as a lieutenant on the *Alfred*, he was given command of the sloop *Ranger* in 1777 and sailed for Europe to harass British trade on His Majesty's home waters. Since the French and the Americans had signed their alliance before Jones arrived in 1778, he was able to use French ports as his bases of operation and to raise havoc in the waters around the British Isles. Giving up command of the *Ranger* on the promise of a more formidable vessel, Jones was disappointed that his new ship was the old 900-ton East India merchant vessel *Duc de Duras*. He promptly rechristened her *Bonhomme Richard* to honor his patron Benjamin Franklin, Ambassador to Paris and author of *Les Maximes du Bonhomme*

Richard (The Sayings of the Gentleman Richard).

Undaunted by this disappointing command assignment, Jones set sail on 14 August 1779 with his squadron: the *Bonhomme Richard*; a new American frigate, the *Alliance*, under an erratic Frenchman named Pierre Landais (an honorary citizen of Massachusetts); three French naval vessels and two French privateers. The squadron attained some success in capturing British vessels. Then, on the evening of 23 September, it fell in with a Baltic convoy off Flamborough Head on the Yorkshire coast. The convoy was guarded by the new 44-gun frigate *Serapis* and a small sloop. Ordering an attack, Jones soon found his companion vessels fleeing the scene, leaving the 42-gun *Bonhomme Richard* to fight the enemy alone.

In the furious duel that followed for three and a half hours, the *Serapis* and *Richard* broadsided one another with their withering fire, reducing both ships to floating wreckage. The *Richard* also suffered broadsides from Landais's *Alliance*, which returned to the scene of battle and began firing on the wrong ship. Finally one of Jones's sailors from the *Richard* crawled out to the end of a yardarm that hung over the deck of the *Serapis*—the two ships by then hopelessly entwined—and dropped a grenade onto the gun deck of the British frigate. The horrible explosion that resulted forced the brave and capable Captain Richard Pearson of the *Serapis* to haul down his colors and present his sword to Jones in surrender of his vessel. The *Bonhomme Richard* was so battered by the battle that she sank two days later.

John Paul Jones's splendid victory created the first and only genuine naval hero of the Revolutionary War. His stirring rejection of Captain Pearson's offer to accept his surrender midway through the battle, 'I have not yet begun to fight,' embodied the embattled spirit of the new nation in an hour of failing fortunes.

After his glorious victory over the *Serapis*, Jones went on to command two other American vessels during the war, then served as a rear admiral in the Russian Black Sea fleet before dying in poverty and obscurity in Paris in 1792 at the age of 45. As a symbol of the spirit of the Revolution, Jones's body was brought back to America early in the twentieth century at the behest of President Theodore Roosevelt (who was promoting a powerful navy in any way he could) and entombed in a marble sarcophagus on the grounds of the United States NavalAcademy at Annapolis, Maryland. After a century of neglect, the brave and resourceful sea captain returned to his adopted country for the honors he deserved as an almost solitary light of fighting hope during the dismal middle years of America's fight for independence.

Through all these years of revolutionary conflict, the effective privateers continued their work, and by 1780 the war was beginning to turn. The French with the assistance of the Spanish, gained command of the Caribbean, as d'Estaing's returned fleet battled Admiral George B Rodney to a draw in those waters in April. In July d'Estaing moved in and took final control of Newport. Rodney would not even challenge his control. The basic strategic reality was that by 1780 the British were involved in a world war against the Americans, the French, the Spanish and the Dutch. This meant that the Royal Navy was attempting to cover the Baltic and North Seas, the north and south

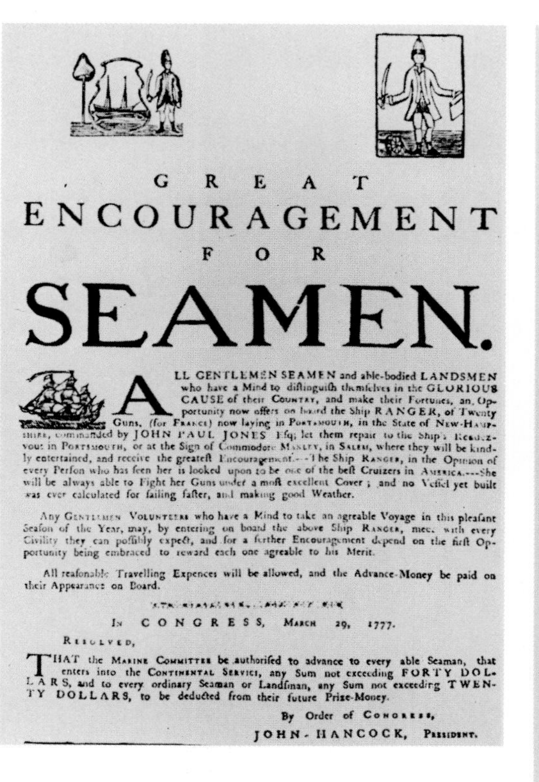

GREAT
ENCOURAGEMENT
FOR
SEAMEN.

ALL GENTLEMEN SEAMEN and able-bodied LANDSMEN who have a Mind to distinguish themselves in the GLORIOUS CAUSE of their COUNTRY, and make their Fortunes, an Opportunity now offers on board the Ship RANGER, of Twenty Guns, (for FRANCE) now laying in PORTSMOUTH, in the State of NEW-HAMPSHIRE, commanded by JOHN PAUL JONES Esq; let them repair to the Ship's Rendezvous in PORTSMOUTH, or at the Sign of Commodore MANLEY, in SALEM, where they will be kindly entertained, and receive the greatest Encouragement.---The Ship RANGER, in the Opinion of every Person who has seen her is looked upon to be one of the best Cruizers in AMERICA.---She will be always able to Fight her Guns under a most excellent Cover; and no Vessel yet built was ever calculated for sailing faster, and making good Weather.

Any GENTLEMEN VOLUNTEERS who have a Mind to take an agreable Voyage in this pleasant Season of the Year, may, by entering on board the above Ship RANGER, meet with every Civility they can possibly expect, and for a further Encouragement depend on the first Opportunity being embraced to reward each one agreable to his Merit.

All reasonable Travelling Expences will be allowed, and the Advance-Money be paid on their Appearance on Board.

IN CONGRESS, MARCH 29, 1777.

RESOLVED,

THAT the MARINE COMMITTEE be authorised to advance to every able Seaman, that enters into the CONTINENTAL SERVICE, any Sum not exceeding FORTY DOLLARS, and to every ordinary Seaman or Landsman, any Sum not exceeding TWENTY DOLLARS, to be deducted from their future Prize-Money.

By Order of CONGRESS,
JOHN-HANCOCK, PRESIDENT.

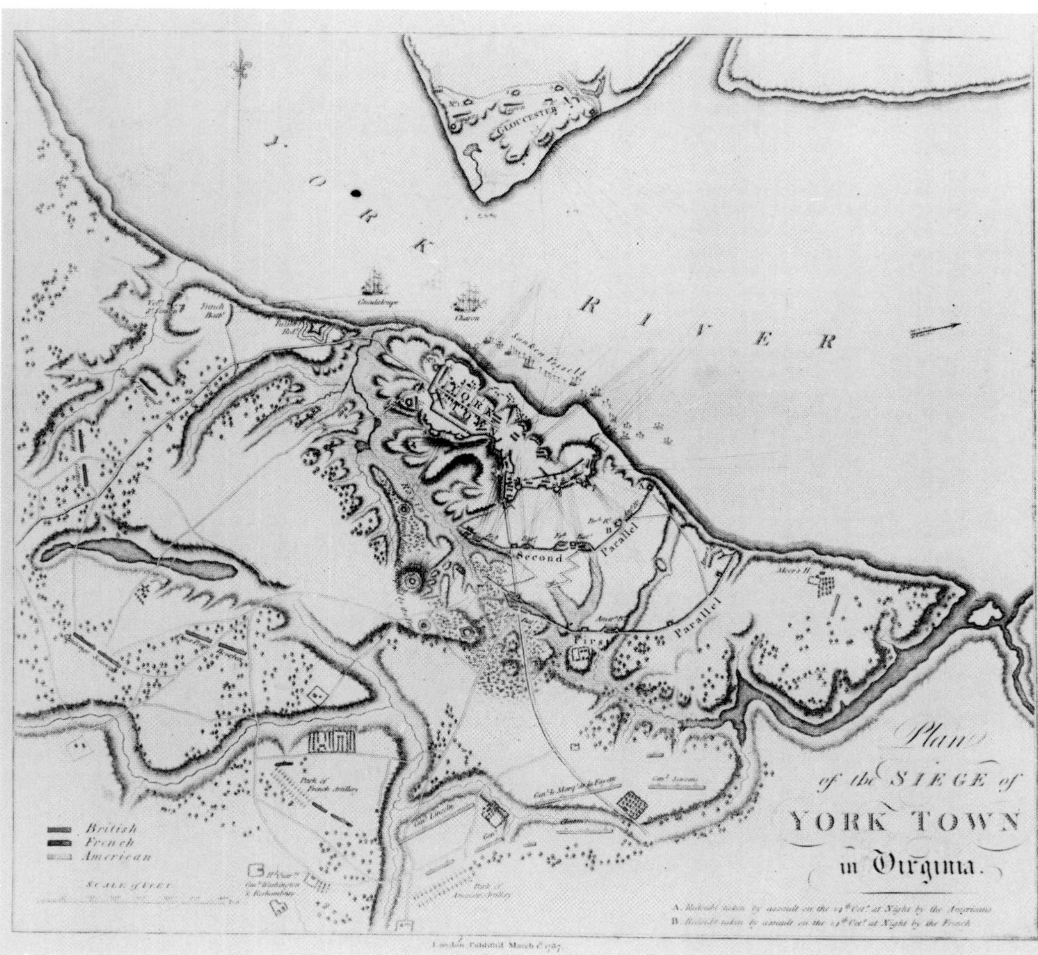

Above: Recruiting poster for the USS *Ranger*.
Right: Map of the siege of Yorktown.
Below right: Esek Hopkins, first commander of the US Navy.

Atlantic, the Caribbean, the Mediterranean Sea and the Indian Ocean. Increasing war weariness at home and rising opposition in Parliament to a prolonged conflict with the nation's best customers, plus Britain's naval weakness, finally spelled crucial defeat for the king and his war party. The occasion was Lord Charles Cornwallis's ostensible 'triumphal march' through the Tory Southern states, which ran into unexpected resistance and moved to Yorktown, Virginia.

Cornwallis had chosen well in moving his army to Yorktown as a base for evacuation by the Royal Navy. He could defend himself against the troops pursuing him, and the harbor could accommodate the fleet that would take him out. But two events occurred which Cornwallis did not count on. First, Washington, correctly estimating the situation, rapidly moved his troops from the New York area—along with those of Lieutenant General de Rochambeau from Newport—and placed Cornwallis's Army under heavy and relentless siege. Second, Admiral Francois Joseph Paul de Grasse, leaving the Spanish fleet to guard the Caribbean in his absence, moved to the Chesapeake to prevent the British fleet from entering to save Cornwallis. When the weakened British fleet arrived off Capes Henry and Charles—Admiral Rodney, then ill, having sailed home with four ships of the line, and six other vessels having been diverted to escort a Jamaican convoy home to England—its commander,

Left: Maps of the British attacks on Charleston, SC, in 1776 (lower) and 1780. American weakness in major vessels prevented intervention in either case.

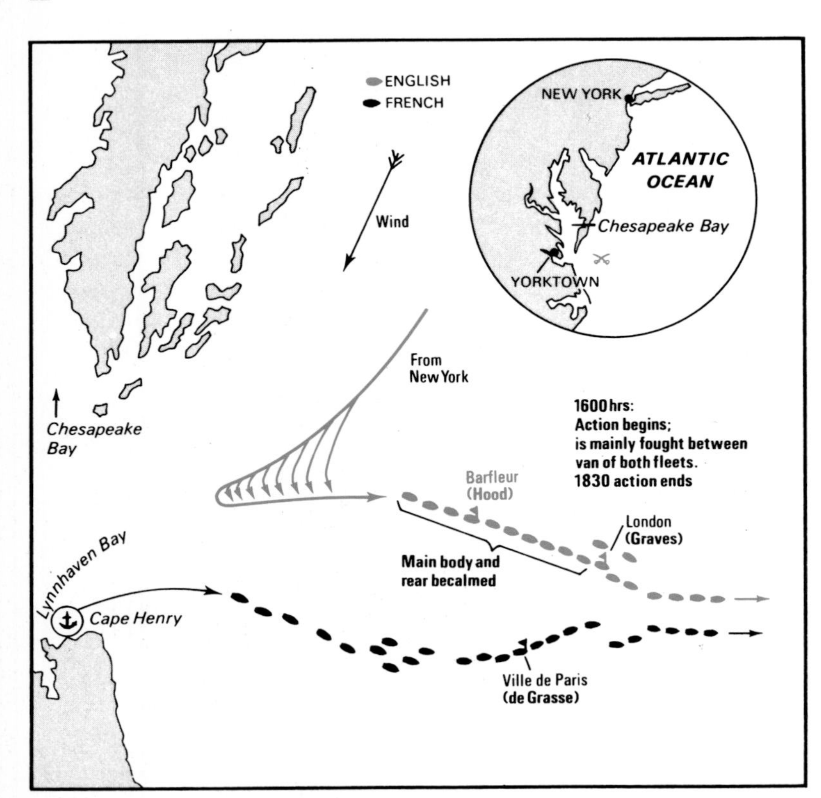

Admiral Thomas Graves, found de Grasse's fleet inside and waiting.

On 5 September 1781 the critical 'Battle of the Capes' was fought. Thanks to British tactical errors—Graves engaged only part of his line of battle—the French Navy's hold on the entrance to Chesapeake Bay could not be broken. Cornwallis's lifeline had been snapped. Furthermore, de Grasse was able to draw off Graves's fleet for five days, allowing a French fleet under Admiral de Barras to slip into the Chesapeake and reinforce the French naval squadron there. Defeated and now outnumbered, Graves sailed back to New York to refit, and as the American and French forces numbering 15,000 men drew the noose tighter and tighter around Cornwallis's 7000 troops, the British commander bowed to the inevitable and asked for terms of surrender. On 19 October 1781 the ceremonies were held. The American war for independence, for all practical purposes, had been won.

Additional fighting at sea took place after that date, most importantly the great British-French sea battle in the Caribbean known as the Battle of the Saints in 1782, but the issue had been decided. The Parliamentary majority that had persisted in the war since 1775 had been discredited, the British nation was deeply in debt, privateers were still wreaking havoc with merchant vessels on the high seas and the vaunted Royal Navy was stretched thin across the face of the earth. The war against the former colonists could be won only by military exertions beyond the willpower and capacity of the nation. It was time to quit.

Dividing the Americans from their French allies, who wanted to pursue the war until lands and rights lost in previous conflicts were restored to the Bourbon Kingdom, the British signed the Treaty of Paris with the American envoys on 3 September 1783. American independence was recognized. The jubilant Americans, now free of the mother country, turned to peacetime pursuits once again. During the war approximately 60 ships had seen service with the Continental Navy. They had captured over 200 enemy vessels. But with the return of peace, it was widely believed that a naval force was both prohibitively expensive and superfluous. Therefore, all the remaining vessels under commission were sold off except the *Alliance*, which would be used to show the flag and protect American trade. But the cost of maintaining even this frigate was soon seen as being too high for the infant nation, so she was sold off on 1 August 1785. With her sale, the Continental Navy came to an end, the state navies having already been disbanded.

Although the leaders of the successful rebellion were extolled for generations as national heroes—as one would expect—quickly forgotten were the military lessons of the war. Chief among these was that the nation had almost lost the war in the first two years for lack of a navy—indeed, would have lost the war if the British Government had shown greater resolution in suppressing the revolt—and that final victory was attained only through control of the sea. Naval power, in this case French naval power, was the crucial ingredient. The new American nation would pay dearly in the years ahead for forgetting these lessons.

Above: Captain John Barry.
Above left: Map of the Battle of Chesapeake Bay which made possible the victory at Yorktown.
Right: Another broadside from the _Bonhomme Richard_ strikes the largely dismasted _Serapis_.

Right: The _Alliance_ fires on the closely engaged _Serapis_ and _Bonhomme Richard_.
Below: Jones' first command for the Continental Navy, the brig _Lexington_.

SERAPIS

FOR NATIONAL RIGHTS AND EXPANSION

Six short years after the Treaty of Paris was signed came an event that was destined to have cataclysmic effects on the European heartland and to pull the infant American nation into another armed conflict. In 1789 the French nation, loaded down with war debts and saddled with a monarchy unwilling or unable to respond effectively to the forces swirling around it, fell into domestic revolution. The French Revolution lasted for ten years, ending only with the rise to power of Napoleon Bonaparte. In the process, the rebellion led to war on all fronts and catapulted the United States into the turmoil of war with first the French, then the British. Between these two conflicts, the new United States was also forced to humble the Barbary pirates from the northern coast of Africa in order to uphold American rights.

The Federalists, the Quasi-War and the Rebirth of the Navy

As the Revolutionary War came to an end and Americans returned to their peaceful pursuits, most of them gave little thought to the nation's lack of naval power. There were problems in that Britain was not living up to all the terms of the Treaty of Paris, Spain was closing the Lower Mississippi to American commerce and the Barbary pirates were plundering American ships on the Mediterranean and holding their crews for ransom. But the fact that a respectable American naval force could help to solve these problems was perceived only dimly, if at all. Besides, the government established under the Articles of Confederation had no real taxing power to support national defense—or any other national interest—and required the consent of nine of the thirteen states to take substantial action on anything. Thus the Navy was nonexistent under the Articles. Fortunately, the fundamental weaknesses of the Articles became apparent to enough states so that a convention was called in Philadelphia in 1787 to alter the Articles in favor of a centralized government more responsive to compelling national needs. The convention altered the Articles right out of existence and created a new central government under a new Constitution: it received the support of the states and came into effect in 1789.

The new national government embodied many fundamental changes in powers, including those of national defense. Under the Constitution, the Commander in Chief of the armed forces was the President, and the Congress was empowered to levy and collect taxes for national defense, although it could appropriate money to the military for only up to two years. Congress was specifically empowered to raise and support an army and a navy. Defense had become primarily a national obligation under the new document.

Although the United States now had the legal power to create an army and a navy, this did not mean that either was forthcoming or adequately financed. The Federalists, under the leadership of Alexander Hamilton and backed by the merchant classes, were clearly in favor of a navy to support and defend the nation's commercial interests. America's shipping, they argued, had to be protected against seizure of its vessels and depredations by the Mediterranean potentates. Coastal shipping and fishing rights in the Atlantic could be upheld only by naval force. A navy, in fine, could enforce the respect America was due as a sovereign power.

The Republicans, however, were opposed to any substantive military power. Drawing their strength from the inland reaches of the country, and fearful of aristocratic power as embodied in an officer corps, besides being ardent friends of France, or Francophiles, the Jeffersonians were in no mood to build a powerful navy. They argued that it would be expensive and unnecessary, since no European power would send a sizable fleet to America's shores. Perhaps a small naval force to punish the Barbary pirates and guard American ports might be acceptable, but any expenditure beyond that would be foolish and superfluous.

Even as Europe slipped into war in 1793 and British and French naval units began to seize neutral American shipping, the Republicans refused to rethink their stance on an American navy; their aversion to land-based forces was also largely un-

Below: **Building the USS *Philadelphia*, *circa* 1800. American frigates were usually larger than other nations' – an obvious advantage.**

Above: **The American ship *Planter* beats off an attack from a French privateer in July 1799 during the Quasi-War.**

changed. The continuing capture of American vessels by the Barbary pirates, and the cavalier attitude of France and Britain toward American neutral rights on the high seas, finally forced the dominant Federalists to re-create a small navy, but only over the opposition of the non-commercial frontier Republicans.

Six new 204-foot frigates, eventually to sail under the names *Constitution*, *Constellation*, *United States*, *Congress*, *President* and *Chesapeake*, were authorized in 1794. Designed by Joshua Humphreys, an experienced Philadelphia shipbuilder, these vessels were to be strong in construction to stand up to enemy equals and swift of sail to escape when outgunned or outclassed. Despite a lessening of tensions with Morocco and Algiers the next year, shipbuilding continued in a dilatory fashion (the *United States*, *Constellation* and *Constitution* were launched in 1797) so that America had some naval muscle to bare when warfare between the British and French spilled over and American rights had to be defended on the high seas.

When John Jay's attempt to settle outstanding problems with Britain met with only partial success—and, indeed, the United States received no assurances from the British that they would stop taking American vessels bound for France on the high seas—France was incensed. The Jay Treaty of 1795 had significantly decreased the danger of war with Britain, but had increased the danger of war with France, which saw it as a pro-British move on the part of the United States. France continued to take American merchant vessels trading with Britain, and President John Adams's attempt to solve the bones of contention with France ended in an aborted attempt at negotiations. Thus America fell into the Quasi-War, or Undeclared War, with France in 1798 when Congress authorized the seizure of armed French vessels.

Although the Quasi-War was of little military significance (the United States eventually seized 80-plus French ships, mostly in the West Indies), it did result in the real rebirth of the US Navy. Congress completed the building of the Humphreys-designed frigates and built, bought or rented more than four dozen other vessels, all of which acquitted themselves well in protecting American convoys and tangling with French vessels. Captain Thomas Truxtun won notable victories in the *Constellation* over the 40-gun *L'Insurgente* in the West Indies (1799) and over *La Vengeance* off Guadeloupe in 1800. Of greater importance in the long run, Congress also created a separate Navy Department in 1798. Benjamin Stoddert, a wealthy Maryland merchant, was appointed by President Adams as its first secretary. Stoddert not only brought the Navy into being as a regular force and directed its operations, but also made plans for new and larger vessels that could stand up to the largest French or British ships of the line. He also planned to build a complete shore establishment of shipyards and warehouses for the fledgling Navy, spreading them along the eastern shore for both defensive and political purposes. When the Undeclared War ended with the Convention of 1800, the United States had a navy, one that had proved its mettle in protecting American seagoing interests. But dark clouds appeared on the new navy's horizon: the fragmentation of the Federalist Party, and popular opposition to the Alien and Sedition Acts, clearly pointed to victory for the anti-navy Republicans under Jefferson.

The Jeffersonians, the Barbary Wars and Trouble with England

Benjamin Stoddert had envisioned a respectable naval force with at least three dozen major vessels, including numerous ships of the line. His Republican successor (after Jefferson's 'Revolution of 1800') had other ideas more in line with his party's values and ideas. Secretary of the Navy Robert Smith, who held the office from 1801 to 1809, presided over the scuttling of Stoddert's plans as unnecessary luxury. Not long after Jefferson's inauguration and Smith's assumption of office, the US Navy had been reduced to six ships and a handful of officers and men.

But Jefferson's dream of a miniscule navy guarding America's coast as proper for a frugal and peaceful people evaporated in the face of renewed Barbary raids on American vessels in the Mediterranean. Soon the attacks by Tripoli, Tunis, Morocco and Algiers forced the land-oriented president to reverse himself and call for a naval force to deter the Barbary Powers. Navy monies were doubled, and an American squadron under the command of Captain Richard Dale was dispatched to punish the Mediterranean pirates. The ineffectual Dale was soon replaced by the equally inept Captain Richard V Morris and finally by Captain Edward Preble. Only then did pacification of the region begin in earnest. The most noteworthy event of this naval police action created a hero for the American public. When Commodore William Bainbridge's frigate *Philadelphia* ran aground off Tripoli on 31 October 1803 and its 307-man crew was captured by the local pasha, Lieutenant Stephen Decatur and a small party worked themselves alongside the hapless *Philadelphia* on a dark night in February 1804 and burned her, thus restoring American honor. While few other actions were of this magnitude, the US naval presence finally convinced the potentates (in 1805) to refrain from attacking American vessels and to return the captured officers and crew of the *Philadelphia*—as long as an agreed-upon $60,000 bribe was paid and America would resume offering annual 'presents' to the African leaders. (Trouble with the Barbary pirates did not end until

Left: **The *United States* at her commissioning ceremony in 1797.**
Right: **Sailors from the USS *Constitution* storm aboard the French privateer *Sandwich* in the West Indies in May 1800.**

1815–16, when squadrons under Commodores Stephen Decatur and William Bainbridge used a show of force to compel Algeria, Tunis and Tripoli to desist.)

The Barbary Wars of 1801–05 demonstrated graphically that naval power, especially when projected into an enemy's home waters, was a very effective protection for national interests. Yet even in the face of British and French violations of America's maritime rights, the Republicans persisted in their anti-naval stand until America stumbled into war all over again —a war that might well have been avoided had the nation been negotiating from strength rather than from weakness.

As of 1805 the American merchant fleet was in a flourishing state. While British and French forces battered away at each other on land and sea (October 1805 saw Horatio Nelson's great victory over the French fleet and that of her Spanish ally off Cape Trafalgar), the Americans were shipping goods from Spanish, Dutch and French colonies in the Caribbean and Far

Right: **Stephen Decatur, hero of actions against the Barbary pirates and the British.**
Below: **The battle between the *Constellation* and *L'Insurgente*, 9 February 1799, from a painting by Charles Patterson.**

Above: **Commodore Richard Dale, one of the first US commanders in the wars with the Barbary pirates.**

All this began to change after the *Chesapeake* affair of 1807. Given the harsh living and disciplinary conditions on British warships, the Royal Navy was forced to man its ships largely by impressment. An impressed sailor was one who was simply seized on land or sea and forced into the King's service. Both impressment and seizure of deserters were allowable under British law, but the *Chesapeake* affair illustrated the peril of enforcing these statutes.

The *Chesapeake* was a new 38-gun American frigate being outfitted at Norfolk on Hampton Roads. A British squadron patrolling in Chesapeake Bay had orders to search for deserters outside American territorial waters and suspected that some British deserters had signed on the *Chesapeake*. Accordingly, HMS *Leopard* passed out of the bay and waited for the American vessel to emerge. As she did so on 22 June 1807, the captain of the *Leopard* informed Commodore James Barron, the *Chesapeake*'s commander, that he would send a crew aboard to search for the deserters. When Barron refused this request, saying that his crew had been recruited in Boston and he knew of no British deserters aboard, the British fired three broadsides into the *Chesapeake*, which was completely unprepared for battle, and forced Barron to haul down his flag to save his ship. The British then boarded the American vessel and took four men as deserters (one of whom was indeed just that). Whatever the legality of the British actions—they had fired a preliminary warning shot across the bow of the *Chesapeake* and Barron had not hove to—the American nation reacted violently to the event. Jefferson ordered all British warships out of American waters and forbade any further entry. Through James Monroe, American Ambassador to England, he demanded reparations and an end to impressment. The British disavowed the actions of the *Leopard*, but steadfastly refused to give up impress-

Right: **The engagement between the *Chesapeake* and the *Leopard*.**
Below: **The USS *Experiment* and the British *Louisa Bridger* in a night battle, 16 November 1800. The *Experiment* believed the *Louisa Bridger* to be French.**

East into Napoleon's France and the ports of his allies. These goods were usually landed in American ports first and then reshipped to Europe (a practice known as the 'broken voyage') in exchange for manufactured goods. American products were also being carried by American ships to the ports of the belligerents, so trade had never been better.

But Britain, fighting for her life against France and her allies, saw no good in such practices. Since she could never raise land armies large enough to conquer Napoleon on the Continent, he would have to be defeated on the seas. That meant stopping American neutral vessels from carrying their cargoes into European ports.

The first incident triggered by American shipping practices came in May 1805 when the *Essex* out of Salem, on a broken voyage from Barcelona to Havana, was seized in the Caribbean by the British. A British admiralty court condemned the cargo, saying it was never intended for the American market, although most of the port duties paid were returned. The Americans were incensed by this action, and a few mariners gave up broken voyages, but most continued on their way.

When France and England subsequently blockaded one another's coasts and ports, American trading vessels were subject to seizure by both sides, but most continued to sail anyway, since great profits could be made by successful vessels. American neutral rights were not being honored by the belligerents, but open war was avoided.

Above: **The *Philadelphia* burns in Tripoli as Decatur and his men escape.**

ment. Within months they had specifically ordered the impressment of all British sailors on any neutral vessel. Insulting as this seemed to the Americans, the British were fighting a war for survival, and the Treaty of Tilsit of that year (1807), whereby Russia became an ally of France, made their situation even more perilous. British survival took precedence over American neutral rights in their eyes, and America, without a navy to challenge these practices, would simply have to live with the consequences.

Below: **A party from the *Enterprise* set out to board a Tripolitan pirate in 1801.**

Even at this, Jefferson could not be convinced of the need for a strong navy, but proposed instead that the nation should only guard her shores against foreign naval encroachments. Accordingly, Congress appropriated money for 188 small gunboats ('Jeffs,' as they came to be called) for inshore patrol. Only 50 feet long, with two 32-pound cannons and crews of 20, the tiny crafts' gunwales were only two feet above water when fully loaded. But the gunboats were cheap—a major consideration. They could also be stored under sheds when not deployed. They were useless against any regular enemy naval force, but might at least be used to keep American vessels in port during an embargo, even if they could not keep enemy vessels out. Thomas Jefferson continued to put his faith in moral persuasion and withholding of American ships and goods, rather than in armed force.

Jefferson's attempts at economic embargo were exercises in futility. His Embargo Law of December 1807, designed to cut off the British from American foodstuffs and raw materials, stopped all exports from the United States by land and sea. Unfortunately for this short-sighted policy, his embargo leaked like a sieve and brought great hardship, not to the British, but to those Americans who depended upon foreign trade and the merchant marine for their livelihood. And Jefferson's gunboats and miniscule navy could not begin to make the embargo effective, no matter how they tried. Faced with an embarrassing and frustrating defeat, Jefferson decided to change to a selective embargo instead. It worked no better than his previous attempt at economic coercion.

The War of 1812

President James Madison, Jefferson's successor, could do no better. The Non-Intercourse Act of 1809 and Macon's Bill Number Two of 1810 only made matters more confusing without guaranteeing American rights. American ships and cargoes were still being seized. Nor did a new short-term full embargo in the spring of 1812 seem to work. But, ironically, it was working better than the Americans realized. On 16 June 1812 the British revoked their Orders in Council authorizing the seizure of American ships, because crop failures at home made American foodstuffs imperative. But two days later, not knowing of this British action, the American Congress declared war on Great Britain. Seizures of American ships, continued British impressment of American seamen, an agricultural depression that the Western farmers blamed on British interference with trade, the desire of the 'War Hawks' in Congress to restore 'national honor' and a belief that the British were stirring up the Indians on the American frontier all combined to lead America into the ill-conceived War of 1812.

Faced with fighting a major power with only sixteen ships in commission, plus the useless 'Jeff boats'—the British had over 600 men-of-war—the navy turned to squadron patrols to harass British vessels on the North Atlantic sea lanes. Captain John Rodgers proved the value of such operations early in the war by drawing the British Halifax, Nova Scotia, naval squadron hundreds of miles to the east to allow American merchantmen to speed safely home to American ports. And American

Right: **Scenes from the battle of HMS *Java* with the *Constitution*. Above, the *Java* loses her foremast in an attempt to board the more heavily armed *Constitution*, becomes unmanageable and is totally dismasted by the *Constitution*'s broadsides, below.**

hopes for naval superiority were raised by the victory of the large 44-gun frigate *Constitution*, under Captain Isaac Hull, over HMS *Guerriere*, 38 guns, off Nova Scotia on 19 August 1812. American privateers were also busy. By the end of 1812, almost 600 vessels were preying on British commerce (including the famous *Rossie* out of Baltimore under Captain Joshua Barney); during the course of the war over 1300 British vessels were claimed.

But despite these efforts by the ship-poor United States, Britain reacted with vigor and had soon clamped a tight blockade on the Atlantic coastal ports and bays. There were occasional American naval victories like that of the USS *United States* under Commodore Stephen Decatur over

***Left:* A privateer captures a British brig, a typical action during the War of 1812.**
***Below:* Close action during Perry's victory on Lake Erie.**

Right: **Thomas Macdonough, victor in the battle at Plattsburgh Harbor, Lake Champlain on 11 September 1814.**

HMS *Macedonian* (25 October 1812) and the USS *Constitution* under Commodore William Bainbridge over HMS *Java* two months later, but the dominance of British seapower was soon obvious. The reinforced British squadrons in American waters had blockaded America's ports. Neither naval nor commercial vessels were able to break out from New York to New Orleans. Not even Captain James Lawrence's spirited duel between his *Chesapeake* and HMS *Shannon* off Boston harbor could crack the blockade strangling the American nation. (This was the engagement in which Lawrence, in the midst of defeat, bravely encouraged his crew by shouting 'Never strike the flag of my ship!' 'Don't give up the ship!') The British Navy controlled the seas and even received supplies from American citizens opposed to the war, especially in New England where numerous American vessels continued to sail under British license. The British also demonstrated graphically the importance of their strategic advantage by sailing up Chesapeake Bay to attack and burn Washington and then bombard Baltimore in August 1814.

Only on inland waters did American forces have notable success. On 10 September 1813 Master Commandant Oliver Hazard Perry, with a home-built fleet, defeated a British lakes squadron off Put-in-Bay. He immortalized the Battle of Lake Erie by transferring his motto flag, 'Don't Give Up the Ship,' from his battle-wrecked *Lawrence* to the *Niagara* to continue the fight until victory was won. Perry's victory, marked by his stirring message 'We have met the enemy and they are ours,' was also a great strategic victory for the United States, ensuring control of the Northwest Territory. Perry then proceeded to transport American forces under General William Henry Harrison across Lake Erie to Ontario, where they won an impressive land victory over the British in the crucial Battle of the Thames the following month.

A home-built American naval force also won well-deserved laurels in the Battle of Lake Champlain in September 1814. A 10,000-man British force had marched down from Montreal via the Richelieu River to Plattsburg, New York, the key to control of Lake Champlain. The commander of the British forces, General Sir George Prevost, sent a naval force of 14 gunboats under Captain George Downie against an equal contingent under Captain Thomas Macdonough to seize control of the lake. Gaining the tactical advantage by superior maneuvering of his vessels, and aided by the fact that his crews were

Right: **American and British privateersmen in a bloody boarding action.**

trained seamen, Macdonough captured most of the British force, retained control of the lake for the Americans and forced Prevost back into Canada. Thus the British were denied the valuable bargaining chip of control extending from eastern Maine to Lake Champlain at the peace negotiations then being held at Ghent, Belgium. American naval forces also played an important role in Andrew Jackson's defeat of General Edward Pakenham at the Battle of New Orleans (fought two weeks after the Treaty of Ghent had been signed on Christmas Eve, 1814) by anchoring Jackson's right flank on the Mississippi River.

As the War of 1812 ground to a halt—a war that tactically and strategically might be termed a draw at best—it was evident that the US Navy had played an unimpressive role in the conflict. The strategies of static defense by small gunboats and the extensive use of privateers against commerce had not brought the British to bay. It was realized that only a powerful trained naval force would command the respect of other nations and defend American interests in time of war. The big heavily gunned frigates had, in fact, done the job, although sheer lack of numbers of these and other first-rate vessels had allowed the British effectively to dominate American coastal waters. Congress, realizing at last the imperatives of command of the sea, authorized the building of seven 74-gun ships of the line in 1816. The year before it had reorganized the navy under a Board of Navy Commissioners (all officers) to advise the secretary of the navy on personnel, shipbuilding and administrative affairs. (The board functioned until 1842, when the bureau system was adopted.) Having won widespread public favor, the US Navy was ready to play a major role in the affairs of the nation.

Standing Down but Keeping Station

Although the Navy stood in this advantageous position at the end of the nation's second great conflict with Great Britain, there was an inevitable decrease in naval defense enthusiasm with no major foes to challenge American interests at home or abroad for the next three decades. In addition, a nationwide fervor for economic development emerged as the United States began to shift to industry in the North, and agricultural expansion in the South and West became boundless. The nation also suffered the severe Panic of 1837. These factors largely account for the Navy's failure to reach its potential in the years prior to the Civil War. The nation did not abandon its Navy—it realized its important role in protecting American commerce on the sea lanes of the world—

Above: **Typical uniforms of the War of 1812. In the foreground a lieutenant carrying a speaking trumpet used for passing orders to men working in the rigging.**

but allowed only a moderate growth of the force. As a result, the Navy made certain notable gains in the period 1815 to 1861 and played a number of key roles in American expansion, but it never enjoyed sufficient public and political favor to develop its full potential as a peace-keeping force.

Ships continued to be built, although the pace was usually dilatory. The seven vaunted 74-gun vessels so enthusiastically authorized by Congress in 1816 were slow in coming: three were still not completed

Above: Captain Isaac Hull of the *Constitution*.
Left and above left: Final scenes in the battle of the *Java* and *Constitution*. The *Java* tries to get under way with a jury sail but, after being forced to surrender and the surviving crew having been taken off, she is blown up.

Left: **'Macdonough Pointing the Gun' (during the fighting on Lake Champlain), from an engraving by F F Walker.**

by 1861. The US Navy could properly boast of the largest warship in the world when the 120-gun *Pennsylvania* was launched in 1837, but the overall pace of building never appreciably quickened. Steam warships also came to the navy during this period: the USS *Fulton*, a 700-ton sidewheeler (1837); the wood paddle-wheel sister ships *Missouri* and *Mississippi*, authorized in 1839; the sloop *Princeton*, which first utilized John Ericsson's screw propeller (1843); and the *Michigan* for use on the Great Lakes, a sidewheeler launched on Lake Erie in 1843 as the first iron-hulled steam warship in the US Navy (she continued to sail the Lakes until 1923). But while the navy occasionally made modest leaps forward, especially during the abbreviated tenures of such naval secretaries as Abel P. Upshur (1841–43) and George Bancroft (1845–46), the overall pace of development was sluggish. The navy was on 'Slow Ahead.'

During these years various squadrons were established for patrol duty: the Mediterranean (1815), the East India (1817), the Pacific (1821), the West Indies (1822), the Brazil (1826), the Home (1843, which absorbed the West Indies Squadron) and the African (1853). Engaged in protecting American commerce, suppressing pirates in the Caribbean, attempting to halt the illegal slave trade from Africa and 'showing the flag' in foreign ports, the naval squadrons quietly conducted the nation's business during thirty years of peace. It was also during this time that Lieutenant Charles Wilkes carried out a very successful voyage of exploration (1838–42) to Antarctica, the South Pacific and the Northwest coast on behalf of the navy and the nation. Also along the scientific line, Naval Lieutenant Matthew Fontaine Maury continued to develop the sciences of navigation and oceanography, which led to his recognition as 'Pathfinder of the Seas.'

Although the number of naval vessels in commission hovered at only about fifty during this period—spread thinly over

the face of the world—naval personnel played key roles in expanding American influence, especially in the Pacific. In 1826 the USS *Peacock*, under the command of Captain Thomas ap Catesby Jones, was ordered to Hawaii to protect commerce there. Jones, on his own, negotiated a treaty with the regents of the child monarch giving Americans certain key rights in the islands. Although the treaty was never even submitted to the Senate, the Americans in the islands and the Hawaiians lived by it anyway. Then in 1842 President John Tyler asserted the 'Tyler Doctrine' of American priority over all other powers in the islands. As a result, Hawaii fell into the American sphere of influence after 1842, a step aided and upheld by the US Navy.

The navy was also present at the opening of China to the Western Powers. The British broke the back of Chinese resistance to the inroads of English trade, especially in opium, in the Opium War of 1839–42 and forced the Chinese Government to open treaty ports to them and to let them trade freely. Commodore Lawrence Kearney arrived in China in 1842 to open negotiations for like privileges for the Americans. He was followed soon after by Caleb Cushing, with four American warships. to resume the negotiations. Cushing, as Commissioner to China, negotiated the Treaty of Wanghia in 1844, gaining trading rights that were very profitable to the Yankee merchants. Although the Chinese were really only bowing to the inevitable in opening their land to outsiders, the navy had played an important role in expanding America's commercial and diplomatic rights in the Far East.

It was also in the crucial decade of the 1840s that the navy took a giant step toward full maturity with the opening of the United States Naval Academy at Annapolis, Maryland. Until then, naval officers had learned their trade at sea, but this time-honored method had many drawbacks, not the least of which was inadequately prepared officers. When an experiment by which young men of promise were sent to sea in small ships ended with the son of the secretary of war and two others being hanged for mutiny in 1842, resistance to a formal academy such as the Army had maintained at West Point since 1802 began to break down. Objections to a

Right: **Perry leaves the badly damaged *Lawrence*, taking his flag to the *Niagara*.**
Below: **The *Niagara* (center) bursts through the British line in the Battle of Lake Erie.**

naval academy as too expensive and too likely to turn out an antidemocratic military caste (a charge long borne by West Point) withered. Under the inspired leadership of Secretary of the Navy George Bancroft, opposition was overcome and an academy with regular courses and a 2–3–1 curriculum (two years at Annapolis, three years at sea and one year on a practice ship) was authorized. Fort Severn at Annapolis was transferred to the navy, all midshipmen not attached to ships were ordered there by Secretary Bancroft, and in October 1845 the Academy formally began its work of educating naval officers. A proud naval tradition had begun.

Men of the USS *Constitution* (right) cheer as their ship goes into action with HMS *Guerriere* (below). Many of the American successes in the War of 1812 were owed to the American emphasis on accurate gunnery, whereas British standards had declined since the victory at Trafalgar in 1805.

War with Mexico

Above: **The landing force at Tabasco comes under fire.**

In the meantime, trouble was brewing to the south. Ever since Texas had proclaimed her independence from Mexico in 1836, relations between the United States and her southern neighbor had been strained. Even though the US Navy had observed strict neutrality toward both belligerents during the Texas war of independence, even allowing the Mexican Government to obtain logistical supplies from New Orleans, Mexico was highly suspicious of American intentions toward the Texas republic peopled largely by ex-Americans, many of whom wanted the new nation in the Union. When, therefore, the United States annexed Texas in 1845 and the two nations began to dispute the location of the new state's southern boundary, the situation went from bad to worse. In January 1846 President James K Polk sent General Zachary Taylor and his men into the disputed territory and, with the help of the navy, Taylor proclaimed a blockade at the mouth of the vital Rio Grande River. When blood was spilled in Mexican attempts to assert its boundary claims, the United States declared war in May 1846. Whatever the rightness or wrongness of American actions in beginning the conflict—fiercely debated then and still debated today—the navy played a key role in winning this war of American expansion.

Once war was declared, the navy discovered that its deep-draft frigates and ships of the line were of limited value, since they could not cross the eight-foot sandbars found at the mouths of the Mexican rivers on the Gulf. Small steamers, schooners and brigs that could be used effectively on close blockade had to be purchased. This was crucial, since Commodore David Connor was under orders to seal off the Mexican Gulf Coast and capture its major ports. However, no challenge to Connor's orders or the navy could come from Mexico, whose navy was too small to engage the American forces. During the course of the war, not one Mexican naval vessel ever put to sea on Gulf waters. The major challenge to the blockaders came from the weather:they kept station outside the Mexican ports in the dry season (October to April) when violent northers caused acute discomfort and in the rainy season (April to October) when the 'vomito', or yellow fever, threatened to immobilize whole crews. But by buying steamers and swift, shallow-draft schooners for tight blockading, the navy was able to seal off the coast to Mexican exports and to supplies from outside.

It took the US Navy two tries to capture the fort at Alvarado, south of the major Mexican port of Vera Cruz—Commodore Matthew C Perry relieving Commodore Connor in the interim—and the taking of

Below: **Steamers tow landing barges across the sand bar before the landing at Tabasco.**

Vera Cruz itself via a joint army-navy effort called for ingenuity and new naval tactics to carry out this giant amphibious landing successfully. Special double-ended, flat-bottomed landing craft forty feet in length and stackable in threes for transporting had to be hurriedly built for the purpose. When an over-the-beach assault by sailors, marines, and soldiers finally took place on 9 March 1847, a line of fire was directed at the shoreline as the surfboats carried the men ashore. The surfboats were then pulled back off the beach by their crews, hauling on ropes attached to kedge anchors dropped offshore for this purpose. All 8600 men were carried ashore in eleven hours without incident—aided by the fact that the Mexicans had decided not to defend the beach. (This was the largest amphibious operation carried out by the navy until World War II.)

As the troops worked their way around Vera Cruz and the forts guarding the northern and southern ends of the city and laid it under siege, the navy was called upon to undertake two vital operations. Naval guns were unloaded from the ships and dragged three miles over the sand into assigned position, from which their crews delivered steady and accurate fire against the city walls. In a two-day stretch before Vera Cruz surrendered, the naval batteries delivered 1000 shells and 800 round shot (45 percent of all ordnance expended) at the city's walls and forts. Meanwhile, naval units in harbor also delivered withering fire on the city, moving directly beneath the guns of the Castle of San Juan de Ulloa to do so. When the city surrendered on 29 March 1847, opening the way for the armies to move inland against the capital of Mexico City, the navy could rightly boast of having played a significant role in the fall of Vera Cruz. During the remainder of the war on the Gulf Coast, the navy continued its tight blockade and sealed off the remaining port cities by taking Alvarado, Tuxpan and Tabasco, the latter two operations requiring movement up rivers and the use of landing parties. By June 1847 the Gulf Coast was secure. The Navy had done its duty in exemplary fashion.

On the Pacific Coast, the war and the navy's part in it was a quagmire of confusion. The first misfire came in 1842, when the commander of the Pacific Squadron, Commodore Thomas ap Catesby Jones, took the port of Monterey under the mistaken belief that war had broken out (the city was returned to Mexican officials with apologies). The squadron comman-

Below: **Another view of the landing at Tabasco. Sidewheelers were very suitable for the Gulf Coast because of their shallow draft.**

der in 1845, Commodore John D Sloat, was reluctant to make any unauthorized moves unless a war was definitely in progress. By June 1846, however, Sloat had become convinced that the war was on and rendered aid to the Americans in California as they proclaimed the 'Bear Flag Republic.' His men occupied Monterey before he found out that Captain John Charles Fremont of the Topographical Engineers, the surveyor-turned-revolutionary, was under no orders whatever to help the rebels. Turning over his command to Commodore Robert F Stockton, who had arrived shortly before, Sloat sailed home.

Cooperating with Fremont, the pompous Stockton made everyone's job more difficult by his inflammatory proclamations to the citizens of California. But he was able to use the crew of his *Congress* to take Santa Barbara, San Pedro and Los Angeles for the American cause. Los Angeles was subsequently lost and had to be painfully retaken, but when San Diego also fell to Stockton's men, California was secure and sewn up in a tight blockade. Subsequently, naval forces under Commodore W Branford Shubrick, who replaced Stockton in January 1847, took key ports in Baja California and on the Mexican West Coast and held them until word was received in March 1848 of the armistice signed at Guadalupe Hidalgo the month before.

Above: **The Stars and Stripes flies over the beach at Vera Cruz as the landing parties continue to stream ashore.**

The navy had done well in the war. Its ships and men had transported the armies to their destinations and had played a major role at Vera Cruz. They had gained control of the seas and prevented reinforcement on both coasts by a tight blockade. Amphibious operations had been learned by trial and error in the Vera Cruz operation. All this had been accomplished despite a lack of supplies and directed coordination. And as a result of the 'Bear Flag' revolt and the taking of California (in addition to the new Oregon Territory to the north), the nation now had a Pacific water frontier and the navy had a bigger job than ever in protecting America's enlarged Pacific interests.

The Opening of Japan

By this time many groups in America were interested in further Pacific expansion, particularly in opening the fabled land of Japan, closed to the outside world for two

Below: **The warships *Levant*, *Savannah* and *Cyane* (R to L) lie offshore as men from the ships land at Monterey, 7 July 1846.**

Above: **Perry and his interpreter in discussion with Japanese commissioner Hayashi.**

centuries. Protestant missionary societies wanted the kingdom opened to spread the Christian gospel among its people; whaler crew members from vessels that had sunk in Japanese waters were being held there; coaling stations were needed for steam vessels plying the sea lanes to China; and Yankee merchants saw great profits in opening the land to American goods. Although America's first attempt to make contact with the aloof kingdom failed miserably when Commodore James Biddle was openly rebuffed in 1846, the Government was determined to try again and turned to the Navy to do the job.

The naval officer chosen to lead the expedition was Commodore Matthew Calbraith Perry, one of the heroes of the Mexican War. Selected because he had diplomatic experience and because President Millard Fillmore liked him, Perry accepted the assignment with enthusiasm and began his preparations in 1852. He would command the sail-steamer *Mississippi* as his flagship, and eventually left from Norfolk on 24 November 1852 with two steam sidewheelers, four sailing sloops-of-war and three supply ships scheduled to join him in the Far East. Perry not only prepared himself thoroughly for his duties by wide reading and talking to whaling captains about the Japanese, but also supplied himself with scientists and artists to observe and record everything they saw. In addition, he carried a letter from the President and gifts for the Emperor of Japan, plus a Frenchman as his chef and an Italian musician as his bandmaster. Armed with credentials as envoy extraordinary and minister plenipotentiary to Japan, Perry sailed in the hope of opening Japanese ports to American trade, obtaining protection for American seamen and gaining coaling stations in the Japanese islands. Making his way across the South Atlantic, then around Africa and across the Indian Ocean to Hong Kong, Canton and Shanghai, Perry provisioned his fleet and left on 17 May 1853 for the Japanese-controlled island of Okinawa in the Ryukyu chain. Using this visit as a dress rehearsal for later negotiations (and to set up talks on a coaling station on Okinawa in case his mission to Japan fell through), Perry approached the Okinawan officials in great pomp and splendor to convince his imperial hosts of his importance. (This Perry believed, was absolutely necessary for impressing the ruling Japanese shoguns.)

On 2 July Perry's fleet of four vessels sailed for Japan. It arrived six days later and anchored just outside Yedo (Tokyo) Bay. This first visit to Japan, which lasted from 8 through 17 July 1853, was designed solely to impress the Japanese officials and their emperor. Negotiations could come

later. Perry would deliver President Fillmore's letter, state his demands, sail away and return the following spring with a greater force of ships when they arrived on station. To impress the Japanese, Perry kept himself invisible from the nation's officials; he was being imperious, not arrogant, by design. He would deal only with high officials in delivering his letter from the President; upon landing to do so, he was accompanied in great ceremony and dignity by 250 sailors and marines, plus the fleet band, to a specially constructed building (under the floor of which ten samurai warriors were concealed in case of trouble). Having delivered the letter, Perry announced that he would return in the spring with more ships to conduct negotiations. Returning to his four-ship fleet, Perry moved it up the bay to test the channel and to show the Japanese he would not be ordered out. He then returned to China.

As promised, Perry returned the following year. He appeared at Yokosuka on 13 February 1854 with ten ships. Again assuming an imperious manner, Perry was now ready to negotiate. Although he originally insisted on the talks being held in the capital city of Edo, Perry compromised and settled on Yokohama, south of Edo, when the Japanese protested that the Emperor would be overthrown if the parley were held in the capital. The commodore made his ceremonious landing on Japanese soil with 500 sailors and marines forming a long corridor of march and the 'Star Spangled Banner' booming from the band. Perry did not forget to order a 21-gun salute to the Emperor, and gifts (including a miniature railway on a 350-foot circular track and a working telegraph setup) were presented by the Americans. Although the Japanese at first refused to open their ports to American trade, Perry persisted in his demands. The resulting Treaty of Kanagawa (31 March 1854) included the opening of two treaty ports for trade, care of American victims of shipwreck and most-favored-nation status (any privilege extended to any other nation was automatically given to the United States). As Perry's fleet sailed away on 10 April 1854, he could well be pleased with his accomplishments. The opening wedge for Japanese trade had been driven by this officer-diplomat who had learned the art of Oriental negotiating. (A full commercial treaty followed in July 1857, with negotiations carried out by Townsend Harris.) As Perry resigned his command and sailed home in September 1854 by commercial steamer, he had earned the accolades heaped upon him. Like the nineteenth-century navy he represented so well, Perry's accomplishments had not been spectacular, but they had been solid. He had served the nation in peace and in war and had helped her become a major expansive power. His achievements, like the navy's had helped engender a deep national confidence in America's future. That national confidence would soon be sorely shaken, as the country found itself in the throes of Civil War.

Below: The USS _Hartford_ photographed _circa_ 1861, three years after she came into service. The _Hartford_ was a typical example of the hybrid steam/sail warships of her day.

CIVIL WAR, AT SEA AND ON INLAND WATERS

The Civil War between the government of the United States and the Confederate States of America was long in coming. The Northern and Southern states had been wrestling with the issues dividing them for over four decades. The question of the expansion of slavery had been argued since 1819, when Southern slaveholders had attempted to expand their 'peculiar institution' into the Louisiana Purchase territories, specifically into Missouri. This move had been strongly opposed by Northern interests who objected to slavery in lands they hoped to develop as free-labor territories and states. This early controversy had been worked out in the famous Compromise that allowed slavery in Missouri but forbade it in all other areas north of the line 36°30′ (the southern border of Missouri), but the issue continued to smolder in the decades that followed.

The Compromise of 1850 and the Kansas-Nebraska Act led to outright border conflict instead of peace; the Supreme Court's Dred Scott decision and the exploits of the abolitionist fanatic John Brown only inflamed the issue further. Northern abolitionists and Southern 'fire-eaters' fueled the controversy, and when Abraham Lincoln was elected President in 1860 as the candidate of the Northern-based Republican party, the Southern states, led by South Carolina, began to secede from the Union. Additional dissension centered on sectional differences over the tariff (the North wanted it higher; the South wanted it lower), aid to the railroads (the North generally pro; the South generally con) and the nature of the Constitution (the North arguing that federal power was supreme, the South that final power resided in the states). Believing they had the Constitutional right to leave the Union, various Southern states passed ordinances of secession after Lincoln's election and proceeded to form a new central government. The issue had finally been joined—despite the unsuccessful efforts of representatives from the border states to bring about a compromise of some kind—and everyone tensely awaited further developments.

The Nation Divides

In the harbor off Charleston, South Carolina, stood Fort Sumter, a federal military installation under the command of Major John Anderson, United States Army. South Carolina, having seceded and joined the Confederacy, claimed that Fort Sumter was now foreign military installation on its sovereign territory and demanded that it be evacuated. President Lincoln, believing that the very act of secession was

invalid because not provided for in the Constitution, argued that South Carolina and the Confederate States were wrong and steadfastly refused to order evacuation of the fort by the federal troops garrisoned there. Undeterred by the fact that a chartered merchant steamer, the *Star of the West*, had attempted to provision and reinforce the troops at Fort Sumter in January 1861 and had been fired upon and turned back, Lincoln ordered reinforcements to Fort Sumter by sea on 8 April 1861. President Jefferson Davis of the Confederacy instructed General P T Beauregard to try to persuade the Federals to leave peacefully before the reinforcements arrived, but Major Anderson refused the request. Accordingly, on 12 April the Confederate batteries along Charleston Harbor opened fire and compelled the Union troops to surrender the next day. Shooting had begun. Both sides, believing they were right, had refused to give in and now called for troops to defend their rights on the battlefield. The Civil War was fated to last for four years and ended only when over half a million men had died and as many had been wounded. It was fought from Texas to Virginia and from Pennsylvania to the waters of the Gulf Coast before the issues had been settled. The US Navy played a major role in the conflict before the hard-fought Union victory was achieved in 1865.

Given the relative economic strength of each section of the country, the South would be hard pressed to emerge victorious. The North had a population of 23,000,000, the South only 9,000,000, of whom about 3,500,000 were slaves whom Southerners dared not put under arms.

MEN WANTED
FOR THE
NAVY!

All able-bodied men not in the employment of the Army, will be enlisted into the Navy upon application at the Naval Rendezvous, on Craven Street, next door to the Printing Office.

H. K. DAVENPORT,
Com'r. & Senior Naval Officer.

New Berne, N. C.,
Nov. 2d, 1863.

Left: Union ships bombard Fort Royal, SC, 7 Nov 1861. After its capture Fort Royal became an important base for the blockade.
Right: Naval recruiting poster.
Below: 9-inch Dahlgren smooth-bore guns, aboard the USS *Hartford*.

In critical railroad mileage the North had 22,000 miles of track, the South only 8000. The North had 90 percent of the nation's manufacturing facilities, crucial to modern warfare, the South only 10 percent. The North owned virtually all the merchant vessels, the South but few. Faced with these discrepancies, the South realized it could win only by fighting a basically defensive war. It would have to force the North into a grand strategy that carried the war into the South to compel submission, a strategy that was expensive in money and manpower. The South also looked for help from abroad, since they believed that the British in particular would be forced to break any Federal blockade to attain their supply of cotton, the South's most important export. If the Southerners could go on the defensive, get outside help and hold out long enough so that the North would tire of the conflict and let them go their way in peace, they could win despite the economic and population differences. It would be a test of will, and the South would win.

Mindful of all this, Lincoln and his planners developed their own grand strategy. First, Union armies would march on the South and cut it into separate pieces while taking a considerable toll of Southern troops, troops very hard to replace in a white population of only 5,500,000. Second, the US Navy would clamp a tight blockade on the Southern coasts, allowing no cotton out and no foreign supplies in, at the same time using river forces to help the army cut the South into pieces by controlling its river systems, especially the vital Mississippi. Thus strangled by the aptly named 'Anaconda Plan,' and hatcheted apart by Northern land offenses, the South would be forced to surrender and the Union would be saved. Thus strategies were set, and each power geared up for a war to the finish which, both sides were sure, would last but a few months at most.

Although the Union Navy was in a weakened state at the beginning of the war due to declining naval appropriations, it was stronger than the virtually nonexistent Confederate Navy. The North had only 42 warships in commission at the start of hostilities (23 of which had steam power), and the number of naval personnel stood at only 7500. These vessels, sporting 455 guns, were spread out on station, however—only 12 in the Home Squadron and the rest in the East Indies and the Pacific. But the Union had at least the nucleus of a powerful navy capable of rapid expansion thanks to the Northern industrial base. The Union Navy also had over 1200 trained officers, even after losing 321 of the 671 officers of Southern background who resigned their commissions when the war broke out. Working on this base, Lincoln's Secretary of the Navy, Gideon Welles from Connecticut, ordered all seaworthy vessels to duty, purchased many others for conversion into war vessels and began construction on others. By December 1861 the Union fleet had over 250 vessels and 22,000 men and continued to expand during the course of the war, adding over 200 new vessels with over 1500 guns to the navy's inventory. These included 74 mighty ironclads.

The South, on the other hand, was hard pressed for naval power as the war began and was unable to add to its sea forces in any appreciable way. Although 321 naval officers in federal service 'went South' after Fort Sumter, they had virtually no vessels or crews to command. Although Southern forces had seized a few small vessels, the entire Southern naval contingent consisted of less than a dozen at hand. But Stephen R Mallory of Florida, the Confederate naval secretary, was undaunted. The former US Senator and chairman of the Senate Naval Affairs Committee, after failing in his attempts to buy ironclad steamers from England and France, ordered the construction of ironclads, floating batteries and gunboats for Southern defense and contracted for the building of swift, heavily gunned commerce raiders in England. It would take miracles to build an effective naval force in the industry-poor South, but Mallory was determined to try. He was heartened by the fact that the Confederates had seized the Pensacola naval yard (even though it was only a small repair yard) and that the important Norfolk (Gosport) naval yard had fallen to the Confederates with little difficulty with its large drydock intact, thanks to the dawdling of old Commodore Charles S McCauley. In the process the South had seized the partially burned screw frigate *Merrimac* and almost 1200 cannon, including 300 powerful Dahlgren guns. It was not enough, but it was at least a start.

Southern Commerce Raiding and Blockade Running

Faced with no chance of building a navy powerful enough openly to challenge the Union Navy in direct combat, the South turned instead to privateering, the traditional response of the weaker naval power. Privateering, or commerce raiding, could accomplish two things. It would gain some supplies for the Southern cause, but, more importantly, it would serve as a very

Below: Union ships withdraw before the Confederate ironclad _Manassas_ and fire ships in an action near the mouth of the Mississippi on 12 October 1861.

effective irritant to Northern commerce, making shipping unsafe and driving marine insurance rates up, thus undermining Northern support for the war. It might well also draw off Union naval vessels from their blockades of Southern ports. Commerce raiding, combined with blockade running and Union defeats at the hands of the Southern armies, would eventually bring victory, it was hoped, to the Southern cause.

Although Southern commerce raiders were always few in number—never more than 30 operating at any one time—some achieved great success and notoriety. The *Florida*, for example, set sail from her building ways at Liverpool in 1862 (thanks to the negligence and even connivance of the British authorities, who allowed Confederate agents to contract for ships and equipment with British builders and suppliers) and in the next two years captured 37 Northern vessels, inflicting a loss of over $3 million on the ships' owners. The *Florida* came to an inglorious end, though. Captured by Union vessels in a Brazilian port in 1864, she was taken to Norfolk, by then in Union hands. When the Brazilian Government rightly protested the taking of the ship in a neutral port, the United States agreed to return her to the South. However, she was 'accidentally' hit by an army transport in Hampton Roads and sank at her moorings when her watercocks were 'accidentally' opened by a Union naval officer. The *Florida* still rests today in the mud off Hampton, Virginia.

The most famous of all Southern privateers was the *Alabama*, also built in England in 1862. She escaped just before the arrival of British Foreign Office orders for her detention (the British finally bowing to American pressure to prevent such non-neutral acts). Sailing the seas of the world, this swift eight-gun barkentine-rigged ship with a retractable propeller enjoyed remarkable success for two years under Captain Raphael Semmes of Maryland. She met her match, however, when she issued a challenge to the USS *Kearsarge*, a steam corvette, in June 1864 off the coast of Cherbourg, France. The *Kearsarge* was heavily gunned and manned by well-trained seamen. In addition, she had an armor belt of chain and heavy planking to protect her vital engines. As the vessels steamed out to do battle on the morning of 19 June 1864, excited crowds watched the epic battle in the making from the Cherbourg waterside and the cliffs. The two powerful vessels steamed in circles, matching broadside for broadside, until the heavy and accurate gunnery of the *Kearsarge* proved too much for the famed *Alabama*. After the wounded were removed, she sank in the early afternoon and Southern commerce raiding and morale suffered a devastating blow.

The testimony at the hearings of the 'Alabama claims' at Geneva after the war

Above: **The *Merrimac* (nearest) makes a clumsy attempt to ram the *Monitor* (right).**

Right: **Farragut stands nonchalantly in the rigging of the heavily engaged *Hartford* at the Battle of Mobile Bay.**

Left: **The Confederate attack on Union forces at Memphis is driven back, 6 June 1862, opening up the Mississippi to the Union advance.**

***Above:* The CSS *Florida* sinks a Union clipper. The contemporary caption describes the *Florida* as a 'British pirate.'**

showed that 11 Southern commerce raiders built in Britain during the war had captured over 250 Northern vessels and caused a loss of over $17 million to American maritime commerce, although by 1863 the British had reversed their policy and had seized Confederacy-bound vessels including two powerful 'Laird Rams' designed to break the blockade. Impressive as these statistics appear, however, the fact remains that while the American merchant marine was sorely wounded by these Southern vessels, with many shipowners 'fleeing the flag' to foreign registry, and marine insurance rates skyrocketed, the commerce raiders never drew the blockading vessels off station or affected the war in any major way. They were an irritant and a source of Southern pride to be sure, but they did not play a significant role in the outcome of the war.

The same was true of the blockade runners. Although the Federal blockade of the Southern coast was proclaimed by May 1861, from the Virginia Capes to the Rio Grande, for the first year of the war there were few ships on station and blockade running involved little risk. But from 1862 to 1864 more ships arrived to fill out the four blockading squadrons (North Atlantic, South Atlantic, East Gulf and West Gulf), and the practice became hazardous indeed. In the final year of the war the remaining Southern ports of Mobile, Savannah, Charleston, and Wilmington, North Carolina, were added to the US Navy's list of captured ports—New Orleans having been taken in 1862—and blockade running came to a complete halt.

Yet even during the early years when successful blockade running was possible, it failed to help the Confederate cause in any appreciable way. Using the Southern ports of New Orleans, Mobile, St Augustine, Savannah, Charleston and Wilmington as bases of operation, blockade-running captains sailed to such neutral ports as Nassau, Havana and Bermuda to exchange Southern cotton for goods needed in the South. Even though the US Navy kept these neutral ports under surveillance, blockade runners were able to sneak in and out at night using local pilots for navigation and steam power for speed. The fast, shallow-draft paddle-wheelers, sometimes with telescoping funnels and painted gray, were usually able to best the Navy's blockades at both ends of their runs and carry into the Southern ports not only 'hardware' (munitions) but, significantly, silks, laces, linens, corset stays and other goods in high demand. Of the 84 steamers in the trade between 1861 and 1864, 37 were captured, 25 met with debilitating accidents and 22 continued to operate. While they operated, the blockade runners made fabulous profits for their owners and crews. Shipowners could repay the cost of their vessels by only one or two successful voyages, captains could make as much as $5000 per month, and crew members could receive $100 per month plus a $50 bonus per trip (a Confederate soldier was paid only one-tenth of this amount).

The reasons for these high profits and wages reveal the weakness of blockade running as a Southern stratagem. While

the Southern cause desperately needed iron, steel, copper, guns, ammunition, engines and medicines, more money could be made in carrying luxury items to the Southern populace than in bringing in war items for the Confederate Government—to be paid off in depreciated Confederate dollars. Salt that could be purchased by enterprising blockade runners in Nassau for $7.50 per ton could be sold at Richmond for $1700 per ton. Coffee that sold in Nassau at $240 per ton brought $5500 per ton in the Confederate capital. Wilmington, North Carolina, held weekly auctions that drew speculators from all over the South to its wharves to bid on goods brought in through the blockade. There the speculators paid premium prices for coffee, tea, fresh meats, fine cloth and corset stays. Try as it might, the Confederate Government could not stop this trade in luxury goods. While only a fraction of Southern cotton was able to reach its market, the return trips by the blockade runners were marked by venality of the worst kind. Thus the Southern war effort gained little by this increasingly dangerous but profitable trade and was forced to depend on its own marginal resources to sustain its armies in the field.

Above: **The action at Memphis. The *Van Dorn* was the only ship to escape the Union victory.**

Union Strategy of Blockade

While the commerce raiders and blockade runners produced some hope for the Confederate cause in the early stages of the war, the Federal strategy of seizing Southern ports and imposing a strict blockade gradually became effective and inexorably drew a noose around Southern imports and exports, thereby dooming the rebellion. Initially utilizing Fort Monroe in Virginia at the entrance to the Chesapeake Bay as its base of operations, the North gradually began to attack, seize and shut up the 89 harbors, ports and bays along the 3500-mile Atlantic and Gulf coastlines that marked the South's water boundaries and its sea link to the outside world. In August 1861 a joint army-navy expedition left Fort Monroe to seize Fort Clark on Hatteras Inlet and its companion installation Fort Hatteras, thereby to deny exit by Confederate vessels from Albermarle and Pamlico Sounds. After a four-day bombardment and an amphibious assault, Fort Clark fell to the Union forces. Fort Hatteras fell to the attackers three days later, and the North Carolina waters were cut off from use as an outlet to the Atlantic sea lanes. Two months later an expedition was mounted from Fort Monroe against Port Royal, South Carolina, headed by General William T Sherman and Captain Samuel F Du Pont. When the city fell to the Union forces on 7 November 1861, the blockading squadron had a secure base to use against Savannah and Charleston. Other ports were taken along the Atlantic in subsequent months so that

Below: **The CSS *Atlanta*, which surrendered to the USS *Weehawken* at Warsaw Sound in the Wilmington River, Georgia, in June 1863.**

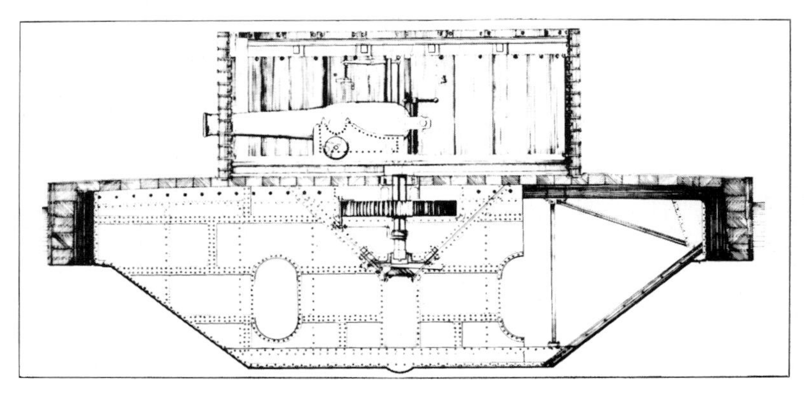

Above: **Secretary of the Confederate States Navy, Stephen R Mallory.**

by March 1862 only Savannah, Charleston and Wilmington were left on the Atlantic coast, although the major ports of Mobile and New Orleans were still open on the Gulf. An attempt to put Charleston out of action without military confrontation had failed. In December 1861 and January 1862, the Union Navy had brought 35 old hulks to Charleston (mostly old whalers) to be sunk in the harbor channel to seal it off to shipping. Towed into position in the outer harbor, the stone-ballasted vessels were sunk in place. Unfortunately for the Union cause, the old hulks disintegrated and the harbor currents cut new channels around them—thus the 'Stone Fleet' experiment proved a failure and the vital port of Charleston remained open.

But if the Union attempts at blockade showed signs of eventually strangling the South, the Confederate leaders held out high hopes for a new naval weapon that could break the Union blockade. It might also assure Southern control of Chesapeake Bay, thereby opening Richmond via the James River to the sea, hampering Union military operations in northern Virginia, and menacing the Federal capital at Washington. That new weapon was the ironclad *Virginia*.

Monitor vs *Virginia (Merrimac)*

When the Union forces abandoned the Gosport navy yard in April 1861, they left behind the scuttled 40-gun steam frigate *Merrimac*, which had been burned to the waterline. The Southern forces raised her hull and placed her in drydock where marine engineers worked to salvage her engines. By July 1861 orders had been issued to naval constructor John L Porter and Lieutenant John M Brooke to convert her into an ironclad. Accordingly, a 170-foot shed with angled sides of 45 degrees was constructed on her cut-down hull. The angled walls were of pine two feet in thickness covered by four inches of plate iron. As she neared completion in February 1862, the ship measured 257 feet in length and 57 feet in beam, drew 23 feet of water, had six smoothbore Dahlgrens and two rifled guns broadside and two rifled guns fore and aft. She could make six knots. Captain Franklin Buchanan, founder of the Naval Academy and an experienced officer, was given command of the rechristened CSS *Virginia* and drew a crew from army and navy ranks. The new ironclad had only to be tried in combat.

Early on the morning of 8 March 1862, the *Virginia* made her way down the Elizabeth River from Gosport and entered

Top: **The *Monitor* in July 1862 showing the dented turret from the battle with *Merrimac*.**
Above: **Midships section through the *Monitor*'s twin turret showing the raft construction.**

Hampton Roads. On blockade duty there were numerous Union vessels: the 50-gun frigate *Congress*, the 50-gun *St Lawrence* and the 24-gun sloop *Cumberland*, backed up by the steam frigates *Roanoke* and *Minnesota*, each of 46 guns. As the *Virginia* moved into range by early afternoon, the Union vessels found that their broadsides only bounced off the Confederate ironclad, and the land batteries along the shore from Newport News Point to Hampton, plus the guns of Fort Monroe and Fort Wool nearby, could do no better. The *Virginia* moved in, broadsided the wooden *Congress* and *Cumberland*, rammed the hapless *Cumberland* and slowly destroyed the resisting Union vessels under merciless fire. The *Roanoke* and *St Lawrence* never got into position, and the *Minnesota* was never in range. Finally the lowering tide forced the victorious ironclad back to base to continue the one-sided fight the next day. But as the sun rose the next day over Hampton Roads, a new combatant had entered the field of battle on the Union side. The second phase of the Battle of Hampton Roads was about to begin.

Sitting under the protective guns of Fort Monroe on that clear Sunday morning of 9 March 1862 was the tiny *Monitor*. Knowing of the Confederate plans for the *Merrimac* from espionage reports and even from Southern newspaper accounts, the Federal Government had belatedly begun work on its own iron vessel. John Ericsson drew the plans as building went along in the Greenspoint shipyard on Long Island, and the diminutive vessel was completed in only 100 days. It was 172 feet in length and 41 feet in beam, drawing only 10 feet of water. On its flat deck almost at water's edge was a revolving turret nine feet high and twenty feet in diameter, with openings for two retractable 11-inch Dahlgrens. Steam powered, the small iron vessel left New York City on 6 March under the command of Captain John L Worden with a crew of 58 men. Although it nearly foundered in heavy seas on its trip south, the *Monitor* arrived at dusk on 8 March as the day's battle was ending, and Captain Worden was ordered to engage the *Virginia* the next day if she appeared.

As the two ironclad vessels approached one another that mild Sunday morning to begin the battle, they soon found that neither could gain the advantage. The *Monitor* was difficult to hit, and when a shot did strike her turret it just bounced off. Likewise, the *Virginia* suffered no damage as shots merely glanced off her sloping sides. After a prolonged exchange of fire, each tried to ram the other, but Worden's *Monitor* missed the *Virginia*'s vulnerable propellers, and the *Virginia* (now under Lieutenant Catesby ap Roger Jones, replacing Captain Buchanan who had been wounded the day before) rammed the *Monitor* only to see her slip out from underneath her thrusts. Finally both vessels withdrew, each claiming victory. The *Virginia* had clearly won the battle on 8 March, but the battle of 9 March was at best a draw. Nevertheless, the *Monitor* had prevented the destruction of the remainder of the blockading fleet and her presence precluded any chance of the Confederates moving up Chesapeake Bay. She must be credited with a strategic victory despite the tactical draw.

In the weeks that followed, the *Monitor* refused to be drawn into a second round with the *Virginia* and kept her station under the guns of Fort Monroe as guardian of the Chesapeake. The *Virginia*, on the other hand, defended the James River and the water approaches to Richmond until Union forces descended on Norfolk as part of the Peninsula Campaign. To prevent her capture, she was scuttled in the lower James on 11 May 1862, never to be recovered. At the end of the year the

Above: **The unsuccessful Union attack on Fort Sumter, 7 April 1863. Five ships were put out of action including the flagship *Keokuk*.**
Below: **S F du Pont, the previously highly successful commander of the South Atlantic blockading squadron, was relieved after the failure at Fort Sumter.**

Above: Officers of the USS *Kearsarge* photographed at Cherbourg in June 1864. Captain Winslow is third from left.
Left: One of the *Kearsarge*'s 11-inch Dahlgren smooth-bore guns seen on the same occasion as the picture above.
Below: Ship's crew of the USS *Choctaw*.

Monitor foundered in a storm off Cape Hatteras as she was being towed to Charleston by the steamer *Rhode Island* to take part in operations there. (She has recently been discovered and efforts are being made to preserve her as an underwater historical site if she cannot be rescued from her watery grave.)

Although both the vessels that had broken new ground at the Battle of Hampton Roads were lost soon thereafter, they played a major role in the evolution of modern navies. They introduced into naval architecture the revolving turret, protective armor plate and the protective deck, rifled guns and all-heavy-gun vessels. They proved that while iron might not be able to beat iron, iron could clearly beat wood in naval warship construction. Ironclads went on to play a significant role in naval construction for the duration of the war and, in the long run, iron (and then steel) vessels would replace the 'wooden walls' of the world's traditional navies. Iron plus steam would spell the eventual end of the old sailing navy. Technology was the ultimate winner of the Battle of Hampton Roads.

Fall of the Southern Ports

Meanwhile Northern attempts to close Southern ports by capture and blockade continued apace. Even as the ironclads were dueling in Virginia waters, a Union fleet was assembling off New Orleans, preparing to capture that vital Southern port at the mouth of the Mississippi. It was built around Flag Officer David G Farragut's flagship, the screw sloop USS *Hartford*. Located at the mouth of the river were Forts St Philip and Jackson, 90 miles south of New Orleans. These would have to be taken first. When mortar bombardments of the forts failed to reduce them, Farragut determined to run by them at night, leaving them isolated and vulnerable. Accordingly, after two gunboats had broken a boom of logs and chains stretched across the river, Farragut made his move past the forts on the night of 24 April 1862. His large ships having been dragged over the mud bars at the mouth of the river, the squadron proceeded in line-ahead fashion to run the gauntlet of Confederate guns. The 17 Union naval vessels had their precious steam engines protected against shot with hay and planking, and the ships suffered no appreciable damage. Since army troops had meanwhile been transported via the bayous to a point five miles above the forts, Forts St Philip and Jackson were besieged and neutralized. New Orleans itself was then easily taken by 1 May, when the troops of General Benjamin F Butler garrisoned the town. Believing that defense of New Orleans was unnecessary, since Union forces could not pass the forts, Richmond had made no further provisions for defending the most important port of the Confederacy.

The second great Gulf port city, Mobile, Alabama, fell to the Union Navy in August 1864. Again the naval commander was David Farragut. In his flotilla were four ironclads of the *Monitor* type and 14 wooden vessels. Mobile Bay was guarded by the Confederate ironclad *Tennessee*, three wooden paddlesteamers and 180 'torpedoes,' or floating kegs filled with gunpowder. Forts Morgan and Gaines also guarded the bay.

On 5 August 1864 Farragut, standing high in the rigging of the *Hartford* to direct the battle, ordered his ships into action to force their way into the bay. When the steam sloop *Brooklyn* came to a halt on seeing the floating mines, Farragut called out, 'Damn the torpedoes. Go ahead!' and the invading force pressed on. Although the ironclad *Tecumseh* was destroyed by one of the mines, the other vessels proceeded and within three hours had passed the forts and were anchored in Mobile Bay. The Confederate ironclad *Tennessee*, captained by Franklin Buchanan, who had commanded the *Virginia* on the first day of the Battle of Hampton Roads, approached to do battle. It was disabled after an hour of fierce fighting, and Union control of the bay was complete. By 23 August the forts had been bombed into submission by Union warships and land batteries, and Mobile was taken out of the war.

Savannah fell to a combined Union naval-army force three months later. The joint expedition was headed by General William T Sherman and Admiral John A Dahlgren. When Sherman's forces captured Fort McAllister guarding the sea approaches to the city on 13 December 1864, it was obvious that Savannah would fall to the Union forces. Complete surrender of the Georgia port city was attained by Christmas. Even while the siege of Savannah was taking place to the south, joint army-navy operations had begun against Wilmington, North Carolina. Wilmington was very important to both sides because of its direct railroad connection with Richmond. Leading the naval squadron was the fiery Admiral David Dixon Porter. In December an initial land attack on Fort Fisher guarding the harbor failed, because the army could not make good its attacks on the doughty fortress; the next month Porter carried out an intense three-day bombardment of the fort followed by a two-pronged land attack. While the 2000 Federal sailors and marines on the east side of the island failed to breach the walls and fled in panic, the action there drew most of the defenders to that side of the fortress, allowing the soldiers to breach the west wall and compel surrender. Wilmington was finished as a Southern port, leaving only Charleston open for the Confederate cause.

By February 1865 it was Charleston's turn to fall under the intense pressure of Union Army-Navy power (an aborted attempt had been made to take the city by the navy alone in 1863). After a sustained naval-battery bombardment against Fort Moultrie on Sullivan's Island on 17 February 1865, landing parties found it deserted. Land operations by the army were gradually successful, and the Union troops first broached the defensive lines around the city and then took Fort Johnson and

Above: **Rear Admiral David Glasgow Farragut photographed in 1863.**

Above: **The Union fleet forges on relentlessly during the Battle of Mobile Bay.**

finally Fort Sumter. The fall of this fortress where hostilities had begun four bloody years before was more than symbolic. When Charleston fell, the South had lost its last useful port. It was sealed off completely from the sea and from outside help. Successful Union Army offenses in Virginia during these months, and General Sherman's slashing march to the sea, ensured that the south could not resist much longer. The Anaconda Plan and the piecemealing of the South by Union armies had worked.

Ironclads on the Western Waters, 1861–62

In the meantime the Union armies' successes on the battlefield, which ultimately brought the Confederates to their knees in 1865, had been aided in many ways by naval power. The Mississippi River and its major tributaries were crucial waterways both to Southern resistance and to Northern offensive operations. Lincoln called the Mississippi 'the backbone of the Rebellion' and was determined to seize it. Accordingly, Union strategy on the inland waters called for working down the river from Cincinnati and Cairo, Illinois, and up the river from the Gulf of Mexico to snap the backbone of the South.

A squadron under Flag Officer Andrew Foote was assembled in November 1861 at Cairo—but under the authority of the War Department, not the navy, since this was to be a land operation and the ships of the squadron were to assist the army. It consisted originally of eight new ironclad gunboats 175 feet in length and drawing only six feet of water for riverine use. Mounting 13 guns, and with bows, machinery and paddlewheels protected by two-and-a-half-inch iron plating, the gunboats, named for cities along the Ohio and Mississippi Rivers, were expected to play a vital role in assisting the Union armies as they penetrated the South.

The first use of gunboats to support the Northern armies came at Forts Henry and Donelson, only twelve miles apart on the Tennessee and Cumberland Rivers. Each had been designed to halt penetration upstream into Tennessee and the middle South. In January 1862 General Henry W Halleck, in command in the West, ordered Flag Officer Foote to attack Fort Henry on the Tennessee with his gunboats while General Ulysses S Grant and his troops cut it off from the rear. The joint attack took place on 6 February and was successful, but the Confederate commander had meanwhile removed his troops to Fort Donelson. Nevertheless, the Union gunboats chased the protecting Confederate gunboats all the way up the Tennessee to Florence, Alabama, capturing three steamers in the process and forcing the Confederates to burn six more. The combined army-navy attack on Fort Donelson on the Cumberland eight days later was also successful, the Confederates being forced to surrender over 12,000 troops, but Halleck would not permit Foote's gunboats to proceed upriver against Nashville. Consequently, the Union lost a splendid opportunity to seize that unprotected vital rail center. When Halleck changed his mind two days later, Foote was back in Cairo and the chance to take Nashville was gone. Nevertheless, the geographic heart of the South had been penetrated, and the land war switched to its rivers for the next year.

Meanwhile, joint army-navy operations continued on the Mississippi. In March 1862 naval gunboats played a key role in taking Island Number 10 near the Kentucky-Tennessee border. The South had made this tenth island on the Mississippi below the mouth of the Ohio a virtually impregnable bastion of defense. Located on the upper part of a double hairpin turn, the island had a low fortress with five artillery batteries. This fortress was supported by five batteries on the Tennessee side of the river plus a floating battery. Well dug in, the Confederates resisted for two weeks and thereby kept General John Pope's Union Army on the west side of the river. Finally, in early April 1862, two of Foote's gunboats, the *Carondelet* and the *Pittsburg*, ran the gauntlet through the Confederate batteries, got behind the fortress and silenced the Southern guns, allowing Pope to cross with his troops. The capture of Island Number 10, one of the strongest Confederate fortifications, took place at the same time the Federals beat off a spirited counterattack at Shiloh, Tennessee, with the help of two wooden steamers

and began a move toward the vital rail center at Corinth, Mississippi. The water-land road to gaining the Mississippi and adjoining lands to the east was opening, but many months of hard warfare remained before the river and her eastern shore-lands fell to Union forces.

Two months later the Union Army-Navy forces took Fort Pillow, halfway between Island Number 10 and Memphis, but only after a fierce gunboat ram attack by the Confederates on the Union gunboat squadron had been beaten off and after the Confederates had abandoned the site—Union forces had taken Corinth, making the fort untenable. The Union forces then moved downriver to Memphis.

On 4 June 1862 one of the most spectacular battles of the river war took place before the city. The Union ironclads were now under the command of Flag Officer Charles Davis (Foote had been wounded at Fort Donelson and was relieved of command, never to return to action). They were aided by an Army Ram Fleet under Colonel Charles Ellet. The Ram Fleet consisted of steamboats converted to ramming vessels, with the ram running from bow to stern for greater strength. In the colorful battle before the enthralled citizens of Memphis, the Confederate gunboat fleet lost three vessels by fire or ramming. The remaining gunboats fled downriver. The defenseless city was forced to surrender, and Union gunboats controlled the Mississippi except for the great citadel at Vicksburg, Mississippi. Union naval vessels controlled the upper and middle river and convoyed steamers with troops and supplies along its waters. They also held New Orleans and the lower Mississippi, but as long as Vicksburg was in Confederate hands the South was not cut in two and could continue to resist Northern encroachments on its territories.

Above: **The twin-turret monitor USS *Monadnock*.**

Right: **Rear Admiral David Porter, highly successful commander of the Union Mississippi Squadron in the Vicksburg campaign.**

Vicksburg and Victory

Vicksburg was located on a high bluff on the eastern side of the Mississippi, just below a hairpin turn. With the winding, entangling Yazoo to the north and a mass of impenetrable bayou rivers to the west, it was a source of unending frustration for Grant, his generals and his troops. Beginning in November 1862, the Union

Below: **The wooden hull of an ironclad is burned on the stocks as the Confederates abandon Savannah, 21 December 1864.**

Above: **The USS *Malvern*, flagship of the North Atlantic blockading squadron, in 1865.**

forces tried three times to cut channels through the watery bayous across the river to get south of the city. Each time they failed. One attempt by Union gunboats to sail down the swollen Yazoo to the solid ground north of Vicksburg was also beaten back. Finally, Grant decided to march his men along the western shore of the river to well below Vicksburg, but this meant that the Federal gunboats would have to run the fierce barrage of Confederate batteries high above them to get below the city and protect the troops as they crossed back to the eastern shores.

The daring maneuver, led by Rear Admiral David Dixon Porter, was carried out on the night of 16 April 1863. A flotilla of nine gunboats, one ram and three steam transports, with coal barges lashed to their sides and wet hay stacked around their boilers, made the dangerous run past the guns of Vicksburg. Despite the hail of artillery raining down upon them, the squadron steamed through, losing only one steamer in the process. On 22 April the maneuver was repeated, this time with six steamers loaded with supplies, and again only one vessel was lost. These courageous moves allowed Grant to land south of Vicksburg and then to put it under siege, after taking the capital city of Jackson to the east and beating off the Confederates at Champion's Hill as the Union forces moved back west. The merciless siege placed both the Confederate troops of General John Pemberton and the civilian population under prolonged and relentless artillery fire from army units on land and naval units below the city. Vicksburg finally fell on 4 July 1863—one day after the great Union victory at Gettysburg, Pennsylvania—with 31,000 men, 172 cannons and 60,000 rifles surrendered to the Union forces. Four days later Port Hudson, south of Vicksburg, also fell, and Abraham Lincoln proclaimed that 'The Father of Waters goes again unvexed to the sea.'

General Grant gave full credit to the naval forces for his incredible victory. The Mississippi River was now in Union hands. The South had been cut in two. Its western states would gradually die in isolation,

Below: **The Confederate blockade runner *Lord Clyde* was captured and renamed first USS *Advance* and later USS *Frolic*.**

their precious men and supplies being denied to the Confederate cause. Union land forces could now move to sunder the remaining Southern states, while bringing their crushing weight down upon General Robert E Lee's Army of the Potomac. This would take almost two years, but the Confederate foundation had been broken. The dual Union strategy of blockading the Confederate coastline and isolating the embattled Southern states was working ever more effectively. It was now only a matter of time. The end came in April 1865 when General Lee, after leading the Southern forces in splendid resistance to the advancing armies of U S Grant in the east, surrendered at Appomattox Court House in Virginia. The Civil War was over.

The US Navy had amassed a sterling record during the four-year conflict. Expanding its number of vessels to 671, its officer corps to 9000 men and its enlisted ranks to 51,000, it had captured or destroyed over 1500 Southern vessels of all types. It had co-operated with the massive Northern land armies on both the seacoasts and the inland waters, and it had clamped an effective blockade on the South that had cut her off from outside help and left her to her own inadequate resources. In the process, the Navy had learned valuable lessons: that unprotected wooden vessels were now obsolete against ironclads, that passive defense of harbors was completely inadequate in modern warfare, that a successful blockade could be imposed only by clear command of the seas, that steam was beginning its conquest over sail power and that modern navies could no longer be created in a short time given the demands of modern technology. The Civil War triumphs of the US Navy had catapulted her into becoming a major national defense force. The question was whether or not she could maintain that eminence in the changed conditions in the aftermath of the war.

Above: **USS *Camanche* ready for launch at San Francisco in November 1864.**

Below: The battlecruiser *Guam* at sea toward the end of World War II.

PART II

A NAVAL POWER BORN TO GLORY

THE NATION BUILDS A NAVY

In 1865, at the end of the Civil War, the US Navy had over 700 ships in its inventory, including 65 ironclads; by 1880 it had only 48 capable of firing a gun and stood twelfth in the world in naval power—behind Chile and China. The US Navy had been effectively scuttled in fifteen years.

The American people decided after Appomattox that a sizable navy was simply too expensive. The nation was deeply in debt due to the war and was embroiled in the massive problems of reconstructing the South. These matters—plus labor strife, farmer agitation and political corruption—were perceived as more important than foreign affairs, and, besides, any potential enemies were 3000 miles across the ocean. Peace seemed inevitable, or at least there were no war clouds on the horizon. If peace was assured and money was tight, the solution was obvious: get rid of 'useless' warships. A navy could always be re-created quickly if the need arose, they argued, overlooking the fact that modern naval and weapon technology had made such ideas obsolete.

The Navy's 'Dark Ages'

Gideon Welles continued as navy secretary and presided over the dismantling of the fleet. A total of 400 ships of the blockading fleet had been broken up or sold off within nine months of the end of the fighting. The mighty ironclads were moored and left to rot, while other river craft were disposed of. By the time Welles left office in 1869, only 52 warships were still in commission. And Adolph E Borie and George M Robeson, President Grant's appointees as navy secretaries, left the job of running the service largely to Vice-Admiral David Dixon Porter, who turned his considerable power against existing research and development programs. Monitors (the low-freeboard turreted gunships developed during the war on the design of Ericsson's *Monitor*) and sailing cruisers would serve the navy well. Modern steam-powered vessels would not, as symbolized by the dismissal of chief engineer Benjamin F Isherwood, the father of the Civil War steam navy, in 1869.

This resistance to steam power on the part of the flag admirals in the navy's 'dark ages' (1865 to 1882) is often criticized as an example of pure reactionism, yet it is understandable in view of the times and their current state of technology. For example, the steam-powered sloop of war USS *Wampanoag* was an Isherwood-created vessel that set a world steam speed record of 17.7 knots in 1868. But it was rejected for naval use nonetheless by a special naval board on steam machinery under Rear Admiral Louis Goldsborough in 1869, because it was a coal burner. Soon thereafter it was removed from the active list and sold.

But this action and other examples of the rejection of steam power did not represent mere stupidity or crass defense of a sailing navy on the part of the admirals. Whatever their attachments to a sailing navy, the admirals were also aware that in the case of the *Wampanoag* her steam plant constituted one-third of her total weight, took up almost half her total length below decks and burned over six tons of coal per

hour at top speed. The admirals knew that while commercial vessels could afford to devote a great amount of weight and space to machinery and coal, a fighting ship needed that valuable space for armament and ammunition, to say nothing of crew's quarters, ship's stores and other requirements. Steam power and greater speed could be a boon to a commercial vessel, but might well leave a ship of war sadly deficient in its primary function. Furthermore, the naval decision-makers during this period worried about the fact that spare parts for steam machinery could not be found in most areas of the world in which the ship might sail and could not be fabricated upon the ships themselves. And what of coal supply? Coal stations were not available on the ocean lanes of the world at this time, nor would they be for a number of years. And coal was expensive, an important consideration in times of declining budgets approved by Congress. Furthermore, naval and steam engineering was far from an exact science in these years, and many 'experts' testified that steam had many shortcomings.

Added to these technical and professional factors was the overriding fact that the American people saw little need for any sizable navy, much less a more expensive steam navy, and this attitude was reflected by their representatives in Washington. Domestic problems, expansion to the West and economic hard times took priority over naval concerns in the minds of the people. Only when American economic expansion led to worldwide investments and interests would the nation awaken to its global destiny and support a strong navy again as a necessary means of achieving that destiny. Thus, while Europe's navies turned toward iron, steel, steam and high-technology ordnance, the American Navy stuck mainly to wood, sail and existing gunnery to carry out its limited functions and awaited new leadership backed by new attitudes that would pull it out of the doldrums.

Showing the Flag and Other Duties

During this period of quiescence, however, the now-reduced navy was busy 'showing the flag' and carrying out other important national duties in all parts of the world. In 1866 the monitors built for Civil War service were sent on extended cruises to show the flag. The *Miantonomah* successfully crossed the Atlantic to visit various European ports, ending up in Russia where an attempt was made to sell her to Czar Alexander II for his imperial fleet. The *Monadnock*, after rounding Cape Horn and visiting a number of South American ports, joined the Asiatic fleet. In 1871 Rear Admiral John Rodgers took the Asiatic fleet into 'forbidden' Korean waters to investigate the disappearance of American merchant crews and to attempt to make a treaty of friendship. His efforts came to nothing, however, as the Koreans fired on his squadron while he was achored in the Salee River near Seoul. Rodgers answered with a 600-man landing party of marines and sailors who attacked the offending forts. In this warlike atmosphere, negotiations were impossible (and a typhoon was approaching), so Rodgers sailed away. Only in 1881, a decade later, was a trade treaty agreed upon and the safety of American crews assured when Commodore Robert W Shufelt returned to the 'Hermit Kingdom.'

The only important warlike action taken by the Navy occurred in 1873–74 in what has come to be known as the '*Virginius*

Above: **Old salts yarning aboard the *Enterprise circa* 1887.**

Left: **The USS *Jeannette* sinking after being crushed in the Arctic Ice in June 1881.**
Right: **Officers of the USS *Constellation* pose with welcoming officials during a visit to Cork, Ireland, in 1880.**

Right: **Negotiations during the Korean Expedition in 1871. F Low, minister to China (right).** ***Bottom:*** **Boats from the USS *Tennessee* take a landing party ashore at Panama in April 1885 to protect American property following disturbances.**

affair.' The *Virginius* was an American vessel flying the American flag that was engaged in carrying 'filibustering' mercenaries into Cuba to fight the Spanish authorities there. Spotted by a Spanish cruiser, the *Tornado*, in Cuban waters, the *Virginius* fled with the Spanish vessel in hot pursuit, only to be captured off Jamaica. The Spanish authorities in Santiago, rightly suspecting that the mercenaries had been on their way to Cuba to aid the revolutionaries and that the ship was actually Cuban-owned with false papers, proceeded to have the captain, two members of the crew and 50 passengers (30 of whom were probably Americans) tried and then executed by a firing squad. As the nation reacted in rage to this 'dishonor to the flag,' the navy was ordered to assemble off Key West to fight if necessary—although the mission was virtually impossible, since its ships were armed with smoothbore cannon good only in a close fight and their top speed was only 4.5 knots. The situation was calmed only when the commander of the USS *Wyoming* left Colon in Panama and sailed into Santiago to protest the Spanish Government's actions. Although he took this action strictly on his own initiative, the *Wyoming* was soon backed up by the *Juniata* and the *Kansas*. This ended the threat of more executions and quieted events sufficiently so that diplomacy could take over. The Spanish Government paid an indemnity, even though it proved the origin and intent of the ship and passengers. The affair was ended—to the navy's credit—and war talk faded.

Providing a lighter touch during these years was the saga of the gunboat *Wateree*. While anchored in the harbor at Arica, Peru, in 1868, the vessel found herself sitting on the harbor floor as a giant tidal wave was preceded by a rush of all the water out of the harbor. Looking up from their embarrassing position, the crew of the *Wateree* was terrified to see a giant wall of green water rushing toward them. The tidal wave picked up the small vessel and deposited it high and dry on land 47

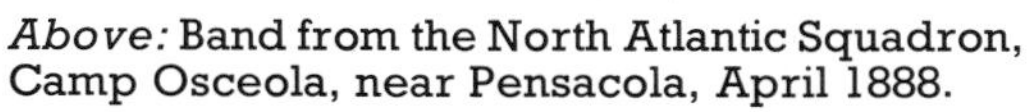
Above: **Band from the North Atlantic Squadron, Camp Osceola, near Pensacola, April 1888.**

feet above the harbor. Although the crew successfully defended the gunboat against attack by local Indians, they were unsuccessful in their attempts to launch her. The enterprising captain, therefore, gave up and sold the *Wateree* to a local businessman who converted the vessel into a hotel while the crew found a way home.

On a weightier note, the navy attempted serious negotiations during this period to gain the islands of Samoa in the Pacific Polynesian group for the United States. Samoa had first been claimed for the nation by Lieutenant Charles Wilkes in 1839 during his memorable voyage of exploration of the Pacific and Antarctica, and the harbor of Pago Pago had been ceded by treaty to the United States in 1873, but the Senate took no action on the treaty. Despite these claims, the excellent harbor was also coveted by the British and the Germans, and all three powers claimed sovereignty and had commercial treaties with the local rulers, the United States gaining hers in 1878. By the late 1880s the disputed ownership had resulted in American, British and German warships being sent to Samoa to bolster their nations' claims. In March 1889 a hurricane struck the islands and the anchorage at Apia, wrecking three German ships and three American cruisers. Great as the loss was, naval presence in Samoa assured American rights; when an agreement was forthcoming later in the year and a joint protectorate was set up over the islands, the nation received valuable Pago Pago and surrounding territories as a coaling station on the sea lane to Australia and later developed it into an important naval base. Thus a naval-diplomatic move in the 1870s bore rich fruit in the decades that followed.

Naval Renaissance

By the early 1880s, certain fundamental economic and perceptual changes mandated a more favorable political climate that created a 'New Navy.' By this time the American economy was growing to full industrial and commercial maturity. American businessmen, solidly backed by the public, were looking beyond the seas for new markets and new sources of foodstuffs and raw materials. They saw no reason why the dynamic American economic expansion should stop at the water's edge. New markets in new lands would lead to greater prosperity and prestige. And, they were coming to realize, new and improved foreign trade meant that the nation needed a navy.

The first naval secretary to respond to

the new economic imperatives was William H Hunt, who served from 1881 to 1882. In his brief tenure, Hunt got things moving by creating a naval board under Admiral John Rodgers to consider the navy's needs and make recommendations on ship types and numbers. Although Congress cut the recommendation severely, it did authorize the construction of three steel cruisers (the *Atlanta*, *Boston* and *Chicago*) and a dispatch boat (the *Dolphin*) in 1883, the famous 'ABCDs' which constituted the first ships of the New Navy. Hunt's work was continued by William E Chandler, his successor, often called the 'Father of the New Navy' for his continued support of the ABCD construction and for fostering the establishment of the Naval War College on Coaster's Harbor Island in Newport, Rhode Island. The War College,

Left: **Officers' uniforms *circa* 1899. From left: Lt JG, Lt and Capt Marines, Chief Engineer, Rear Adm, Commander and Surgeon.**
Below: **USS *Chicago* seen during the New York Naval Review 1889.**

Right: **Enlisted men's uniforms including steward (left) and master at arms, with rifle.**

under Rear Admiral Stephen B Luce, was the beginning of an intellectual renaissance in naval circles, not only because it attracted aspiring officers to learn naval strategy, tactics and logistics in a systematic and demanding environment, but also because Luce brought Captain Alfred Thayer Mahan to the staff.

Mahan, whose father, Major Dennis Hart Mahan, was long a dominant figure in the classrooms of the United States Military Academy at West Point, displayed brilliant insights into naval affairs. He tied them to theories of national power and greatness in his lectures on sea power and history developed over the years at Newport. These ideas were eventually brought to public attention in 1890 with the publication of Mahan's epic *The Influence of Sea Power upon History, 1660–1782*, a book which demonstrated historically his belief that a nation could become great and maintain her strength only if she had sea power to expand and protect her vital economic interests. Mahan's words were tantamount to Holy Writ to the students who sat before him. He influenced not only generations of naval and civilian leaders in the United States, but also military and political leaders of all the major nations. In creating the Naval War College and placing it under Admiral Luce, Secretary Chandler had built more than he ever dreamed.

Chandler's successor, William C Whitney, who served from 1885 to 1889, extended Chandler's work by authorizing 30 ships superior in design, armament, ordnance and speed to any that had preceded them. Included were the two heavy-armored cruisers (or second-class battleships) *Maine* and *Texas* authorized in 1886. Each displaced 6000 tons. Another ship,

Right: **(L to R) *Amphitrite*, *Puritan*, *Montgomery* and *Ericsson* in 1893.**

Below: **The USS *Palos* tows landing barges during the Korean Expedition, 10 June 1871.**

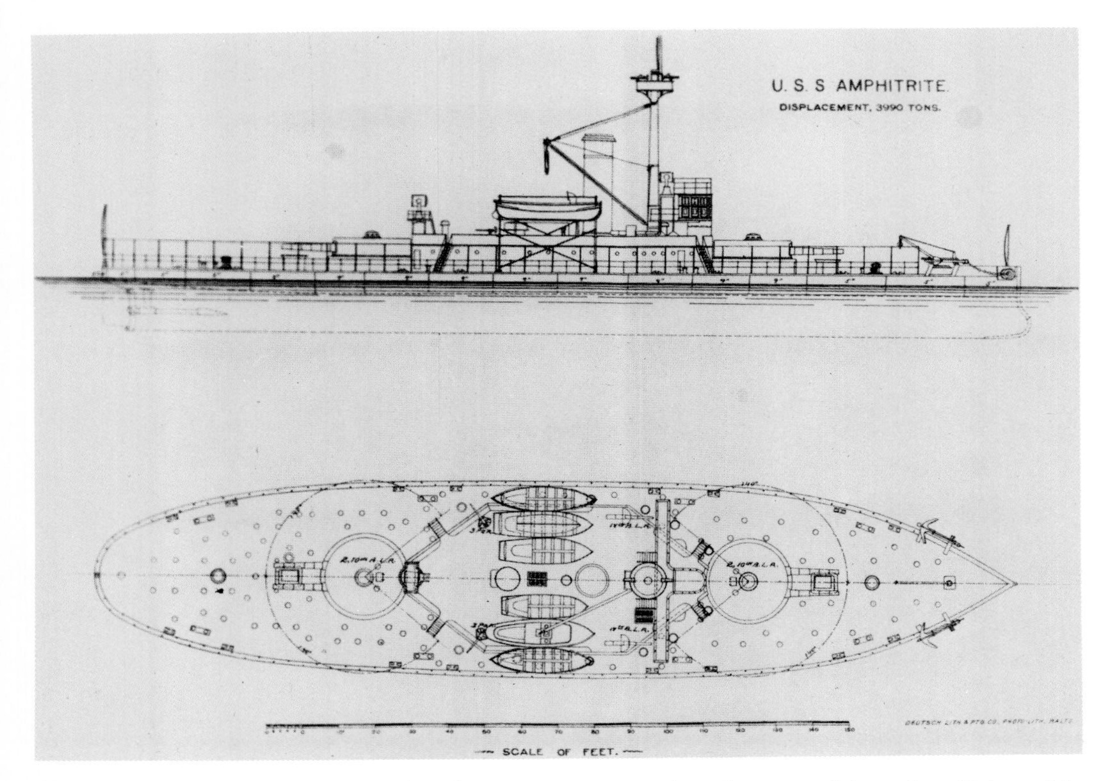

Above: **Plans of the *Amphitrite*, already obsolete when she came into service in the early 1890s.**

the cruiser *Charleston*, authorized in 1885, was the first American naval vessel to sport no sails. Whitney's work, in turn, was extended by Benjamin F Tracy, 1889–93, who was a devotee of Mahan and believed with him that the nation's shores could best be defended by creating a force of capital ships to meet any enemy far at sea. These mighty vessels could also protect American commerce on the sea lanes of the world. To Tracy, this meant armored battleships to destroy enemy fleets and carry the fight to their shores. Even with the help of influential friends in both political parties, Tracy was unable to build two great fleets, as he had hoped (for the Atlantic and the Pacific). But he did gain Congressional authorization for three 10,000-ton armored 'coastal battleships,' the *Oregon*, *Indiana* and *Massachusetts*, followed by the larger and more heavily gunned 11,400-ton *Iowa*. Tracy also obtained authorization for three armored cruisers of 7000 to 9000 tons.

Although the Panic of 1893 temporarily wreaked havoc on naval expansion, Hilary A Herbert, naval secretary from 1893 to 1897, continued the push for an even larger navy. In 1895 Congress authorized the construction of two *Kearsarge*-class battleships of 11,500 tons (the *Kearsarge* and the *Kentucky*) and the following year authorized the building of three more battleships of the *Illinois* class (the *Illinois*, the *Alabama* and the *Wisconsin*). Thus through good times and bad, under Democratic and Republican Administrations, the new navy continued to grow. By the mid-1890s the nation had awakened to its economic interests and saw the Navy as a vital instrument in extending itself upward and outward into the affairs of the world. No longer did European nations have a monopoly on steel-hulled, heavily armored, speedy steam vessels with breech-loading rifled guns and more efficient powders. The United States had a ranking navy superior to most, and looked for the day it would stand equal to Britain's great Royal Navy. Farm boys and city lads left their farms, small towns and great cities to 'join up' and be part of America's expanding naval presence. Shipyards buzzed with the work of creating the behemoths of the seas and their smaller companion vessels that carried American colors to the four corners of the globe. America had 'navy fever' and a pride in her new-found status.

War with Spain

The new navy would get the chance to prove its mettle in the Spanish-American war of 1898. Trouble had long been brewing on the island of Cuba in the Caribbean. For decades the Cubans had been actively resisting their Spanish overlords. Cuba and Puerto Rico were the last New World possessions of the once-great Spanish Empire, an empire that had been steadily slipping from the control of the mother country as one colony after another rose in revolution, beginning in the 1820s. Spain was as determined to retain Cuba as the Cuban people were to gain their independence. But to gain their freedom against a stronger mother country, Cuba needed help, a 'big brother' to equal or surpass Spanish strength. That friend could be the nearby United States, which had declared its right to oversee Latin American affairs as early as 1823 in the Monroe Doctrine. The trick for the Cuban revolutionaries was to get the Americans interested, then involved, in their cause.

This they attempted to do by operating a propaganda headquarters out of New York City where they sold 'Cuban bonds' and generally labored hard to keep the American public aware of the troubles in their homeland. They were aided by the stringent measures that Spanish authorities inflicted on the Cuban people. These were loudly trumpeted by the American newspapers, as they tried to surpass one another in sensationalistic stories of Spanish atrocities. The Spanish military commander in Cuba, General Valeriano Weyler, became well known in American homes under such unfortunate names as 'Butcher Weyler,' 'the human hyena' and 'the mad dog of Spain.'

President Grover Cleveland resisted public pressure and Congressional attempts to get the nation involved in the Cuban revolution, although he warned

Right: **Admiral George Dewey, whose victory at Manila Bay was achieved at the cost of only eight American wounded.**
Below: **The wreck of the *Maine*.**

the Spanish Government that the United States could not tolerate such disturbing events so close to its shores. His successor, William McKinley, a Republican, followed the same policy of avoiding war, but was soon overcome by events. On 9 February 1898 a letter was released to the American press by the Cuban revolutionary 'junta' operating in the United States. Written by Dupey de Lome, the Spanish Minister in Washington, to an editor friend in Cuba, it had been stolen from the post office in Havana and turned over to the junta. The letter contained many slurs against President McKinley and immediately caused a great public outcry, which did not subside even when de Lome was immediately recalled.

One week later, on 15 February 1898, with public opinion still wrathful over the de Lome letter, the USS *Maine*, reclassified as a second-class battleship after launching, was rocked by a terrific explosion while anchored in the harbor at Havana. Some 260 of the 350 men aboard were killed. Captain Charles Sigsbee of the *Maine* stated that the explosion could have been internal or external and urged caution until a complete investigation could be launched. A Spanish board of inquiry determined that from the bent hull plating it was clear that the explosion had been internal. An American naval board of inquiry concluded that the cause of the explosion was probably external, specifically a 'submarine mine' clandestinely fastened to the hull of the vessel, but they could not determine who might have done the deed. This made little difference to the American public, since they soon became convinced from American newspaper accounts that the Spanish were the culprits. The cry 'Remember the *Maine*!' rumbled across the country and into the halls of Congress.

Still William McKinley refused to panic or to urge war, because Spain was willing to make some reforms in Cuba. But finally he collapsed under the frenzied call for war and on 9 April 1898, 'in the name of humanity,' recommended American intervention in the troubled situation. Con-

gress was only too happy to comply and passed a resolution declaring Cuba to be free (but with an amendment by Senator Henry Teller that the United States had no intention of taking Cuba as its own) and authorizing the Commander in Chief to use the armed forces to make Cuba's freedom a reality. When the navy immediately set up a blockade around the island, Spain declared war on the United States; the United States reciprocated the next day, 25 April 1898. The Spanish-American War, the 'splendid little war,' was on.

Having been allocated $30 million by Congress in the crisis, the navy began construction on three battleships plus numerous torpedo boats and torpedo boat destroyers. In short order it also purchased or chartered 50 steamers to be used as transports (about one-half were of foreign registry, a sad commentary on the state of the US merchant marine) and purchased or chartered a number of fast liners to be armed and converted into scouts and auxiliary cruisers. Crewing for the expanding navy was no problem, as naval militia from various states soon stepped forward.

Above: **Examining the wreck of the *Maine*.**
Below: **The battleship *Oregon* rounding the Horn en route to join the fleet at Santiago.**

The initial steps taken by the navy were for defensive purposes. A 'flying squadron' was assembled in Hampton Roads under Commodore Winfield S Schley. Its job was to protect the East Coast from Spanish attack, since it was known that Spanish Admiral Pascual Cervera had left the Cape Verde Islands on 29 April although his destination was unknown. Fearing a bombardment of seaboard cities, many wealthy Americans sent their valuables inland for safety, and all along the coast cities demanded naval protection.

In the meantime, the North Atlantic Squadron under Rear Admiral William T Sampson assembled at Key West to intercept Cervera and begin action in the Caribbean waters as necessary. The Asiatic Squadron under Commodore George Dewey was stationed in Hong Kong and ready for action in the Far East, having been instructed as early as December by the assistant naval secretary—the bellicose and dynamic New York politician Theodore Roosevelt—to stand at combat readiness.

It was this Asiatic fleet that first won a great victory for the American cause. In February, in the midst of the diplomatic crisis, Roosevelt sent a second confidential dispatch to Dewey urging him to be prepared for immediate action. Thus when war was declared, and naval secretary John D Long ordered the fleet to the Philippines to destroy the Spanish fleet stationed in that faraway archipelago, Dewey was ready to go. On 27 April 1898 Dewey left his anchorage at Mirs Bay near Hong Kong and headed for the Philippine capital of Manila. His squadron consisted of four protected cruisers and three auxiliary vessels. Waiting to meet him was a weak Spanish contingent of only two protected cruisers and five obsolete smaller vessels. On the night of 30 April, Dewey's fleet passed the protecting Spanish batteries on Corregidor and El Fraile without incident and anchored in Manila Bay.

The next morning, 1 May, Admiral Dewey said to the captain of his flagship, the *Olympia*, 'You may fire when ready, Gridley,' and the Battle of Manila Bay began. The American fleet made five maneuvers past the anchored Spanish fleet, which did not have turreted guns and so could utilize only half its ordnance.

Above: **The action off Cardenas on 11 May 1898. L to R, the *Winslow*, *Hudson* and *Wilmington*.**

Below: **The bombardment of Matanzas on 27 April 1898 by the *New York*, *Cincinnati* and *Puritan*.**

Below: **The landing fleet lies offshore as men of the 71st Regiment reach the beach at Sibboney on 22 June 1898.**

Even at that, the greater range and accuracy of the American naval guns made the outcome a foregone conclusion. The order was given to cease fire to count ammunition and survey the Spanish fleet, and, as the smoke from the guns slowly lifted, the Americans were astonished to see that almost the whole Spanish fleet had been destroyed. Renewing the fray, Dewey's ships finished off the remainder of the Spanish fleet by 12:30 in the afternoon. The navy had scored a tremendous victory—admittedly against a weak enemy—and America had a new hero named George Dewey, quickly promoted to Acting Rear Admiral by President McKinley.

The Spanish were forced to surrender control of Manila Bay with the destruction of their fleet, but Dewey had sovereignty over the Spanish Philippines only within the range of his guns. Surrender of the capital and of the archipelago would have to wait for an occupying force, so Dewey gathered his squadron before Manila to impose a tight blockade on the Bay—and to keep other foreign powers like Germany out, so they could not make claim to the Philippines. Not until three months later did the US Army arrive and Manila surrender (only to lead to greater troubles, when the Filipino insurgents fighting the Spanish discovered that the Philippines would not be turned over to them). But it had been a memorable and dashing victory, and the navy enjoyed great esteem.

Within two weeks of this engagement in the Far East, reports reached the navy that Cervera's squadron was heading for the Caribbean. Despite the best efforts of Sampson's and Schley's squadrons, Cervera made it safely into the port of Santiago on the southern coast of Cuba. As he was soon discovered by Sampson and Schley and blockaded in the harbor at Santiago, a basic problem surfaced. Cervera could not come out of harbor, as the superior American naval force would destroy him, but the Americans could not get into the harbor to drive him out because of the long, narrow configuration of the harbor and shipping channel and the

Right: Destruction of the Spanish fleet at Manila Bay. At left the USS _Olympia_, _Baltimore_ and _Boston_.
Below: Wreck of the _Merrimac_ in the channel at Santiago.

Above: **The American battleships prepare to engage in the Battle of Santiago.**
Left: **Dewey on his flagship at the outset of the Manila Bay engagement.**

guns positioned on the hillsides to fire against any incoming force. So the navy blockaded Santiago Harbor and waited for the army to arrive and launch a ground attack against the city of Santiago, making Cervera's position untenable.

By mid-June the naval transports had brought General William R Shafter's 17,000 men to the southern coast of Cuba and disembarked them over the surf, the horses being slung over the side by cranes to swim ashore (many swam out to sea). If all went well with the land maneuvers, Cervera's fleet of four cruisers and two

Below: **Battle of Santiago. The** ***Cristobal Colon*** **comes under fire from the** ***Oregon*** **and** ***Iowa*** **(left).** ***Texas*** **(right) is also engaged.**

torpedo boat destroyers would soon be forced to flee—into the guns of the five American battleships, three armored cruisers and two protected cruisers steaming in a giant circle outside the harbor. In order to make their escape impossible, however, a daring plan was concocted. The collier *Merrimac* was to be deliberately sunk in the channel by naval constructor Lieutenant Richmond Pearson Hobson and a skeleton crew. Unfortunately, the *Merrimac* sank off the channel and Hobson and his men were captured, although the Spanish defenders treated them as heroes for their brave attempt.

With the American expeditionary force finally making its way around the city of Santiago, the Spanish military commander ordered Admiral Cervera to make a run for it—although how he would get out and where he would go was far from clear. On 3 July at 9:30 in the morning the Spanish fleet came steaming out and turned west. Although the American fleet had grave difficulty in getting into parallel position—a battleship and a cruiser almost collided in the thick smoke disgorged by the coal-fired warships—the Spanish fleet was soon under intense gunfire. By 1:30 in the afternoon the entire fleet had been either destroyed or beached, the hapless Spanish sailors being shot in the water by Cuban revolutionaries as they swam for shore. This pitched naval battle saw over 600 Spanish killed and another 1700 taken prisoner. American casualties amounted to one man killed and one wounded. It was a most one-sided victory.

Having little to do thereafter, the navy continued to blockade Santiago Harbor until the city surrendered on 17 July. Thereafter, they transported the army troops to Puerto Rico where they were joyfully received. Meanwhile, a fleet had been assembled in Spain and had sallied forth to retake Manila Bay, but when word arrived of Cervera's defeat and of American intentions to send a squadron to the coast of Spain, the fleet was recalled—having already passed through the Suez Canal—by the government. The war was effectively over in both the Philippines and the Caribbean. A peace protocol was signed between the governments of Spain and the United States on 12 August 1898. As later characterized by the American diplomat John Hay, it had been a 'splendid little war.'

Responsibilities Near and Far

What most Americans did not realize as the war came to an end with the Treaty of Paris (signed in November 1898 and approved by the Senate in February 1899) was that the United States had now become a Far Eastern power as well as the major Caribbean power. Despite some misgivings, the United States took the Philippines from Spain—fearing either internal convulsions or outside domination by some other power; it also took Guam. And during the course of the war, American reluctance to take Hawaii (seen as late as 1893 when a 'spontaneous' revolution aided by the marines of the USS *Boston* overthrew the native government and the revolutionists asked for recognition and annexation) had been overridden by the need for a secure coaling station: the islands had been annexed. Uninhabited Wake Island had been taken at the same time and Midway back in 1867; the United States now had a clear line—Hawaii, Midway, Wake, Guam—to the Philippines and the Far East. America was now a Pacific and Far Eastern power, with all this would entail in the decades to come down to the present day. At the same time, she had become dominant in the Caribbean by taking Puerto Rico and placing Cuba under US protection and guidance. None of this had been foreseen as the nation drifted toward war over atrocities against the Cuban people, but it was the new reality. America was no longer isolationist; its responsibilities were rapidly becoming worldwide.

Among other things, this meant that the US Navy had major commitments that followed the flag. The navy was now bigger than ever before, and its impressive victories at Manila Bay and Santiago had forged a special place for it in American affections. It was ready to come of age.

A mark of the navy's new status was that public opinion seemed to support 'a navy second to none but Britain's.' This 'Big Navy' sentiment was strengthened by the presence of Theodore Roosevelt in the White House after the assassination of William McKinley in 1901. Roosevelt was an avid disciple of Alfred Thayer Mahan, and pushed naval primacy as no president had ever done in peacetime through his speeches and appointments. Roosevelt also used the navy to promote his ideas of American dominance in the Caribbean, leading to frequent American intervention in that area.

American naval thinking had clearly abandoned the doctrine of a passive defensive posture plus commerce raiding. Manila and Santiago showed what could be done by taking the fight to the enemy.

American naval strategists and tacticians of the early twentieth century envisioned epic and decisive sea battles in which the stronger, faster and more heavily gunned fleet would emerge victorious. This view was shared by naval strategists worldwide and led to the building of vessels suitable for such climactic duels.

With the construction of the British *Dreadnought* (launched in 1906) all other battleships were rendered obsolescent. The *Dreadnought* was the first giant 'all-big-gun' ship. She was larger (17,900 tons), longer (490 feet), faster (21.5 knots) and more heavily armored (11-inch steel hull and turret coverage) than anything afloat

Below: Painting of the USS _Iowa_ as she would have appeared in 1898 in a typical contemporary paint scheme of tan and light gray.

Scenes from the cruise of the Great White Fleet. *Above*, the *Georgia* (BB.15); *Below*, the fleet leaves Hampton Roads. *Right*, Roosevelt addresses the crew of the *Connecticut* on their return.

or building. All the navies of the world were forced to shift to dreadnought construction to match or supersede her. The United States was no exception. In addition to building battleships, the Navy retained its armored cruisers for scouting, commerce raiding and anti-torpedo duty with the fleets, and added destroyers, submarines and airplanes. The United States not only had a bigger navy by 1914 —including 17 modern battleships built or building—it also had a better navy.

The US Navy was very active in the years 1898–1914, carrying out America's new commitments in the Far East and acting as one of Theodore Roosevelt's 'big sticks' in the Caribbean. Between 1899 and 1902 the navy, operating out of San Francisco, abetted military efforts to put down the Filipino insurgency against American control by support and blockading activities in that wartorn archipelago. In 1900 over 2500 naval personnel joined the international force which put down the nationalistic Boxer Rebellion in China against outside nations' interference in the affairs of that hapless country. In 1903 the Navy played a major role in obtaining the Panama Canal for the United States.

Many attempts had been made to build a canal somewhere across the Central American isthmus, but all had failed for one reason or another. The latest attempt had been made by the bankrupt French De Lesseps Company, which retained the right to build the canal. American interest in a canal intensified during the Spanish-American War when the *Oregon*'s 'dash' from Bremerton, Washington, to Key West, Florida, around Cape Horn took 25 days. From a naval point of view this was clearly unacceptable, because it meant that the United States would have to maintain two fleets, one in the Atlantic and one in the Pacific, unless a cut-through was obtained. Political leaders agreed, and accord was reached with Great Britain in the Hay-Pauncefote Treaty of 1901 that the United States could build an isthmian canal on its own. The problem was Colombia, of which Panama was a part, which held out for the highest possible amount of money. Reacting to Colombian obstinacy, Roosevelt—with the assistance of the French, who wanted their bankrupt company compensated, and with an eye on the 1904 election campaign—inspired a local revolt by the Panamanians, who wanted the canal, against their Colombian overlords. The Navy actively aided the revolution by preventing Colombian ships from reinforcing the tiny garrison in Panama, and the revolutionary regime and its Republic of Panama were recognized three days later, on 6 November 1903, by the United States. Shortly thereafter the Hay-Bunau-Varilla Treaty was

signed, by which the US obtained a 10-mile strip of land for a canal for $10 million and a $250,000 annual annuity. Roosevelt now had a green light to 'make the dirt fly,' and the great task of building the canal began. It was completed in 1914, to the delight of the American people, merchant shippers (who cut 9000 miles off the trip from New York to San Francisco and 6000 miles off the trip from New York to Manila) and the navy, which could now expeditiously move its forces from ocean to ocean by a fast and secure passage.

The navy was also active in 'America's lake,' the Caribbean, during these years in bringing the US Marines to Cuba, Santo Domingo, Haiti and Nicaragua to restore order and forestall European intervention. The navy also bombarded and seized the port of Vera Cruz during the Mexican crisis of 1914, when President Woodrow Wilson moved against the government of General Victoriano Huerta after it attempted to buy a large quantity of arms to use against its domestic enemies.

Wherever and whenever called upon, the navy served well during the years before World War I in carrying out its duty of protecting American interests as determined by US political leaders. And the American people were proud of and confident in the Navy as never before in the nation's history. Indicative of this pride was the Roosevelt-inspired cruise of the Great White Fleet from December 1907 to February 1909, designed to display America's new national and naval power. The fleet of 16 battleships and 10 auxiliary vessels, all painted gleaming white as a sign of peace, assembled at Hampton Roads for a great send-off by the President himself. The tour took the vessels around the coast of South America and up the west coast of the United States, then across the Pacific to Hawaii, New Zealand, Australia, the Philippines and Japan. Wherever it went, the fleet made ceremonious port calls to entertain and be received by political leaders. It created a grand impression, although the American sailors displayed a propensity to sample the 'low' culture rather than the 'high' culture of the port cities. After a fervent welcome everywhere, especially in Japan, the Great White Fleet made its way home via the Suez Canal and the Mediterranean, to drop anchor with synchronized precision in Hampton Roads before a beaming Theodore Roosevelt. It had been a 'good show,' and Roosevelt could leave office that March 1909 with a navy dominant in the Western Hemisphere and coming to power in the Pacific. Roosevelt was proud of his navy. It had come of age. The American people shared his pride and enthusiasm. It was with this self-assurance that the nation soon found itself embroiled in the carnage of World War I.

Above: **Japanese and American officers pose on the quarterdeck of the USS *Missouri* during the Great White Fleet's visit to Yokohama in October 1908.**
Below: **The battleship *Connecticut* (right) and Russian ships in Messina Harbor in January 1909**

Top: The USS *Kentucky* showing the highly unconventional arrangement of the armament with the secondary turrets superimposed above the main weapons.
Above: The *Kearsarge* pictured around the turn of the century.

A PARTNER IN THE GREAT CRUSADE

Building upon the foundation created by Theodore Roosevelt, the navy's most enthusiastic presidential patron and publicist, his successor William Howard Taft continued to support a powerful sea force. Their patronage took the form mainly of support for big battleships, a reflection of the prevailing assumption that control of the seas would be seized and maintained by these titans, locked in mortal gun duels on the high seas.

Battleships and Other Weapons

During Roosevelt's time, the American battleship navy matured and in 1909 the *Michigan* and *South Carolina*, of 16,000 tons and armed with eight 12-inch guns in twin-stacked turrets fore and aft, came off the building ways to join the fleet. These imposing battleships were followed by the 20,000-ton *Delaware* and *North Dakota* with ten 12-inchers. And this was not the end, for the *Arkansas* and *Wyoming* of 26,000 tons and twelve 12-inch guns followed soon after.

Not only were the new battleships more heavily armed than ever before, but their gunnery power and accuracy were greatly improved, due largely to the determined efforts of naval officers William S Sims and Bradley K Fiske. As a lieutenant Sims found American gunnery so deficient at the turn of the century that he began a one-man campaign to improve it. He persisted to the point where his career was almost ruined by conflict with senior admirals on the issue. He was saved by the favorable notice of President Roosevelt, who made him inspector of target practice and then his personal naval aide. Under Sims's leadership, training methods were improved and the navy adopted continuous-aim firing and 'dotters' for training purposes, which measured gun-crew accuracy without expending ammunition. Bradley Fiske invented a valuable telescopic gun sight and the optical range finder. By World War I a gun-control officer perched high on the ship's foremast could aim and fire the vessel's big guns simultaneously to an effective range of almost 20,000 yards (over 11 miles). Thanks to these and other developments, the US Navy's battleships were equal to those of any other nation and received a major share of the limited shipbuilding funds doled out by Congress in the prewar years.

Yet while battleships received most of the attention, the navy did not entirely neglect other weapons then coming into use in the forces of the great powers. Submarines began to join the fleets in the pre-World War I era. The father of the American submarine was a civilian, John P Holland. Although his first boat, the 85-foot *Plunger*, was launched in 1897, it was unworkable because of mandated naval speeds that necessitated a triple-screw

Top: The battleships *Iowa*, *Indiana* and *Massachusetts* on a visit to Kiel in 1911.
Above left: Eugene Ely ready to fly off the USS *Pennsylvania*, 18 January 1911.
Above: The battleship *Illinois* enters a floating dock for repairs in 1902.
Main picture: An early Lake submarine passes the battleship *Kearsarge* during the 1905 review of the Atlantic Fleet.

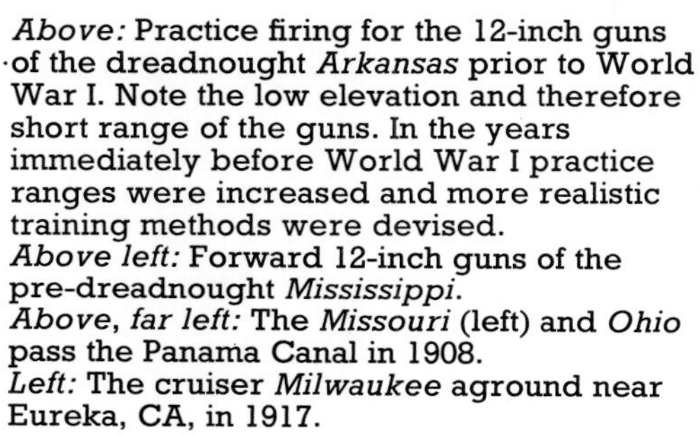

Above: Practice firing for the 12-inch guns of the dreadnought _Arkansas_ prior to World War I. Note the low elevation and therefore short range of the guns. In the years immediately before World War I practice ranges were increased and more realistic training methods were devised.
Above left: Forward 12-inch guns of the pre-dreadnought _Mississippi_.
Above, far left: The _Missouri_ (left) and _Ohio_ pass the Panama Canal in 1908.
Left: The cruiser _Milwaukee_ aground near Eureka, CA, in 1917.

steam plant to allow the submarine to run on the surface at 15 knots. But Holland, on his own, had been developing a simpler model, the *Holland*, which had a single torpedo tube, a surface speed of seven knots and a range of 1500 miles. Although the boat had no periscope, and thus had to surface every few minutes to take bearings, the *Holland* was purchased by the Navy in 1900, and improvements to submarine technology and operations followed swiftly thereafter. The invention of the gyrocompass made underwater cruising possible, and the adaptation of the diesel engine for surface power greatly improved the boats' safety. Life aboard the primitive undersea boats was cramped, unhealthy and always dangerous, and naval doctrine saw no use for submarines except against enemy warships or in protecting harbors, but the submarine had certainly come to stay in the US Navy by the time World War I broke out in 1914.

Air power had also joined the fleet although, like the submarines, only in a minor capacity. As in so many other naval projects, Theodore Roosevelt played a role. As assistant secretary of the navy in 1898, he interested both the army and the navy in the work of Professor Samuel P Langley of the Smithsonian Institution toward an 'aerodrome' (airplane). But the navy would not pursue it further at that time because the apparatus was 'only fit for land service.' Only in 1910, seven years after the Wright brothers' successful flight at Kitty Hawk, was the Navy bestirred to look into the possibilities of air flight from ships. On 14 November 1910, as the cruiser *Birmingham* sat in Hampton Roads, Eugene Ely, a civilian flier, took off in his Curtiss pusher biplane from an inclined platform over her bow and landed safely on the beach. Two months later, on 18 January 1911, Ely took off from shore and landed safely on a platform erected on the stern of the cruiser *Pennsylvania* as she lay at anchor in San Francisco Bay. Ely's plane was brought to a halt on the 120-foot platform by catching his 'arresting gear,' trailing below the plane, on cables stretched over the 'deck,' each cable attached to 50-pound sandbags. One hour later Ely flew off the ship. The basic idea behind the modern aircraft carrier had been proved.

But although it was quickly recognized that the new airplane could perform valuable service to the fleet by acting as its 'eyes' for reconnaissance purposes—miles beyond what lookouts in the fleet could possibly see even with binoculars—and by freeing cruisers from scouting duty, landing an airplane on a deck was still a very dangerous proposition. Accordingly, development turned toward floatplanes, or seaplanes, which could be launched from a shipboard ramp or catapult at sea to do their work, then be recovered by landing near the mother ship on their floats or pontoons. The seaplane

Above: A Goodyear B-type airship in 1917.
Left: Admiral Sims, the notable gunnery specialist, and members of his staff in London in 1918.

would then be hoisted aboard ship by a crane. By 1913 fleet operations at Guantanamo Bay, Cuba and other locales had proved that airplanes could take photographs, sight enemy submarines and surface vessels, perform wide scouting missions aloft for extended periods and be recovered in moderate seas. The next year five seaplanes attached to the naval squadron at Vera Cruz, by President Wilson's investment of the port in his quarrel with the Mexican Government under General Huerta, proved that air reconnaissance over hostile territory was invaluable. Although air power would subsequently play only a minor role in naval operations during World War I, it had won a place for itself—albeit a limited place—in the emerging navy even before the conflict began. It was not until the 1920s and 1930s that naval air power really came into its own.

The naval weapon that did come to play the major role in World War I was the lowly and unglamorous destroyer. The destroyer was a smaller vessel that had evolved as a counterweapon to the torpedo boat. Initially it was referred to as a 'torpedo boat destroyer.' Torpedo boats had come into use since the 1870s, when the invention of self-propelled torpedoes had been wedded to small, fast boats designed to deliver them against fleet vessels. The torpedo boat destroyer was the answer to stopping the small maneuverable torpedo boat, because it had greater size, speed and firepower than its prey. It could also perform valuable duty by screening the larger vessels while underway. The first American destroyer

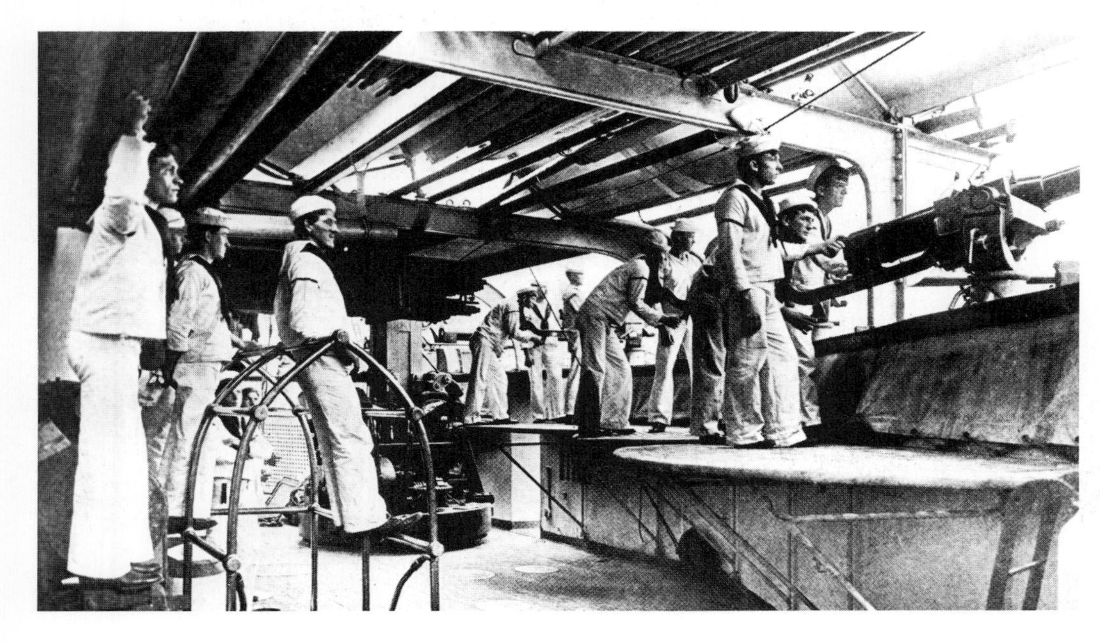

Left: Practice with 6-pounder anti-torpedo boat guns on the *Illinois* before WWI.

joined the fleet in 1902—the 420-ton *Bainbridge*. It had two 3-inch guns and two 18-inch torpedo tubes and could make an amazing 29 knots. By 1914 the destroyer had been significantly improved in size and seaworthiness, and the navy had three dozen of these trim vessels on duty. Thus by the outbreak of war in 1914, the navy, while heavy in battleships and comparatively lacking in cruisers, had taken significant steps in developing submarine and air power. It had also begun to balance out its fleet with destroyers. Like the great European navies, it saw great surface-ship warfare as the probable scenario in the event of hostilities. But, as events were to prove, it could give a good account of itself when the fortunes of war forced it to make significant changes.

Europe Goes to War

'The Great War' to Americans living through it—'The War to End All Wars' and to 'Make the World Safe for Democracy' in the mind of President Woodrow Wilson—began in the summer of 1914 with the assassination by Serbian terrorists of the Austrian Archduke Franz Ferdinand in the little Bosnian town of Sarajevo. Austria, to gain satisfaction for the death of the heir apparent and end Serbian agitation against her, made impossible demands on the Serbian Government, which looked to her ally Russia for aid. Germany, backing Austria, sought assurances from Russia and France that they would not enter the dispute. When neither would comply, Germany—fearing a two-front war, and relying on its Schlieffen Plan of hitting France first and then turning toward Russia in case of conflict—declared war on both powers. In attacking France, Germany moved across Belgium, and this brought Britain into the conflict. Soon the secondary nations joined in, and a world war was on. Imperialism, an inflated sense of national pride, an entangling alliance system, and, critically, a desire finally to 'have it out' led to bloody warfare that would leave millions dead on the battlefields of Europe before ending in 1918.

The great land strategies of the European powers soon broke down. The rapid German sweep across northern France, designed to encircle and destroy the vaunted French Army, slowed, then stalled and finally ground to a halt on the Western Front. On the Eastern Front plans also went awry, resulting in Germany's fighting on two fronts. Even joined by Austria and Turkey, Germany was too weak to win and too strong to lose, and the war quickly settled into a bloody stalemate with the combatants, especially in France and Belgium, engaged in merciless, unending trench warfare.

On the seas, too, grand strategies did not work out as planned. Britain, as an island power with a great navy, was faced with the necessity of keeping her sea lanes open against commerce raiders, containing the German High Seas Fleet and blockading Germany's ports. Germany, on the other hand, technically superior to the British fleet although numerically inferior, had to shut off British commerce with her Dominions and all neutrals, especially the United States. Both saw the North Sea as the critical water mass to command while waiting for the great sea battles that would give them naval domination and eventual victory.

After some preliminary confrontations in the North Sea, in the Falklands in the far South Atlantic and in the Dogger Bank, the great test of sea strength came on 31 May and 1 June 1916: in the Battle of Jutland,

Above: **Secretary of the Navy Josephus Daniels addresses a meeting in 1917.**

Below: **The SS *Albert Watts* on fire near Genoa in November 1917. Note the guns fore and aft denoting the presence of a USN armed guard.**

Above: **A U-boat's torpedo strikes home on a freighter. Merchant ships sailing independently were easy victims.**

the Germans tried to break the British blockade and humble her fleet in one grand engagement. The German High Seas Fleet of 22 battleships and 77 other vessels was commanded by Vice-Admiral Reinhard Scheer, the British Grand Fleet of 28 battleships and 120 other ships by Admiral Sir John Jellicoe. In this first real test of the great battleship fleets, the Germans attempted to draw the British into a trap off the coast of Denmark and managed to win a narrow victory in a shifting series of surface combats. Cutting through the British fleet, Scheer's forces returned safely to port, but the importance of the battle lies chiefly in what occurred thereafter. The British, having failed to defeat the German High Seas Fleet, were forced to keep their Grand Fleet concentrated in home waters and the North Sea (with 100 valuable destroyers in support that could have been used against submarines) in case the High Seas Fleet re-emerged to do battle. The Germans, unwilling to risk their valuable surface fleet again in head-to-head combat, turned to the submarine as a means of destroying supplies coming into Britain and breaking the British blockade of their homeland. Thus the stage was set for the United States, as the leading neutral trader and supplier to Britain and her allies, to be drawn slowly but inexorably into the war.

When hostilities broke out in Europe in the summer of 1914, President Wilson declared American neutrality, giving the United States the legal right to trade with any and all belligerents. But Wilson himself, an ardent Anglophile, was hardly neutral and was inclined to downplay British violations of neutral rights (such as redefining contraband lists to suit their purposes, mining the North Sea, opening private mail and 'blacklisting' firms that traded with Germany). He focused his attention—and the nation's—on German use of submarine warfare. Wilson's attitudes, plus American trade with England and France, American investments in the Allied cause and well-publicized stories of German 'atrocities' against civilians, turned America more and more against the Central Powers.

In February 1915 the German Government announced that the waters around the British Isles would be considered a war zone and enemy ships traveling through them were subject to sinking without warning. Although Germany backed up its words with repeated sinkings, Americans continued to travel into these waters on Allied vessels, disregarding the warnings. On the afternoon of 7 May 1915, the British Cunard liner *Lusitania* was sunk within sight of the coast of Ireland by the German submarine U-20. She sank in 20 minutes, taking with her to her watery grave 1198 victims, including 128 Americans. Whether or not the *Lusitania* was indeed carrying munitions and thus liable to attack, the Americans and President Wilson were incensed at the callous deed. The German Government agreed to pay an indemnity and to stop unrestricted submarine warfare, but the damage had been done. The memory of the *Lusitania* and its victims was burned into the American consciousness. There it smouldered until early 1917 when Germany, sensing the time was right with the Eastern Front about to collapse because of the impending revolution in Russia, broke the military deadlock. Believing that any American military aid would be too little too late—the ratio of British merchant ships sunk to

Above: Admiral Mayo, C-in-C US Atlantic Fleet (left) and Rear Admiral Strauss seen during a visit to a hospital in Scotland.
Above right: The minesweeper *Tanager* at work in heavy seas.

German submarines lost was then 15:1 and Germany estimated that Britain could be overcome in five months if the subs were unleashed—Germany resumed unrestricted submarine warfare in January. This finally brought America into the war on 6 April 1917 at President Wilson's request, and the United States stepped to the side of the Allied powers.

Above: A US Navy airship patrols over a convoy en route to Europe.
Below: US 'four stacker' destroyers on convoy duty.

America Joins the Crusade

But as it did so, it found that the US Navy was hardly ready for all-out war. Part of the reason was Wilson's naval secretary, Josephus Daniels, a land-lubbing small-town newspaperman from North Carolina. Wilson had little respect for military men and their opinions, and his choice of Daniels was unfortunate in many ways. Known for his reformism, pacifism, populist agrarianism and support of Prohibition, Daniels brought some controversial ideas to the navy. He introduced compulsory basic education courses on every ship and at every duty station and, to make the service more 'democratic,' cut out the officers' wine mess in July 1914, since the enlisted men's grog had been curtailed during the Civil War. Daniels also fought in Congress against the establishment of an office of Chief of Naval Operations with any real power, believing that civilian control would be endangered. On the other hand, Secretary Daniels made some positive contributions prior to 1917. First, he fought for the naval preparedness program as embodied in the Naval Act of 1916, which called for the construction of 156 ships (including 10 battleships, 16 cruisers, 50 destroyers and 67 submarines) in three years—although he resisted all efforts to construct ships for ASW (anti-submarine warfare) duty and dallied on preparing existing vessels and crews for combat. Second, he chose as assistant naval secretary Franklin D Roosevelt, a New York politician and naval enthusiast looking for a way to further his blossoming career; Roosevelt was a disciple of decisive naval power. He did a fine job as a buffer between the officers and Daniels and the politicos both before and during the war and studied the navy well in the process. This experience would benefit both him and the navy after 1933, when Roosevelt would be Commander in Chief.

Thus when the war began in 1914, the US Navy under Daniels was building but ill prepared for major conflict. There were no war plans (Wilson had forbidden the military to make contingency plans), few ASW vessels, and no apparatus set up to co-operate with the British; only one-third of the navy's vessels were fit for duty and 90 percent of its ships were inadequately manned. Despite this, the Navy went to its task and played a substantial role in winning World War I.

By the time the United States entered the war, Germany's unrestricted warfare with her 120 subs was taking a tremendous toll of British merchant vessels. In the first three months of 1917, almost 1,300,000 tons of shipping had been sunk, and the toll was rising fast. Britain faced starvation if the German submarines could not be contained or destroyed. That was the message received by Admiral William S Sims, sent to London by President Wilson to survey the naval situation, when he met with Admiral Sir John Jellicoe, the First Sea Lord, on 10 April 1917 at the Admiralty. If sub-seeking destroyers were not sent to contain the menace, Britain might lose the war. Although the British had 200 destroyers, 100 were attached to the Grand Fleet at Scapa Flow in the Orkney Islands on the northern tip of Scotland, and the remainder were spread thinly in patrolling the waters around the British Isles, in the Mediterranean and in the North Atlantic. This was simply not enough.

Above: **A Curtiss H-16 flying boat at Queenstown Naval Air Station, Ireland in 1918.**

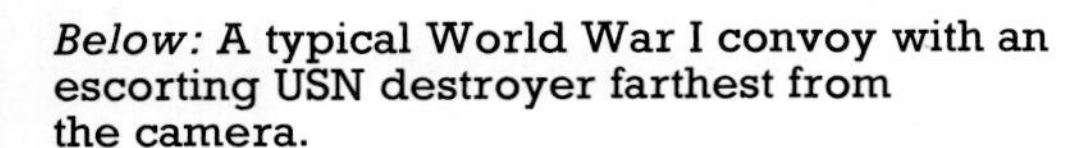

Below: **A typical World War I convoy with an escorting USN destroyer farthest from the camera.**

Above: The USS *Covington* sinking off Brest on 2 July 1918 after being torpedoed by the German submarine U-86.
Left: King George V and Admiral Rodman inspect the crew of the *New York*.

Destroyers, Convoys and Mines

Sims moved quickly in two directions. First, he cabled home to the navy to send every available destroyer to Britain. Despite the reluctance of Secretary Daniels and Admiral William S Benson, Chief of Naval Operations, to make such a commitment, the government finally decided to honor Sims's request. On 4 May 1917 six American destroyers constituting Destroyer Division 8 arrived at the Queenstown naval base in Ireland. They were commanded by Joseph K Tausigg, Commander, USN, and were the first of dozens that would follow in the months ahead. With destroyers available, the German submarines could be sunk or neutralized. Second, Sims convinced the British and the French that they must convoy ships carrying men and supplies. Although the Admiralty had first rejected this on the grounds that convoys were limited in speed to that of the slowest vessel and merchant captains could not maintain their positions, the Allies finally became con-

vinced in May 1917—after a trial run by a convoy from Gibraltar—that the stratagem would work with more destroyers available for escort duty. They further found that merchant captains could keep station very well. Convoying thus became standard practice, with the Americans playing an important role in protecting the vessels under escort.

Soon American destroyers, operating from bases from the Mediterranean to Scotland, were co-operating well with their British counterparts under the overall command of Vice-Admiral Lewis Bayly of the Royal Navy. Under Captain Joel Pringle, as Bayly's US Chief of Staff, the destroyers operated smoothly as part of the British naval defense force, with Bayly proclaiming his affection for the Yank destroyermen by referring to them as 'my Americans.' This co-operation, plus the use of the newly developed contact mine (equipped with copper wire tendrils that exploded the device on contact with metal) and depth charges (steel cylinders containing 300 pounds of explosives and detonated by the increased water pressure as they sank), gradually contained the submarine menace, and Britain could hold out and fight back. Sinkings of Allied ships declined from 875,000 tons in April 1917, to 458,723 tons in October 1917, to 277,934 tons in April 1918. The submarines were clearly on the run, and American destroyers and companion submarine chasers were proving their worth. The work was not glamorous for the officers and crews of the workhorse vessels, but it was helping to win the war on the sea.

The US Navy also made a major contribution to the sea-war effort by helping to lay a great minefield across the North Sea from Norway to Scotland, a distance of 240 miles: this kept the German U-Boats from getting out to sea, 'shutting the hornets up in their nests,' in the words of President Wilson. Mining the North Sea was originally rejected by the British because it would call for an impossible total of 400,000 mines, but when the copper-wire tendril mine (invented by Ralph C Browne of the United States) became available, the picture changed. Now 100,000 mines would do the job. Accordingly, the operation was carried out between June and October 1918, the Americans laying over 56,000 mines and the British over 13,000. Although it is impossible to determine how many German vessels fell victim to the mines, the barrier effectively closed the North Sea and had a great negative psychological effect on the German people and on the German Navy. The US Navy also contributed a division of five battleships to the Grand Fleet at Scapa Flow, and a few US submarines served in European waters as well. These vessels, along with the naval cruisers on convoy duty in the western Atlantic protecting the American merchant marine's 'bridge of ships' to the war zone, played a crucial supporting role in the naval war against the Central Powers.

As the Germans and their allies began losing the war at sea, they were also being slowly pushed back on the Western Front as French, British and American army units threatened to break their defensive lines and move into the fatherland itself. There revolutions threatened to break loose in reaction to starvation and the prolonged war effort. The Imperial Government had to call a halt. Kaiser Wilhelm II left the country, and a new interim government asked for an armistice: when it was agreed to, the fighting ended.

The Great War was over. The US Navy had proved its mettle again from the highest admiral to the lowest seaman. The crews of the bobbing, sub-chasing destroyers stalking their prey; the men on the great dreadnoughts at anchor in Scapa Flow awaiting an enemy that never came; the more than 6000 American naval aviators who flew planes and blimps on reconnaissance and convoy-protecting missions; the 12,000 'yeomanettes' who supported the men at sea by donning US Navy uniforms; and the 14-inch-gun crews in France wearing the 'Woozlefinch' insignia, whose railroad-mounted guns lobbed 1400-pound shells onto the German front lines—all had served meritoriously as part of America's naval contribution to the 'war to end all wars.' Peace arrived to general rejoicing at 11:00 on the morning of 11 November 1918.

Above: The submarine *L-3* leads a flotilla into an Irish base in 1918.
Right: Admiral Strauss, Commander Mine Force, and members of his staff.
Below right: Tugs help the USS *Mount Vernon*, damaged by torpedo, to dock at Brest.
Bottom right: Naval railway battery in France.
Below: The destroyer *Shaw* after a collision.

RETRENCHMENT AND REBIRTH

One of the most dramatic events of modern naval history took place in June 1919 at Scapa Flow, Scotland, home port of the British Grand Fleet. Pursuant to the provisions of the Treaty of Versailles, the defeated German High Seas Fleet had sailed into the Forth in perfect order on 21 November 1918 to be turned over to the victors. Ten battleships, 17 cruisers, 50 destroyers and 102 submarines made up the incredible armada which eventually anchored at Scapa Flow. Then, on 21 June 1919, obeying the command of Vice-Admiral Ludwig von Reuter, the captain of every ship ordered its seacocks opened: all 179 vessels began to sink to the bottom of the Flow in protest against the victors' Treaty. Only four ships were salvaged. The German Navy was no more.

This gesture of defiance meant that only the United States was now in a position to challenge Britain's control of the seas. But perhaps the scuttling at Scapa Flow had a greater and unintended symbolic value, for in the early 1920s a movement arose, especially in England and the United States, advocating that all the world's navies should be scuttled, or at least scaled back drastically in the name of peace. The 1920s, a time of self-imposed American isolation from world affairs, became the decade of naval disarmament; the 1930s would become the decade of naval rearmament, as the nation began to realize its worldwide obligations once again in the face of the growing tensions inspired by Hitler's regime and the clear territorial ambitions harbored by Japan.

Disarmament Cripples the Navy

In early 1919 the US Navy had 16 dreadnoughts and 13 more building. It was awaiting 12 new battle cruisers authorized in 1916. Britain, with 33 dreadnoughts and nine battle cruisers, was preparing to build four great 48,000-ton battle cruisers and four more battleships. Japan was looking toward two great naval squadrons of battleships and battlecruisers—one squadron of each—to be completed by 1928. A capital-ship naval race was underway even though the war was over. In all three countries movements designed to halt such building and to scale down the naval budgets sprang up. Peace could not be gained by more weapons of war, argued

Below: **The battleship USS *Washington* under construction in 1922. She was cancelled before completion under the terms of the Washington Naval Treaty.**

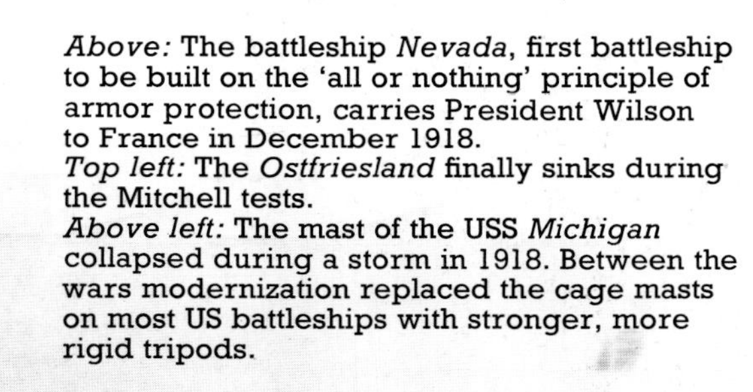

Above: The battleship *Nevada*, first battleship to be built on the 'all or nothing' principle of armor protection, carries President Wilson to France in December 1918.
Top left: The *Ostfriesland* finally sinks during the Mitchell tests.
Above left: The mast of the USS *Michigan* collapsed during a storm in 1918. Between the wars modernization replaced the cage masts on most US battleships with stronger, more rigid tripods.

the pro-disarmament forces, and prosperity demanded a relief from the crushing tax burdens they imposed. By 1921 the pressure for disarmament had become irresistible.

An invitation to a worldwide disarmament conference to cut back the world's navies and to clear the air over Japanese intentions in the Far East was issued by the Harding Administration in August 1921, after a resolution by Senator William Borah of Idaho had crystallized popular support for such a meeting. As the delegates from nine nations assembled in the nation's capital the following month, the American secretary of state, Charles Evans Hughes, electrified the conferees in his opening speech by saying that the United States would be willing to scrap 30 battleships (15 built and 15 building, for 845,740 tons) if the other powers would move in the same direction. Hughes went on to propose that the British and the Japanese follow suit and outlined exactly how they should do it. Britain was to scrap 19 capital ships (583,375 tons) and Japan 17 ships (447,928 tons). Since no agenda had been agreed upon previously, Hughes's breathtaking suggestions became the basis for negotiations, and eventually three separate agreements were made before the Washington Naval Conference adjourned in February 1922.

Two of the agreements dealt with Far Eastern problems. The 'Four Power Treaty' bound the United States, Great Britain, France and Japan to recognize and

Left: A phosphorus bomb explodes above the old battleship _Alabama_ during tests in 1923. _Right:_ Nieuport 28 flying off a battleship (probably _Arizona circa_ 1921).

respect one another's possessions in the Far East and to settle any disputes that arose by joint conference. The 'Nine Power Treaty,' accepted by the same four nations plus Italy, China, Belgium, the Netherlands and Portugal, pledged to maintain the 'Open Door' in China, a doctrine first promulgated by American secretary of state John Hay in 1899 to protect China's integrity. The third treaty dealt with naval disarmament.

This 'Five Power Treaty' agreed to on 6 February 1922 called for a ratio of 5:5:3:1.75:1.75 in capital ships (the nations involved according to their ratios being the United States, Britain, Japan, France and Italy). In standard displacement tonnage the agreement specified 525,000 tons, 525,000 tons, and 315,000 tons for the greater powers and 175,000 tons each for France and Italy. In addition, no capital ships (battleships and battle cruisers) could be constructed for ten years and no capital ships retained could be over 35,000 tons or carry ordnance greater than 16 inches. The aircraft carrier ratio was set at 135,000 tons, 135,000 tons, 81,000 tons, 60,000 tons and 60,000 tons, with no carriers except for any two per country to be over 27,000 tons. The two excepted carriers could go to 33,000 tons apiece, but under no circumstances could any nation's maximum tonnage be topped. No cruiser could be over 10,000 tons or be armed with more than 8-inch guns. And no battleships or carriers could be replaced before twenty years of age. This treaty was to remain in effect for ten years, any nation seeking to disavow its provisions being bound to give two years' notice. Thus the Five Power Treaty brought a virtual end to capital-ship construction and postponed any naval building rivalry for fifteen years, even though Japanese movements into China in the early 1930s made a mockery of the other two treaties.

Cutting Back

The desired naval-limitation agreement having been gained, the Harding Administration went to work cutting back the US Navy to treaty strength through naval secretary Edwin C Denby, although Congress deserves the major blame for putting the axe to the navy in these years. Congress made it almost impossible even to modernize personnel and refused to fund 16 cruisers needed by the navy. Denby did manage to get the collier *Jupiter* converted to the navy's first carrier (the inadequate *Langley*) and instituted plans for converting the hulls of two battle cruisers into the new 33,000-ton carriers *Lexington* and *Saratoga*. But given Congress's control of the purse strings, there was little else he could do.

The navy did not fare better under President Calvin Coolidge, who knew little about it and showed no signs of wanting to cure that deficiency. In newer vessels it received only the two carriers, 10 light cruisers and three submarines, plus the five battleships authorized at the end of the war, but little else. Coolidge also called for a second disarmament conference to limit cruisers, submarines and destroyers. It met in Geneva in 1927 but came to nothing, due partly to skillful lobbying by William B Shearer representing American shipbuilding interests. Coolidge, angered by the failure at Geneva, called for building more cruisers of the treaty tonnage

Main picture: **A battleship lets loose a full broadside during firing practice in the mid-1920s.**

TEXAS
IDAHO
MISSISSIPPI
ARKANSAS
MELVILLE
WYOMING
STODDERT
BIRMINGHAM
PARTRIDGE

Left: The battleship *California* fitting out at Mare Island Navy Yard, CA, in 1920. The *California* was armed with twelve 14-inch guns and saw service throughout the Pacific War after being badly damaged at Pearl Harbor.

limit of 10,000 tons each and backed a Navy General Board call to bring the navy up to treaty strength. But neither he nor his naval secretary, Curtis D Wilbur, made a spirited fight for the newer vessels, and a '15-cruiser' bill was signed only in February 1929, as Coolidge was about to leave office.

Herbert Hoover, his peace-loving Quaker successor, was a disaster for the US Navy. Believing that the failure of the Geneva conference would result in another arms race, he met with British Prime Minister Ramsay MacDonald to discuss the problem; this resulted in the London Naval Conference of 1930. Meeting in the shadow of the Kellogg-Briand Peace Pact, wherein warfare had been denounced as an instrument of national policy, this conference set to work to limit all naval vessels not covered by the Washington Naval Conference, especially cruisers.

From the London Naval Conference came limitations on light (6-inch-gun) and heavy (8-inch-gun) cruisers, an agreement on parity among the three powers present regarding submarines, and a ratio of 10 (United States):10 (Britain):7 (Japan) on destroyers. Battleships were further reduced to 15:15:9, and the capital-ship building holiday was extended to 1936. Thus naval building programs had finally been contained—or so it seemed. But the London Naval Treaty also contained Article 21, which allowed any signatory to scuttle its limitations if threatened by any nonsignatory power, and if one signatory went beyond its limits, all others could do so. This 'escalator clause' was an open door to self-willed expansion, especially as Japan, in 1933, announced her intention to withdraw from the treaty when it expired. Japan had begun her conquest of Manchuria in 1931, and none of the signatories to the three Washington Naval Conference agreements had moved to stop her. Since the subsequent League of Nations Disarmament Conference of 1932–34 and the London Naval Conference of 1935–36 were both failures, it was clear to all by the mid-1930s that naval arms limitation was falling apart in the face of national aggressions. Only then did the United States turn again to rebuild its truncated navy to deal with the realities of world power politics.

The US Navy in general was sadly lacking in 1933, with only 101 newer vessels, 9000 officers and 81,000 men. It had not even been built up to treaty limits in the decade since the Washington Naval Conference, standing at only 65 percent of authorized strength. President Hoover had told his naval secretary, Charles Francis Adams, to cut spending and return appropriated funds in an attempt to cut expenses during the deepening Depression. The year 1932 was the nadir of the modern US Navy. Only one branch of the navy had been growing in strength throughout the period of decline. This was naval aviation.

Left: Ships of the Atlantic and Pacific Fleets at anchor in Panama Bay in January 1921.

Naval Air Power

The Navy's experience with air power during World War I was limited, as we have seen, but the public and air enthusiasts were enthralled by the relatively high rate of damage (for the low expenditure of money) promised by air power (an approach that would later come to be called 'more bang for the buck'). With tactical and strategic theorists worldwide making fabulous claims that airplanes would soon render both armies and navies obsolete, the navy could hardly turn away from a weapon which, at the least, could aid them appreciably in fleet operations. But well-publicized tests off the Atlantic coast in 1921 against ships—including bombing attacks by Army Brigadier General Billy Mitchell's crews on the old German battleship *Ostfriesland*, and later on the modern battleship *Washington*—were largely inconclusive. Ships were hard to hit from the air and when properly compartmentalized could take tremendous damage and remain afloat—a lesson that had to be taught to such myopic devotees of air power as Mitchell, who drew his ideas from the theories of General Giulio Douhet of Italy. The navy was not about to reject air power; it was too busy adding it to its fleets.

Common sense won out over those

Below: The airship *Los Angeles* landing on the aircraft carrier *Saratoga*. The long endurance of airships was useful for patrolling.

admirals who still envisioned great sea battles with big-gun vessels slugging it out to a decisive conclusion, as well as over those admirals who saw the airplane as making the armed vessel obsolete. The navy took the middle course. In the 1920s such carriers as the *Langley*, then *Lexington* and *Saratoga*, came on line, and carrier pilots were being trained at Pensacola. From the naval aircraft factory at Philadelphia came better catapults, arresting gear and metal alloys for the 'skins' of the planes. Fighter planes and torpedo and dive bombers were built, tested and added to the carrier squadrons, and long-range scouting and patrol planes joined the air inventory to replace the great dirigibles as scouts. (Three of the navy's four great lighter-than-air ships unfortunately crashed in storms, one of which claimed as a victim Rear Admiral William A Moffett, chief of the Navy's Bureau of Aeronautics.) Between 1926 and 1930 the navy purchased over 100 airplanes, and Pensacola could not possibly train all the young ensigns who wanted to add gold wings to their uniforms. Pensacola was also overrun with senior officers who sought their pilot or aerial-observer wings as a means of promotion. The 'Pensacola admirals' were 'having their tickets punched,' a practice not unknown since the beginning of command and seniority structures. The Navy somehow survived the 1920s, even adding an air arm; the 1930s saw its renaissance.

Far left: The aviator Charles Lindbergh pictured in 1929 aboard the carrier _Saratoga_. In the background, one of the ship's 8-inch gun turrets.
Left: US fleet at Colon in 1933. At right the carriers _Saratoga_ and _Lexington_.
Below: Battle line during maneuvers in the 1920s. The 32,000-ton battleship _Pennsylvania_ is the leading ship.

Resurgence in the Face of Danger

The impetus for rebuilding the US Navy after 1933 came from three factors: President Franklin D Roosevelt's commitment to naval power; the grim necessity of putting men back to work after the Great Depression, with shipbuilding playing a significant role in New Deal recovery efforts; and the deteriorating world situation, as aggression became the rule of the day in Europe, the Mediterranean area and the Far East. The first two require little explanation, since Roosevelt had demonstrated his naval enthusiasm and know-how as assistant secretary during World War I. The renaissance in ship-

Above: Battleships maneuvering off Hawaii in 1925, a photograph taken from the *Oklahoma*. Next ahead is the *Nevada*.
Top: The *Tennessee* fires a full 14-inch broadside.

building got under way in June 1933 under a $238 million National Recovery Administration program to build 32 warships and continued from that point. The third factor requires amplification.

As of 1933 Germany had fallen under the leadership of Adolf Hitler and his Nazi cohorts on a platform of repudiating the Versailles Treaty and seeking to regain German superiority in European affairs. A decade before, Italy had fallen under the rule of the Fascist dictator Benito Mussolini who wanted to re-create the Roman Empire in the Mediterranean whatever the cost. In Russia, Josef Stalin was firmly entrenched in power and dedicated to spreading Marxist Communism throughout the world. And in Japan a military clique had already taken Manchuria as part of its public goal of establishing a great Far Eastern Empire at the expense of its neighbors. All these developments contained overt challenges to world peace and to the ideals and traditions of the American people. If power was not checked by power, the face of the world would be sadly altered by the grim hand of totalitarian aggression.

As the 1930s continued, aggression escalated. In 1933 Japan took the northern provinces of China. In 1935 Mussolini's mechanized troops overran the hapless natives of Ethiopia. In that same year Hitler announced he was repudiating the arms restriction on Germany imposed by the Treaty of Versailles and announced a submarine-building program. The next year he marched boldly into the demilitarized Rhineland. In 1936 Spain fell into civil war and the Russians, Germans and Italians hastened to help the combatants. In November of that year Japan and Germany joined forces in the Anti-Comintern Pact, with Italy standing close by as an ally. In 1937 Japan continued its attacks on China, and an American gunboat, the USS *Panay*, was attacked and sunk on the Yangtse River by Japanese planes. In 1938 Hitler took control of Austria by his famous *Anschluss* and forced the Czechs to give up the Sudetenland (with the approval at Munich of England and France). The following year, despite his promises, he took the Czech provinces of Bohemia and Moravia. In April 1939 Italy invaded tiny Albania, and the Germans and Italians joined hands as the Axis Powers. Russia gave Germany the green light to move east on 23 August 1939 when she signed a non-aggression pact with Hitler—she was also promised half of Poland—and Hitler responded on 1 September by invading Poland. Britain and France finally decided to curb Germany by honoring their guarantees of Polish independence. World War II began.

Through all of this President Roosevelt was walking a tightrope between military preparedness and the overwhelming desire of the American public to stay out of the troubles of the world. As the situation deteriorated in Europe and the Far East, the isolationism of the 1920s came to full flower, as the American people balked at being pulled into Europe's troubles again. This sentiment received new life in 1934, when the report of the Senate committee chaired by Gerald P Nye stated—on very slanted evidence—that American munitions makers and bankers had conspired to drag the United States into World War I. The next year Congress passed a neutrality act that forbade American exports of arms and ammunition to any belligerents—be they aggressors or victims—and allowed no American vessels to carry armaments to any belligerents. It also restricted travel by Americans on the vessels of belligerents. While this amounted to a *de facto* surrender of America's rights on the high seas, the neutrality law would ostensibly keep America out of any situation that might embroil her in war. That was the whole idea. And as the events of the middle 1930s made the world situation ever more dangerous, with Germany, Japan and Italy on the move, American opinion showed continued determination to stay out of war, and neutrality legislation was only marginally liberalized. Roosevelt, as a result, had to 'sell' naval rearmament until 1939 as a make-work boost to the economy, and thereafter as a means of protecting American interests in an increasingly lawless world. In this he was eminently successful. The US Navy grew at an ever-accelerating pace from 1933 to 1941.

During the 1920s, as mentioned, the navy was allowed to add to the fleet to some extent, especially in cruisers. While

***Main picture:* Battleship Division 5 at firing practice off San Diego in 1925–26. The leading ships are *Maryland*, *Colorado* and *West Virginia*.**

Above: Fleet at anchor in Guantanamo Bay, Cuba, for maneuvers in 1927.
Left: Curtiss R-type floatplane being hoisted aboard the carrier *Langley*.
Right: UO-1 observation aircraft, in service in the 1930s.

completing work on 10 *Omaha*-type cruisers of only 7500 tons, the Navy laid down eight heavy cruisers of 10,000 tons, and in 1929 began work on Coolidge's 15 heavy cruisers, six of the *Phoenix*-class 'treaty cruisers' of 10,000 tons and nine of the 10,000-ton *Portland* class. Work also began that year on the *Ranger*, a smaller carrier of 14,500 tons. Thus by early 1933 the Navy had 342 ships (1,000,270 total tons) with another 16 vessels being built (78,060 tons). These 342 ships included 15 battleships, three carriers, 20 cruisers, 222 destroyers and 82 submarines.

Rebuilding the Fleet

Impressive as this might seem, the navy was hardly at adequate strength to defend the nation's worldwide interests, and so benefited greatly by the building programs of the 1930s. Under the National Recovery Administration funding of 1933, the navy was authorized one heavy and three light cruisers, and, most importantly, two new aircraft carriers of 19,900 tons, to be named the *Enterprise* and the *Yorktown*. The Vinson-Trammel Act of 1934 called for a US Navy of full treaty strength in all types of vessels and authorized construction of new battleships and carriers. The carrier *Wasp* was authorized in 1936 and the *Hornet* followed; the new battleship *North Carolina* was laid down in 1937.

In 1935 Congress funded 24 destroyers and 12 submarines, and in 1936, in addition to funding the *Wasp*, provided monies for two light cruisers, 15 destroyers and six submarines. As the world situation continued to deteriorate, Congress passed the Vinson Act, or 'Twenty Percent Naval Expansion Act,' in 1938 calling for an increase in naval tonnage of 20 percent (46 warships and 26 auxiliaries) and funded eight more destroyers and four subs. Money for more vessels followed in 1939: by July of that year the resurgent US Navy had 373 ships in its inventory (15 battleships, 5 carriers, 37 cruisers, 221 destroyers and 94 submarines) in an aggregate tonnage of 1,277,290. Building were 77 vessels of another 458,880 tons, including 8 battleships, 2 carriers, 4 cruisers, 43 destroyers and 20 subs. In a little over six years, the US Navy had increased its tonnage by over 25 percent, modernized existing vessels and now had a more balanced fleet of faster and more heavily gunned ships. Furthermore, a dozen bases were being constructed or improved throughout the navy's areas of concern.

But Europe's war and Japanese aggressions prodded Roosevelt to do even more to prepare the US Navy for trouble if it came. In June 1940 Congress authorized a 21-vessel battleship fleet and the next month, in the Vinson-Walsh Act, or the 'Two-Ocean Navy Act,' authorized another increase in warship tonnage, this time by another 70 percent, up to 3,049,480 tons. Included were the giant *Essex*-type carriers of 27,000 tons, plus *Iowa*-class battleships, heavy cruisers, destroyers and 1500-ton fleet submarines. Under the prompting of Roosevelt and the perilous state of world affairs, the Navy was being pushed to combat readiness if war could not be avoided.

Aiding the Nation's Friends

World events were not waiting on the navy, while President Roosevelt maneuvered to render all possible aid to the Allies without getting America directly involved in the war. In October 1939 the United States and 21 Latin American nations signed the Declaration of Panama, declaring Western Hemisphere waters to be inherently free from hostile acts by warring nations and establishing a 300-mile neutrality zone off their shores. These waters would be patrolled by warships and planes to enforce the Declaration. That

Right: **The carrier *Langley* in Pearl Harbor in 1928. The *Langley*'s navigating bridge was at the bow under the overhang of the flight deck.**
Below: **Flotilla vessels and cruisers of the Pacific Fleet in March 1925.**

2

Left: Martin T4M-1 torpedo-bombers landing on the carrier *Lexington* in January 1929.
Right: Curtiss F6C fighters and Martin T3M torpedo planes aboard the *Lexington* during the carrier's maiden cruise in April 1928.
Below: The minesweeper *Owl* under way during the Fleet Review, 4 June 1927.

Above: **The airship *Los Angeles* and two blimps in flight over the light cruiser *Raleigh* during maneuvers in October 1930.**

same year saw American neutrality legislation altered to permit the sale of American arms, but only for cash and only on the buyer's vessels. However, the changes also forbade American merchant vessels from carrying arms and barred US citizens from combat zones. America would protect its own turf, but was still strenuously avoiding war.

This ambivalence became more difficult to maintain in late 1939 and early 1940, as Poland, then Finland, were overrun, followed by Germany's invasion in quick order of Denmark, Norway, the Netherlands, Belgium and France—the latter coupled with an Italian invasion from the south. Things looked bleak for the Allied Powers when the evacuation of 300,000 British troops at Dunkirk left the home islands in dire straits, France capitulated to Germany on 22 June 1940, leaving Hitler astride the Continent from the English Channel to the plains of Poland, and Japanese aggression continued virtually unchecked in China. The United States Government responded by joining the Latin American nations in the Declaration of Havana of June 1940, in which the signatory powers stated that an act of aggression by any non-American nation upon any American nation would be considered an act of aggression on all. In September 1940 the US passed the Burke-Wadsworth Bill instituting the peacetime draft for all men between the ages of 21 and 35 (although the law specified that draftees could not be used outside the Western Hemisphere except on American possessions).

While these measures brought America much closer to preparedness and drew a line around the territory which the Axis Powers were forbidden to cross, they offered no help to the hard-pressed British facing the onslaught of German power, especially on the seas, where British resistance met mammoth pressure in the form of German submarine attacks on vital commerce.

With this in mind, Franklin Roosevelt and British Prime Minister Winston Churchill worked out an agreement known as the 'destroyer deal.' As announced by the President on 3 September 1940, 50 older American destroyers would be transferred to Britain by executive agreement in return for 99-year leases on eight Western Hemisphere bases belonging to Britain, one in Newfoundland and seven in the Caribbean. Roosevelt, furthermore, extended American neutrality patrols farther out to sea in search of submarines, the pilots reporting any sightings on open radio frequencies so that British ships could pick up the information. After his successful re-election to an unprecedented third term in office that fall, Roosevelt, in his 'Four Freedoms' speech of 6 January 1941, called for America to supply ships, planes, tanks and guns to nations fighting for those freedoms against 'aggressors' (there was no room for doubt about the identity of these protagonists).

America took other crucial steps toward full involvement in the war in the Lend-

Right: **The crowded flight deck of the *Saratoga*. The *Lexington* and *Saratoga* were designed to carry 78 aircraft and could comfortably fit in more.**

Lease Act of March 1941, wherein the 1939 provision of 'cash and carry' was dropped for nations fighting the aggressors; in forming an agreement with Denmark for America to construct air bases in Greenland for patrol duty; and in Roosevelt's extending the area of the ships and planes of the neutrality patrol up to 2000 miles from the American coast. This was well within the area defined by Germany as the war zone earlier that year. Furthermore, American scout planes within the zone were informing the nearest British base when a German ship or sub was spotted, so that convoys could avoid the area and British planes and ships could seek to destroy it.

It was a decidedly pro-Allied neutrality game that Roosevelt was playing in the North Atlantic, marked by the shifting of many US Navy vessels from the Pacific to the Atlantic. By the fall of 1941—the 'Atlantic Charter' decrying Nazi tyranny having been drawn up by Roosevelt and Churchill in Newfoundland—the United States was in an undeclared war on Germany through Roosevelt's extended neutrality patrol.

The US Navy was virtually the only American force carrying on the undeclared war. When the USS *Greer* was attacked in the North Atlantic by a German submarine on 4 September 1941, Roosevelt told the Navy to 'shoot on sight' any hostile craft attacking American ships or any ships under American escort. Whatever the legality of the last part of the order, the naval war in the North Atlantic was becoming very dangerous. The attack on

Below: **The *Yorktown* (CV.5) pictured in Hampton Roads in October 1937.**

the *Greer* was followed by attacks by German subs on the destroyer *Kearney* (after the *Kearney* had dropped depth charges) and on the destroyer *Reuben James* in October 1941. The attack on the *Kearney* prompted Roosevelt (who did not reveal to the public the circumstances of the incident) to say, 'We Americans have cleared our decks and taken our battle stations.' The sinking of the *Reuben James* prompted Congress to allow American merchant vessels to be armed and to sail to any and all belligerent ports. America, already in an undeclared naval shooting war, stood at the threshold of all-out involvement in warfare against Nazi Germany. Then devastation fell from the skies onto the US Navy base at Pearl Harbor in the Pacific, and the undeclared naval war against Hitler's Germany in the North Atlantic turned into a conflict against all the Axis Powers worldwide. The US Navy faced its greatest challenge as the smoke from the devastated Pacific Fleet marked the incredible destruction of the 'day that will live in infamy.'

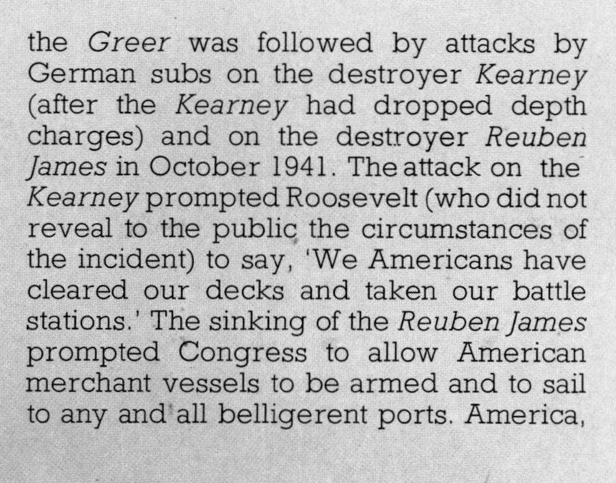

REGAINING THE PACIFIC SEAS

Japan had long been determined to extend its holding and influence in the Far East, and the year 1940 saw a resurgence of this aggressive expansionism. As a spokesman for the Japanese militarists, Prince Fumimaro Konoye announced the area of Japanese interests as the expansive Greater East Asia Co-Prosperity Sphere, stretching from the home islands and Manchuria south through the Dutch East Indies and into central Pacific waters. In the very heart of this projected Japanese empire were the Philippines and the American island of Guam in the Marianas. Then in September 1940 an agreement was made with the Nazi-dominated Vichy regime in France for the Japanese to take over Indochina, and the Imperial Japanese Government became a partner in the Axis military alliance.

No letup occurred in 1941. Despite President Roosevelt's freezing of all Japanese assets in the United States as a warning to Japan to cease its march of conquest, the Japanese moved into Indochina, and the war-minded General Hideki Tojo became Prime Minister. The American Government, with its attention focused on the deteriorating military situation in Europe—Hitler turned his fury on Britain to gain final control of the Continent for his 'Thousand-Year Reich'—shored up US military forces in the Philippines as best it could. This included placing all US Army forces in the Far East under the authority of the imperious Lieutenant General Douglas MacArthur—top man in his West Point class, World War I decorated hero, former Army Chief of Staff, experienced Far Eastern military leader, and hitherto Field Marshal of the Philippine Army. A few submarines were also sent to the Philippines to reinforce the Navy's Asiatic fleet under the command of Admiral Thomas C Hart. But, all in all, it would be a pitifully weak army-navy defensive team that would face the Japanese if, as expected, their primary target was the Philippine archipelago. In the meantime, Washington carefully watched events in the Pacific and tried to perceive Japanese intentions.

Pearl Harbor

The Japanese leaders were looking at another objective. Their original Pacific plans had, indeed, called for a sweep through the Philippines en route to the conquest of the rich Dutch East Indies, fending off American naval attacks on their left flank as they moved south. But these plans were scuttled in favor of a more daring strategy that came from the mind of Admiral Isoruko Yamamoto, Commander in Chief of the Combined Fleet. Pearl Harbor, America's great naval base in the Hawaiian Islands, was chosen as the new primary target. With the American fleet at Pearl Harbor destroyed, the Japanese would have virtually no opposition as they moved south; before the Americans could challenge them, their position in the Pacific would be impregnable.

Accordingly, plans were drawn up for a lightning air strike on the American naval and air bases on Oahu. An advanced cover force would lead to the target area a strike force of six carriers, two battleships and three cruisers plus escorts. This impressive armada began to gather in November 1941 in Hitokappu Bay in the Kuriles; on 26 November, under strict radio silence, the vessels steamed out of the bay to sail east, southeast, then south. The target: Pearl Harbor and the unsuspecting American fleet. Target date: 7 December 1941.

Moving steadily on their charted course, the phantom fleet was refueled en route. Late Japanese intelligence reports indicated that eight US battleships, nine cruisers, 20 destroyers and 41 other vessels were anchored at Pearl Harbor. Diplomatic negotiations between Washington and Tokyo being deadlocked, the coded message 'Climb Mount Niitaka' ('Proceed with attack') was sent out. On 7 December 1941 (Hawaiian date) between 6:00 and 7:15 in the morning, 360 planes (81 fighters, 104 horizontal bombers, 40 torpedo bombers, and 135 dive bombers) took flight from the decks of the six Japanese carriers 200 miles due north of the islands, formed up, and headed for Pearl Harbor. At 7:55 they attacked the quiet naval base with full fury. The greatest surprise attack in history had begun.

Between 7:55 and 9:45 the American fleet and air bases—not sufficiently warned despite ominous signs of trouble with Japan—underwent a devastating air raid without being able to put up a creditable defense. With little difficulty, the Japanese dive bombers first neutralized the airfields on Oahu; the American planes had

Below: **Japanese Zero fighters ready for take off from a carrier at the start of the Pearl Harbor attack.**

Right: **The destroyers *Cassin* and *Downes* and (behind) the battleship *Pennsylvania* in the flooded dry dock at Pearl Harbor after the attack.**

Above: A large column of smoke fills the sky above Battleship Row as the Japanese attack reaches its height.

Above: Rifle-armed soldiers and sailors keep watch for a renewed Japanese attack as the ships of Battleship Row burn in the background.
Below: Damage-control parties strive to control fires aboard the battleship *Nevada* at Pearl Harbor.

been neatly lined up in rows as a precaution against sabotage. At the same time the first waves of torpedo planes zoomed in at low altitude to ram their deadly ordnance into the hulls of battleships and cruisers moored side by side along the docks, the outside vessels taking the worst punishment. Pearl Harbor became an inferno of blazing ships as surviving crew members tried desperately to save the vessels and to man their antiaircraft weapons. After the initial half-hour attack, a 15-minute lull ensued; then the chaos of death began again at 8:40 as the Japanese horizontal bombers went to work, followed by a second wave of torpedo bombers. At 9:15 the dive bomber attacks resumed, lasting for an agonizing half hour. By 9:45 it was all over. The Japanese planes—only 29 of which had been lost—returned to their carriers, leaving behind them the burning wreckage of the Pacific Fleet.

In less than two hours the Japanese attackers had sunk or severely damaged eight battleships, three cruisers, three destroyers, four other vessels and 188 American aircraft. The Navy and Marine Corps suffered over 2000 men killed and over 700 wounded that day; the Army had almost 200 killed and over 400 wounded. The only consolation the American military leaders could draw from the dreadful day of death was that the Japanese had not destroyed the fuel storage tanks and naval repair shops on Oahu and that the three American carriers all happened to be deployed away from Pearl Harbor. The Pacific Fleet could be rebuilt to fight back.

Early Actions

Within three days of Pearl Harbor America had declared war on Japan, Germany and Italy had declared war on the United States, and the United States had declared war on Germany and Italy. America had now joined the Allies in the worldwide fight against the Axis powers. By 1 January 1942 the Allies had confirmed their wartime intentions in the Declaration of Washington, which included the decision to concentrate first on Hitler and the Atlantic front. This priority was set because the German war machine, extended on four fronts, was a greater immediate danger. In the Pacific the Americans would wait until Europe had been taken care of, holding all the territory they could while slowing down the Japanese movements. American Forces went on the offensive in the Atlantic and on the defensive in the Pacific.

To lead this demanding military mission for the Navy, the stern taskmaster Admiral Ernest J King was brought in as Commander in Chief, US Fleet, on 30 December and the next month was also given the job of Chief of Naval Operations. King's man in the Pacific after 31 December was Admiral Chester W Nimitz, Commander in Chief, Pacific Fleet (Cincpac), moved up from Chief of the Bureau of Navigation to replace Admiral Husband E Kimmel, in disgrace and under investigation in the aftermath of the Pearl Harbor debacle. Time would show that this was a brilliant appointment. Admiral Hart was retained as commander of the Asiatic fleet for the time being as he was fighting a fine delaying action against the strong initial Japanese movements south. This team would be in charge of stalling the Japanese juggernaut in the Pacific. If they could not do the job, the way back to victory would be virtually impossible. Nimitz's task as Cincpac was to see that the Navy's job in the Pacific was done and done right.

Despite the rebuilding programs of the 1930s, the Navy had a mammoth job to gear up both men and ships for the fight ahead. Within a year of Pearl Harbor, 900,000 volunteers had been added to the prewar naval ranks of 325,000 officers and men. This called for rapidly expanding the four existing training sites and building three more. The additional officers needed would come partly from the V-5 (aviation cadet), V-7 (reserve midshipmen) and V-12 (general officer) programs on the nation's college campuses. Maintaining adequate trained manpower for the fleet was not a major problem for the Navy throughout the war once the multitudinous training programs had been set up.

Naval shipbuilding received top priority from the wartime administration, as industry turned to building the American war machine. Faced with the loss of virtually its entire Pacific battleship fleet at Pearl Harbor, the Navy was left with its carriers as the nucleus of Pacific power (the Atlantic Fleet had eight battleships and four carriers). Accordingly, it had only seven big carriers available for both oceans, although several large *Essex*-class flat-tops were building. The Navy turned to converting merchant vessels into 'baby flat-tops' or 'jeep carriers' for convoy escort, airplane transport and fleet support roles. Light also in cruisers, destroyers, submarines, landing craft, fighters, dive bombers and torpedo bom-

Opposite: Map of the Battle of the Coral Sea.
***Below:* The Japanese carrier *Shokaku* under attack during the Coral Sea battle.**
***Bottom:* The crew of the *Lexington* abandon ship, Coral Sea, 8 May 1942.**

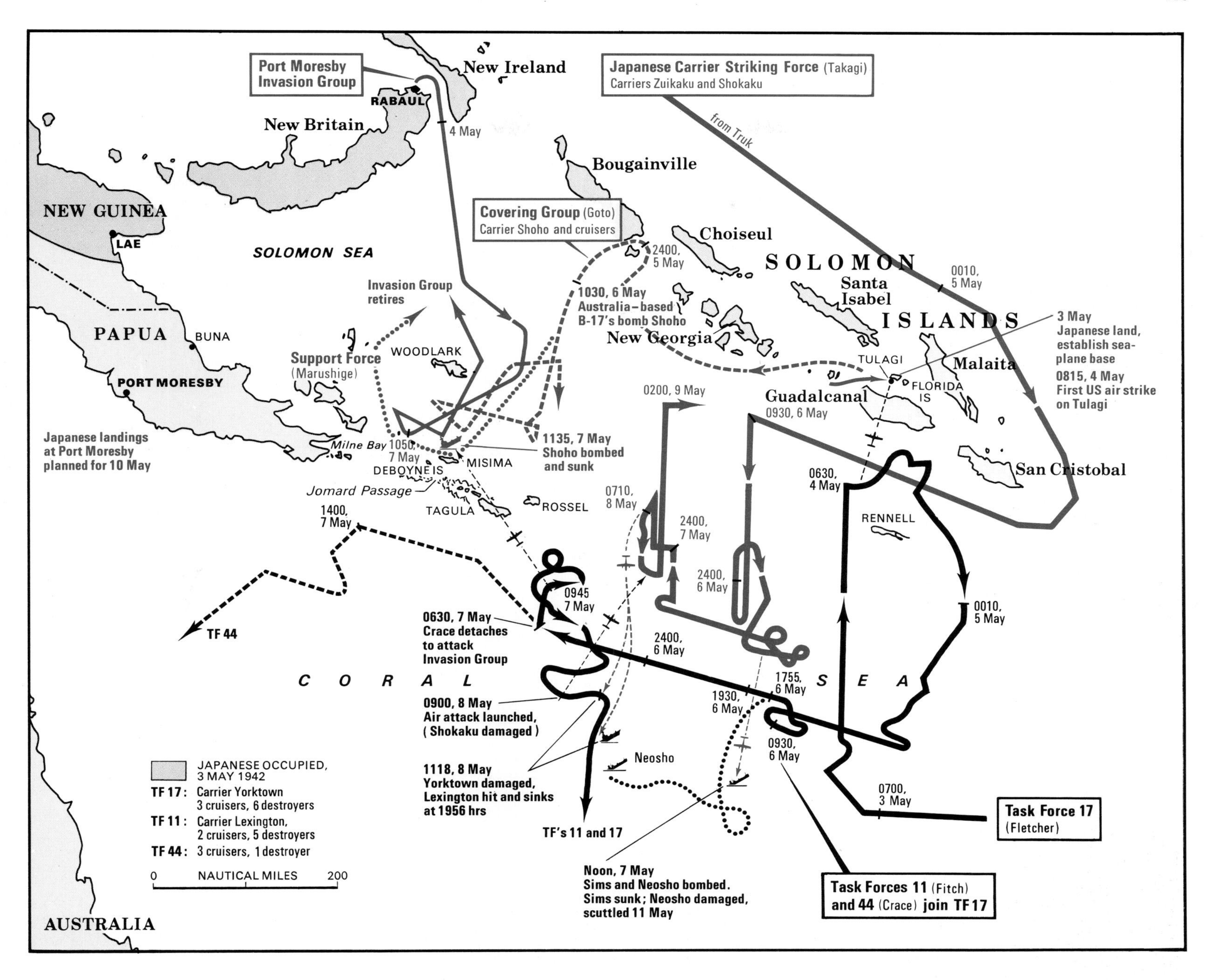

bers, the Navy began or accelerated building programs on all types of vessels and airplanes, so that by late 1942 it was gaining the muscle it needed. By 1943 giant fleets built around fast carriers would begin to dominate Pacific waters, but in the meantime the Navy was buying time until the balance of naval power could swing its way.

During the first six months of the war America's Pacific forces were fighting with their backs to the wall. Guam, Wake and Hong Kong were taken shortly after Pearl Harbor, and the Japanese marched down the Malayan Peninsula toward Singapore; the American Philippines were another prime target. Seeking to slow down the enemy a British naval force consisting of the new 35,000-ton battleship *Prince of Wales* and the battlecruiser *Repulse* threw themselves in the way of the Japanese fleet moving down through Malayan waters on 10 December, only to be sunk by Japanese bombers and torpedo planes. In January 1942 four old American destroyers launched an attack on the Japanese in the Makassar Strait west of Borneo and sank five ships in an amazing display of gallantry. The following month a weak Allied naval force under Rear Admiral Karel Doorman of the Royal Netherlands Navy tried valiantly to stop the Japanese in the Battle of the Java Sea. All the Allied cruisers, including the USS *Houston*, were lost. With the Allied defensive fleet gone, the Dutch East Indies were soon in Japanese hands.

In the critical Philippines the American forces grimly awaited their turn. Soon Army and Filipino ground forces were encircled on the Bataan Peninsula, and the 4th Marine Regiment was holding out on Corregidor at the entrance to Manila Bay. With the Philippines about to fall to the Japanese juggernaut, General MacArthur was ordered out to make his way to Australia, from which point he could direct a counteroffensive. What remained of the American forces surrendered in May 1942, and General Jonathan Wainwright and his 70,000 men were forced to undergo the infamous Bataan Death March.

While this was taking place, the Japanese in the early months of 1942 had moved far south into the Solomon Islands and northern New Guinea and threatened both Port Moresby on Papua New Guinea and Australia itself. If these fell, defeat of the Japanese would be virtually impossible. No one knew this better than the Pacific fleet commanders.

To gain some idea of Japanese strength along the sea lanes to Australia and to lift civilian morale by showing that somebody was 'doing something,' an American carrier force built around the *Enterprise* under the command of Vice-Admiral William F Halsey staged a raid on the Marshall and Gilbert Islands halfway between Hawaii and Australia in February 1942.

They followed this up the same month with a raid on Wake and Marcus Islands in the central Pacific. In March a task force that included the *Lexington* and *Yorktown* raided northern New Guinea. None of

Top: A destroyer comes alongside the damaged *Lexington* to help take the crew off. *Above:* The *Lexington* finally blows up. Better damage-control procedures might have saved the ship.

these raids caused significant damage, but they did lift morale at home. The same is true of Lieutenant Colonel James Doolittle's raid on Tokyo of 18 April 1942. The 16 B-25 Army bombers that lifted off the deck of the *Hornet*, 650 miles out at sea, to bomb Tokyo and then fly another 1100 miles to China did little damage, but they did give Americans a great deal of much-needed hope in the dismal early months of 1942.

When the Americans discovered, by breaking the Japanese naval code, that the enemy was launching invasion forces against Port Moresby in southern New Guinea and the island of Tulagi in the Solomons to the east, they decided to thwart those plans as best they could. The result was the Battle of the Coral Sea of 7–8 May 1942. Rear Admiral Frank Jack Fletcher and the *Yorktown* task force, and Rear Admiral Aubrey W Fitch in command of the *Lexington* task force, were ordered to strike at the two enemy task forces. Halsey, with the *Enterprise* and *Hornet* (back from the Tokyo raid) was ordered to follow. He arrived too late. The opposing American and Japanese forces found one another on 7 May and launched their attacks. This was the first naval engagement in history in which surface ships never fired a shot at one another and, indeed, never saw one another. When it was over after two days of air attacks on the fleets, the Japanese had lost the new small carrier *Shoho* and another had been badly damaged. The Americans saw the *Yorktown* badly damaged and lost a tanker, a destroyer and the *Lexington* on the second day—the *Lexington* the victim of two torpedoes plus an enormous explosion caused by ruptured aviation fuel lines. (Most of the crew were saved.) The Battle of the Coral Sea was a strategic victory for the Americans despite their heavy losses because it stopped the invasion of Port Moresby. But now the Americans had only four carriers left in Pacific waters (*Yorktown*, *Hornet*, *Saratoga*, *Enterprise*); the Japanese had nine. Within one month this imbalance had been largely nullified in the Battle of Midway, the Navy's greatest victory in World War II.

The Battle of Midway

The Japanese wanted the island of Midway as a forward base for an attack on Hawaii; they also wanted to lure the American fleet out to its own destruction. The First Carrier Striking Force of four carriers (*Akagi*, *Kaga*, *Hiryu*, *Soryu*) plus two battleships, three cruisers and 11 destroyers was under the command of Vice-Admiral Chuichi Nagumo, who had led the attack on Pearl Harbor. Its mission was to attack Midway by air and devastate the American fleet if it showed up. The Midway Invasion Force (Second Fleet) under Vice-Admiral Nobutake Kondo would move in from the west with 5000 men in 12 transports with two battleships, a light carrier and numerous cruisers and destroyers as escorts. A third armada, the Second Carrier Striking Force, would move on American positions at Attu, Adak and Kiska far north in the Aleutians as a diversion. It would consist of two light carriers, three cruisers and six destroyers. In the rear would come the Main Force (First Fleet) of nine battleships plus numerous cruisers and destroyers under the command of Admiral Yamamoto himself, who had personally approved the invasion-entrapment plans. In addition, 16 submarines would station themselves between Pearl Harbor and Midway to the northwest. If the Americans came out to do battle, Yamamoto had more than enough firepower to put them down (although he believed that the *Yorktown* as well as the *Lexington* might have been sunk in the Battle of the Coral Sea and that the *Hornet* and the *Enterprise* were still in the Solomons area). If not, the submarine screen could stop them or at least give warning if any carriers sallied forth.

Unknown to Yamamoto, Admiral Nimitz had learned both his plans and his target date: 4 June 1942. This was due to the

Above: The small Japanese carrier _Shoho_ takes a torpedo hit from an American aircraft, 7 May 1942.
Below, main picture: A Japanese Val dive-bomber attacks the USS _Hornet_ during the Battle of Santa Cruz, 26 October 1942.

Above: **The *Yorktown* on fire after the first Japanese attack during the Battle of Midway. These fires were brought under control.**

superior sleuthing of cryptologist Commander Joseph Rochefort and his assistants at Pearl Harbor. Nimitz knew that he had only two carriers (*Hornet* and *Enterprise*), plus the damaged *Yorktown* if she could be patched up in time, with which to stop the attack. The recently repaired *Saratoga* was at San Diego to form a new task force and undoubtedly could not get back in time. Against these the Japanese could throw perhaps 10 carriers, plus 23 cruisers and 11 fast battleships. Rather than scatter his fleet to protect Oahu, Nimitz decided not to take the bait of the Aleutians invading force and concentrate his forces on the Japanese left flank. If the four carriers of the First Carrier Striking Force were to be taken out of action, the Midway invasion force and the combined fleets would be without air cover. Put the carriers down and the whole Japanese operation would fail. It was a long shot, but Nimitz had no choice. If he scattered his thin fleet, the Americans could do nothing to stop the Japanese.

Accordingly, when Task Force 16 including the *Hornet* and *Enterprise* returned to Pearl Harbor on 16 May, Nimitz gave command of the force to Rear Admiral Raymond Spruance (Halsey being hospitalized with a skin ailment) and told him to put himself on Nagumo's flank and hit him while his planes were off raiding Midway. Task Force 16 left Oahu on 28 May. When Task Force 17 returned to Pearl Harbor under Admiral Fletcher, Nimitz gave the repair crews three days to get the *Yorktown* ready again (the estimates had all concluded it would take 90 days). Three days later, on 30 May, the *Yorktown* and Task Force 17 left the Pacific base to meet Spruance and Task Force 16 at the rendezvous point 200 miles north of Midway. The stage was set for a titanic clash.

As the American task forces arrived on station, it became a matter of waiting. In the meantime Rear Admiral Robert A Theobald's North Pacific Force was steaming north to intercept the attack on the Aleutians, but Theobald, believing the Aleutians landing was a ruse and that the enemy would hit Dutch Harbor far to the east or else Alaska, placed his force 400 miles south of Kodiak: as a result, he was out of the fight altogether. As the *Saratoga* task force left San Diego on 1 June, it would arrive too late to help.

Although all this was not known by Nimitz, Spruance and Fletcher at the time, it was clearly up to the two carrier task forces, plus some Army B-17s on Midway, to stop the invasion. Yet Nimitz had a glimpse of victory. His Operation Plan No. 29–42, while stipulating an attack of attrition on the Japanese striking force, included the enticing idea that, with luck, maybe the Japanese fleet could be caught while recovering its attacking planes, thus grounding the remaining Japanese carrier planes until recovery of the fuel-shy first wave was completed. Furthermore, the Japanese might still believe the carriers were far south in the Solomons (a US cruiser in the Coral Sea was broadcasting on carrier air-group frequencies to give that impression). Then complete surprise would be possible. As the battle turnd out, this is exactly what happened. A shot of luck, unbelievable gallantry and correct command decisions won the day for the undersized American naval forces.

On 3 June the Japanese invasion fleet was spotted 700 miles west of Midway: Army B-17s attacked the enemy ships, although no damage was done. But at least Admiral Nimitz knew the Japanese were coming right on schedule and could be expected the next day.

At six o'clock on the morning of 4 June Navy Catalina scout planes found the Japanese strike force 180 miles northwest of Midway and coming down hard at 135 degrees. Nimitz correctly surmised that they had launched their first wave and did not know of the American carriers on their flank, since they were not turning to meet them. By 6:25 Midway was under heavy air attack. A half hour later Spruance launched his planes from the *Hornet*, *Enterprise* and *Yorktown*. By 8:20 Nimitz knew that Nagumo would either have to launch his reserves (if his search planes had discovered the American carriers), leaving the returning first-strike planes in the air on low fuel, or he would have to

Above: **Japanese torpedo bombers pass near the already damaged *Yorktown*.**
Below: **The Japanese *Hiryu* shortly before she was sunk.**

recover, refuel and rearm the first strike planes for a second strike, leaving the second-wave planes waiting. If he chose the first, he would lose planes to the sea; if he chose the second, he would lose at least an hour. He chose the latter. If only the American planes arrived on time, Nimitz knew, the Japanese would be in an extremely vulnerable position.

Although 35 dive bombers from the *Hornet* could not find the Japanese fleet and flew on to Midway, the 15 old TBD Devastator torpedo bombers from the *Hornet* sighted the enemy at 10:25 am and attacked with no fighter cover. They skimmed in over the water to launch their torpedoes, with Japanese fighters and antiaircraft guns contesting them every inch of the way. Ten of 14 torpedo bombers from the *Enterprise* joining in the attack were shot down; 35 of 41 from the *Yorktown* met the same fate; all the torpedo bombers from the *Hornet* were lost. And they had done no damage whatever. But their gallant sacrifice won rich dividends, because they had pulled the Japanese fighter cover down just as dive bombers from the *Yorktown* and *Enterprise* happened to discover the Japanese fleet. No fighters were up to oppose them. Down they plummeted through clear skies. The *Akagi* was hit by three bombs and soon turned into a raging inferno of fuel oil and torpedoes left on deck in rearming the first wave for a strike on the American carriers. Admiral Nagumo was forced to transfer his flag to a nearby cruiser, and the survivors of the fiery holocaust abandoned ship. She sank the next morning.

At almost the same time the *Akagi* was hit, the *Kaga* and *Soryu* were struck by the American dive bombers. Again the ships quickly became infernos from the bombs, torpedoes and aviation fuel. Nagumo had refused to launch an attack on the American carriers with his reserves as soon as he discovered they were in the area; he had waited until the first wave was recovered, re-fueled and armed with armor-piercing bombs and torpedoes. This took two hours. Just as his carriers were turning into the wind to launch, the *Yorktown* and *Enterprise* bombers hit them. It was like throwing a match into a powder keg.

Shortly thereafter, at 10:50 am, Japanese dive bombers from the fourth and trailing carrier, the *Hiryu*, were launched against the American carriers. They found their prey—the *Yorktown*. Eighteen dive bombers hit her with two bombs that stopped her dead in the water. Within

Above: **An escorting cruiser moves in to assist the burning *Yorktown*.**

minutes Admiral Fletcher had shifted his flag from the doomed vessel to the cruiser *Astoria*. But the *Yorktown* refused to go down. Two hours later her men had repaired her boilers and she was making 20 knots and preparing to launch her fighters. At this point she was attacked again by torpedo planes; a third wave hit her once more an hour later and she was abandoned. But for a second time she refused to go down, and was not sunk until three days later while being towed to Pearl Harbor. A Japanese sub evaded her destroyer screen to put her down.

The *Hiryu* may have been carrying on gallantly as the last carrier in the group, but at 5:00 in the afternoon of 4 June her turn came. She was hit by 24 American planes in four waves, took four bomb hits and had to be abandoned. She was deliberately sunk the next morning by a Japanese submarine.

Four Japanese carriers were sunk or sinking: the American flank attack had worked perfectly. But the battle was not over. What if Yamamoto detached his fast battleships and cruisers from the Midway Invasion Force to attack the American carrier task forces in their state of exhaustion? Correctly guessing that this would happen, Spruance and Fletcher moved to the east. The Japanese battleships and cruisers came on in hot pursuit the night of 4 June, but had to abandon their search early the next morning for fear of being caught in daylight without air cover. As they turned back west, American air-search crews reported that all Japanese ships were moving northwest; Yamamoto had called off the invasion.

But Spruance was not done. He came barreling through to catch the fleeing Japanese fleets and put them under air attack. The next day, 6 June, American air strikes sank the cruiser *Mikuma* and battered the *Mogami* unmercifully. Still Yamamoto could salvage at least a partial victory if Spruance kept coming. Task Force 16 could run into a trap of bombers stationed on Wake Island plus the firepower of his First Fleet (at this point, indeed throughout the entire battle, the Pacific command had no idea that the First Fleet was in the rear area). Yamamoto even had English-language distress signals sent out to lure the Americans into the trap. But Spruance refused to take the bait. Fearing attacks on his task force from the land-based bombers, he turned back east 400 miles from Midway. The battle was over, even though the Japanese from the Second Carrier Striking Force landed and took Attu and Kiska the next day, 7 June—while Theobald's Force was 1000 miles away.

Above: **A Hellcat fighter comes in to land on a new *Essex* class carrier.**
Above right: **R to L, Admiral Halsey, Secretary Knox and Admiral King.**
Right: **A landing officer brings a plane in to land on the carrier *Wasp*.**
Below: **The Japanese heavy cruiser *Mikuma* sinking after the Battle of Midway.**

Above: **Dauntless dive bombers head for the Japanese aircraft carrier fleet at Midway. What seems to be a burning Japanese ship can be seen below.**

When the score was tallied up, the American Navy had won an overwhelming victory, perhaps the greatest in its history. While losing the *Yorktown*, one destroyer, 147 aircraft and 307 men, American naval forces had pounded the Japanese with heavy losses: four carriers and one heavy cruiser sunk, one heavy cruiser wrecked, one battleship and three destroyers damaged, 322 aircraft lost and 2500 men killed. This last factor was especially crucial, since among the casualties were the elite of Japanese naval pilots. Time would prove that they could never be adequately replaced—a critical factor in a naval war dominated by the antagonists' air power. Admiral Yamamoto, in trying to obtain two objectives, Midway and the American fleet, had gained neither. The Battle of Midway reversed the entire course of the Pacific war: the US took the offensive. It was the Navy's finest hour in World War II.

Battles for Guadalcanal

The Japanese military forces had reached their farthest point of expansion by the summer of 1942, although no one realized it at the time. But both sides understood clearly that if the Japanese secured complete control of the Solomon Islands east of New Guinea, they would be able to cut the supply lines to Australia and wreck Allied plans for a counteroffensive from that base of operations. Furthermore, the Americans wanted to wrest Guadalcanal in the south Solomons from the Japanese to establish a base for the right arm of a two-pronged movement north through the Solomons. (The left arm under General MacArthur would move from Australia along the coast of New Guinea, then turn right to take the large Japanese base at Rabaul on New Britain Island). Accordingly, the first giant amphibious operation of the war was planned with the islands of Guadalcanal and Tulagi, Ganutu and Tanambogo, twenty miles to the north, as the targets. It was set for early August 1942. Two Navy task forces were to aid 19,000 Marines in the landing: an air support force built around the carriers *Hornet*, *Wasp* and *Enterprise* and an amphibious support force built around seven cruisers. The Marine landing on 7 August went well, and by the next day Tulagi, the other tiny islands and the airfield on the north edge of Guadalcanal had been taken (renamed Henderson Field, it was the focus of fighting for the next four months). The Navy's SeaBees (Construction Battalions) went to work to finish the field for American use. But early next morning, a Japanese strike force of seven cruisers and a destroyer came racing down 'The Slot' through the

Below: **The carrier *Wasp* sinks after a torpedo attack from the Japanese submarine *I.19* in the Solomons in September 1942.**

Right: The flight deck of the carrier *Saratoga* at dawn before an attack on Rabaul in November 1943.

***Above:* President Roosevelt examines a captured Japanese flag, taken after an amphibious operation.**

waters of the central Solomons and attacked the unsuspecting amphibious force as it lay south of Guadalcanal—the carrier fleet having been pulled back by Admiral Fletcher for refueling.

In the resulting Battle of Savo Island, the Allied amphibious fleet was severely mauled, losing four cruisers in a matter of hours. Unaware that the American carriers were not in the area, Vice-Admiral Gunichi Mikawa withdrew before attacking the unprotected transports. A severe defeat could easily have been a disaster. But Rear Admiral Kelly Turner, expecting more trouble for his battered men and ships, withdrew the naval amphibious support force before the supply ships were completely unloaded, leaving the Marines and SeaBees to their own devices on Guadalcanal. After a ten-day stage of rebuilding by both combatants, marked by light attacks by each side, the Japanese returned in force. Six sea battles were eventually fought before the control of the south Solomons was finally decided.

The first of these, the Battle of the Eastern Solomons of 24 August 1942, was fought 150 miles east of Guadalcanal. As a Japanese occupation force and two screening forces moved toward the island, Admiral Fletcher's planes from the *Enterprise* and *Saratoga* attacked the enemy forces and sank the small carrier *Ryujo* and a destroyer. This blunted the planned attack, although the *Enterprise* was badly damaged by Japanese aircraft. The Japanese were forced to abandon their attempt to recapture Guadalcanal at this time. The second engagement, the Battle of Cape Esperance, took place on 11–12 October. An American naval force—less the carriers *Saratoga* (damaged by a torpedo on 31 August and forced out of action for three months) and *Wasp* (torpedoed and sunk by a Japanese sub on 15 September)—took on a Japanese force that was part of the 'Tokyo Express'—cruisers and destroyers that moved in nightly to reinforce Japanese positions and shell American troops on Guadalcanal. The American cruiser-destroyer task force sank a Japanese cruiser and destroyer, losing one destroyer in the battle. Undeterred, the Japanese continued to resupply and reinforce their Guadalcanal forces. The situation was growing critical as they fiercely contested the American presence on Guadalcanal. The Navy had to gain control of the air and water around the island, or America's toehold in the Solomons would be lost.

Two weeks later, sensing the time was right for a massive move to expel the hard-pressed Americans, Admiral Yamamoto sent a giant force of four carriers, four battleships, 14 cruisers and 44 destroyers to deliver a knockout blow to the Navy and push the Marines off Guadalcanal. Admiral Halsey, now in command in the area, sent Admiral Thomas C Kinkaid to meet them with two carriers, two battleships, nine cruisers and 24 destroyers. The resulting air melee, known as the Battle of the Santa Cruz Islands, took place on 26 October 1942 and ended with American loss of the *Hornet* and new damage to the *Enterprise*. In this carrier-plane battle the Americans suffered a tactical defeat when Kincaid was forced to withdraw, but they won a strategic victory in that over 100 Japanese planes and crews went down—a crucial loss to the Japanese Navy. While this third battle was taking place, the Marines were beating off Japanese reinforcements. The Guadalcanal campaign was beginning to turn around, despite the losses in the Battle of the Santa Cruz Islands.

The fourth and fifth battles, known as the Naval Battles of Guadalcanal, took place on

Above: The assault transport *McCawley* on exercises in 1943.
Right: Arming a Dauntless dive bomber aboard the *Enterprise* in August 1942.

12–15 November. The first was a wild brawl of only 14 minutes, in which an American force of five cruisers and eight destroyers under Rear Admiral Daniel J Callahan attempted to derail the Tokyo Express and its 13,500-troop replacement force bound for Guadalcanal. The Japanese lost one battleship and two destroyers in the furious and desperate fighting; the Americans lost the cruisers *Atlanta* and *Juneau* and four destroyers. But the Jap-

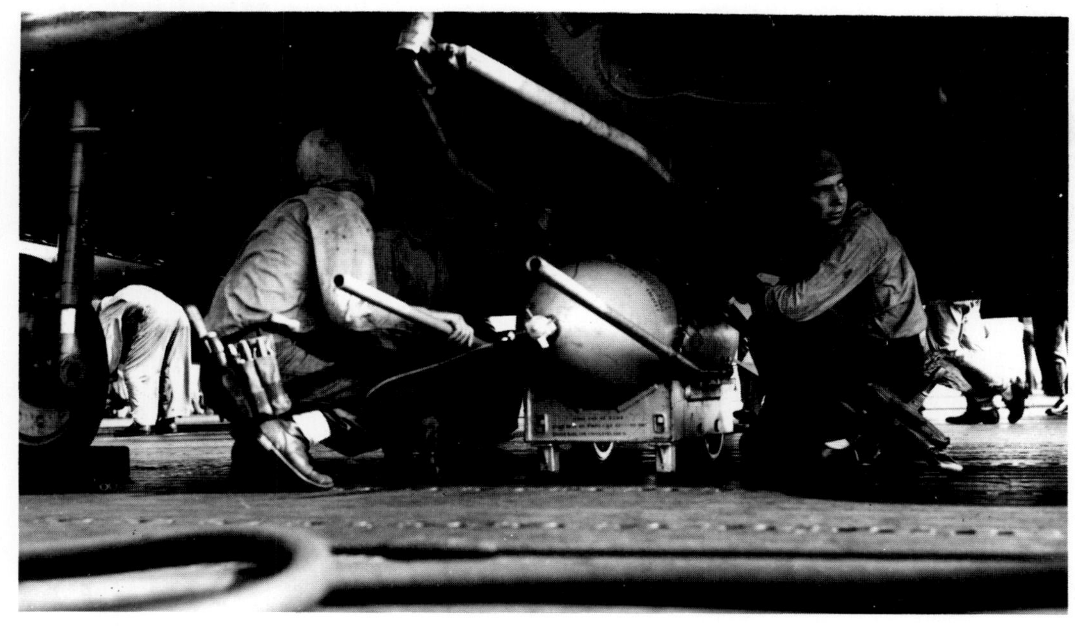

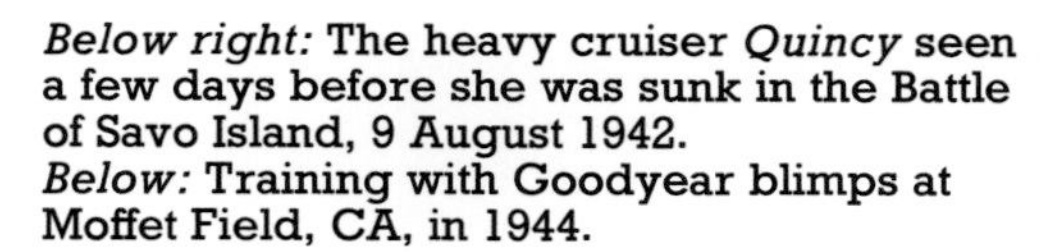

Below right: The heavy cruiser *Quincy* seen a few days before she was sunk in the Battle of Savo Island, 9 August 1942.
Below: Training with Goodyear blimps at Moffet Field, CA, in 1944.

anese were forced to retreat without reinforcing Guadalcanal. The second battle took place on 14 November. Again the Japanese were attempting to reinforce Guadalcanal, and again the American naval forces were assigned the task of stopping them. In this surface ship-to-ship battle American and Japanese units pounded at one another again, both sides suffering heavy losses, but as the Japanese invasion force scattered, Guadalcanal was secure at last.

The sixth engagement, the Battle of Tassafaronga of 30 November 1942, was a clear Japanese victory of eight destroyers over an American cruiser-destroyer force in the dark of night, but it made no appreciable difference in the campaign. American naval forces had gradually but definitely gained control of the sea and air in the southern Solomons to the point where the Japanese could no longer contest them. So many ships had been sunk in the waters just north of Guadalcanal that the area was given the nickname 'Iron-bottom Sound.' When the Army took over Guadalcanal from the Marines with 50,000 troops in January, and the Tokyo Express was finally derailed at the same time by patrol torpedo (PT) boats and aircraft, the dogged battle for Guadalcanal was over (9 February 1943). American military forces now had their staging area in the southern Solomons and could begin to move north.

Island Hopping

For the next year and a half, combined American forces in the Pacific carried out a giant ocean-wide, two-pronged movement against the Japanese possessions. The left prong of the movement consisted of General Douglas MacArthur's Southwest Pacific Forces clearing the enemy from the north shore of New Guinea and moving into the Bismarck Sea. As he moved, his right flank was covered by the South Pacific Forces under Admiral Halsey fighting their way through the Solomon Island chain to meet MacArthur's forces in the Admiralty Islands. The two would then roll northwest toward the Philippines. In the meantime, the right prong, the Central Pacific Forces under Admiral Spruance, moved from Pearl Harbor in a westerly and southwesterly direction to take the Marshall, Gilbert and Marianas island chains from the Japanese, then advanced west to meet the left pincer at the Philippines, while also driving to the northwest toward the Japanese home islands. During this gigantic offensive campaign the Japanese would be pushed inexorably back by a series of amphibious landings on certain key islands and bases while the Allies deliberately neutralized or bypassed others to let them 'die on the vine' with severing of their supply lines to the rear.

To carry out its Pacific-wide strategy successfully, the US Navy had to expand constantly, procuring more ships, men

Above: The battleship *Iowa* and a sister ship at sea in 1944.
Left: Crewmen of the carrier *Yorktown* in May 1943. Several of the US ships sunk early in the war were remembered in the names of more modern replacements.
Below: The *Massachusetts* during a shore bombardment.

and equipment from the shipyards, factories and homes of America. These were forthcoming in abundance. By mid-1943 the fast carrier task force had been formed and was proving a powerful weapon. Usually consisting of up to a dozen heavy and light carriers with hundreds of planes on board, as many as six great battleships for firepower and dozens of escorting cruisers and destroyers with necessary support vessels, these mighty armadas cruised at 25 knots, taking the war to the Japanese with devastating force. By that same year the Navy had 18,000 aircraft of improved quality; during 1944 the number reached 30,000. Grumman Avenger torpedo bombers, Grumman F6F Hellcats and Vought Corsairs and their crews could match and excel anything the Japanese could launch. Navy personnel approached three million in 1943, including 100,000 WAVES (Women Accepted for Voluntary Emergency Service). Utilization of scientific inventions made the armadas' ships and weapons even more effective. The use and improvement of radar, sonar, variable-timed fuses, rockets and hundreds of other developments made the deadly work of the Navy more effective than ever before. Behind all this the ever-improving logistical stream of unglamorous oilers, transports and freighters carrying the millions of tons of supplies and hundreds of thousands of soldiers and Marines facilitated the mission of pushing back the Japanese. As the Pacific conflict turned into a war of strategy, firepower, manpower and logistics—in short, into a war of attrition—the Americans began advancing as a gigantic force across the broad waters of the Pacific.

By the summer of 1943, the Americans and their Australian and New Zealand allies were prepared to begin 'island

Below: A Navy Liberator patrol aircraft takes off from Guadalcanal on a photo-reconnaissance mission in 1943.

Above: **Final briefing for pilots aboard the *Lexington* before a mission during the Gilberts operations in December 1943.**

hopping toward the Philippines and the Japanese home islands. They were indirectly aided by the death of Admiral Isoruko Yamamoto (18 April 1943) shot down by an Army P-38 pursuit plane over Bougainville in the Solomons. The great strategist of the Japanese Pacific war was out of the fight, the victim of an intercepted code message and an ambush. His replacement was more defensive-minded than the great Yamamoto—a fact much to the Allies' advantage.

The summer/fall 1943 objective for the left prong of the Pacific strategy was the central Solomons. Munda, Kolombangara and Vella Lavella were taken or neutralized, and the great Japanese base at Rabaul on New Britain was pounded by American planes, neutralized and finally bypassed. To the west, Bougainville with its 60,000 defenders was invaded by amphibious forces on 1 November after its airfields had been knocked out: it was secured in two months. In all these operations the US Navy carried out very successful preliminary air attacks to soften up the enemy positions, covered the landings with bombardments and air cover, and supplied and protected the land forces as they struggled toward their objectives. The Army, Navy, and Marines were learning that precisely co-ordinated preparation and execution were critical in amphibious warfare. The summer of 1943 also saw the Aleutians wrested from the Japanese by American naval and army units with co-operation from Canadian forces. US Navy bombardment and landing-support operations were as critical to Allied amphibious victory here in the north as they were in the South Pacific.

The central Pacific right prong of the grand strategy began to move in the fall of 1943. After intermittent air attacks through October and early November from the new giant *Essex*-class carrier fleets, American forces moved to take Makin and Tarawa in the Gilbert Islands in mid-November. After heavy air and sea bombardments of the islands, the Army landed on Makin and the Marines hit Tarawa on 20 November. Makin, lightly defended, was relatively easy, but Tarawa was a nightmare. The attacking waves of Marines came up against reinforced pillboxes, bunkers and dugouts virtually untouched by preliminary bombardment. They suffered very heavy casualties. Only when the naval air and sea bombardments were resumed were the Japanese dug out of their fortified emplacements. But the Americans learned their lessons from the Tarawa experience. Armor-piercing shells and rockets were needed against reinforced fortifications, better across-the-beach landing craft were required, and improved preinvasion reconnaissance of the enemy's defenses was absolutely essential. Tarawa was a grim teacher of the realities of amphibious warfare.

By early 1944 MacArthur's forces had worked their way across the coast of northern New Guinea and had turned west to take the Admiralty Islands. With Rabaul bypassed and the Admiralties taken, the Solomon Island chain was in American and Allied hands. Success was achieved by seizure of key bases, leaving others to wither without support; this was possible because the Japanese Navy could no longer contend with the ever-increasing power of the US Navy, which concentrated increasingly on supplying air cover, sea bombardment and transport and landing support to invading soldiers and marines. The Pacific war was gradually turning around as naval offensive and support power developed into an unbeatable weapon of modern amphibious warfare.

As MacArthur advanced in the South Pacific, Spruance and the Central Pacific Forces continued westward. The major islands of the Gilberts secured, the target shifted to the Marshall Islands to the northwest. Little was known of the Marshalls, which consist of over 1000 atolls and five major islands, because they had been

Above: **Flight-deck scene aboard the light carrier *Monterey* in late 1943. *Monterey* and her sisters were converted from hulls laid down for light cruisers.**
Right: **The light cruiser *St Louis* leaves Tulagi Harbor.**

taken by Japan from Germany after World War I and been closed to all outsiders since 1935. It was rightly believed they had been converted into a complex of naval and air bases. The decision was to concentrate on Kwajelein Atoll in the southwest Marshalls, since it could be converted into a giant staging area, and on Eniwetok at the far northwestern edge of the group. Learning from previous experience, on 20–21 January 1944 Kwajalein was bombed and shelled as no Japanese stronghold had ever been hit before. It paid off: over three-fourths of the Japanese defenders died before any Americans began to hit the beach on 31 January. Although the soldiers and Marines assaulting Kwajalein Atoll took heavy casualties, the Japanese lost over 8000 men in one week. Kwajalein was taken. Eniwetok fell two weeks later. Overwhelming naval bombardment and air power, plus flinty determination by the land forces, had brought the Marshalls into American hands.

Next stop in the central Pacific was the Mariana Islands 1000 miles due west and only 1500 miles from the Japanese home islands. First Saipan, then Guam and Tinian, would be assaulted. On 11–12 June 1944 the airfields and defenses of all three islands came under murderous bombing from the planes of the American fast-carrier task forces moving into the area. Two days of concentrated shelling of Saipan and Tinian from the vessels of the surface fleet followed. On 15 June the Marines landed on Saipan, on the 16th, soldiers of the 27th Army Division. They were faced by 30,000 determined Japanese defenders. It took three weeks of hard fighting to secure an island of only 72 square miles, the last days being marked by the horror of over 3000 Japanese suicides, mostly civilians who chose to die by leaping from the bluffs of the northern coast to the rocky shore 830 feet below rather than submit to capture. (They had been told the Americans would torture and execute them if they surrendered.)

Tinian and Guam were the next targets, and the Mariana Islands would soon be in American hands and prepared as staging areas for the next offensives. Giant airfields in the Marianas would put Japan itself within reach of long-range American bombers.

Above: **Aircrew aboard the *Ticonderoga* relax in the carrier's ready room in November 1944.**

For the Japanese, the successful American onslaughts in the Gilberts and Marshalls had been serious reverses, but now the Americans simply had to be stopped. From the Marianas they could link up with MacArthur's forces moving north from New Guinea to assault the Philippines. And they could swing north, using their bomber and naval power to attack the islands off the Japanese coast, like Okinawa. From there, the Allies could launch frequent, death-dealing air attacks on Japan's home islands. With the whole war effort endangered, the Japanese Navy was called upon to stop the Americans in the Marianas before the whole Japanese outer defense perimeter collapsed. The result was the Battle of the Philippine Sea of 19–20 June 1944.

Below: **A Japanese patrol boat sinking after being torpedoed by the submarine *Seawolf* in April 1943.**

Warned by his scouting submarines that a Japanese carrier group was approaching the Marianas, Admiral Spruance detached Rear Admiral Marc A Mitscher's Task Force 58, consisting of 15 carriers and seven battleships, to meet them. On the morning of 19 June the Japanese launched an initial 69 planes against the American force, and 'The Great Marianas Turkey Shoot' began. Navy Hellcats shot down 25 of this first wave of planes before they even saw the American fleet. Most of the remaining planes fell victim to American antiaircraft guns fitted with the new VT (proximity) fuses that detonated anywhere within 70 feet of the target. Yet wave after wave of Japanese planes—piloted by very inexperienced crews due to a critical shortage in the fleet—tried to penetrate the American defenses. About 320 Japanese planes went down or were wrecked on landing, to only 27 American planes lost; American submarines sank two carriers during the battle. The Japanese withdrew, but Mitscher's air crews found them late the next day. Two hundred and sixteen American planes took to the air and caught up with the retreating Japanese fleet. One carrier was sunk and another damaged. Critically low on gasoline, the carrier pilots returned to Task Force 58 after sunset. Many could not find the fleet and landed in the dark. Seventy-three planes were lost in the murky Pacific waters, but all except 16 pilots and 33 crew members were rescued. Despite the danger of being sunk by submarines if the lights were turned on, Mitscher saved his remaining pilots by ordering full illumination, and the Battle of the Philippine Sea came to a successful conclusion. The Japanese sea menace in the Marianas removed, Tinian fell on 1 August and Guam nine days later. From the newly constructed airstrips on Saipan, Army B-29s would begin bombing the Japanese home islands by November.

Submarine Warfare

While American surface ships were waging their giant two-pronged offensive against Japanese naval and military units across the Pacific waters, American fleet

Right: **Planes of the carrier *Enterprise* during the raid on Marcus Island in 1942.**
Below: **Enlisted men exercise on the deck of the *Yorktown* during operations in 1943.**

3
3
10
10
7
7
12
11
11
5
5
4
4

LCM 53

Far left: US personnel inspect the battered shoreline of Kwajalein after its capture from the Japanese in February 1944.
Left: One of the battlecruiser *Alaska*'s Curtiss SC-1 float planes taxis in to be recovered during the Iwo Jima operation in March 1945.
Main picture: The oiler *Cahaba* refuels the battleship *Iowa* and an aircraft carrier in the Pacific in 1945.

Above: **A pilot of VF.17 describes a successful air battle near Rabaul to one of his buddies in February 1944.**

submarines of the 311-foot *Gato*, *Balao* and *Tench* classes were achieving their own remarkable victories. American submarines early in the war were few in number, and captains and crews were frequently frustrated by too few torpedoes and by failures of the magnetic exploder, depth-control mechanism or contact exploder in the standard Mark 14 torpedoes. These flaws made the torpedoes run below their target or fail to detonate, but improvements in both boats and weaponry soon turned the submarines into one of the most effective classes of weapons in the American naval arsenal.

American subs had no hesitancy in attacking Japanese warships. They also served invaluable rescue and intelligence-gathering functions across the Pacific and even in Japanese home waters. Fleet-movement and weather information gathered by submarines played a valuable role in the Navy's Pacific strategy. But the primary mission of the submarines was to destroy the Japanese merchant marine.

Japan, an island nation, was as vulnerable to economic strangulation as Britain. Without its merchant fleet to bring in raw materials from its far-flung subject states and to supply its garrisons defending the empire, it could not even function, much less win the war. Japan had to import 24 percent of its coal, 88 percent of its iron ore and almost 90 per cent of its oil. Strangely, given this vulnerability, the Japanese had never developed effective antisubmarine warfare (ASW) resources and did little to remedy the deficiency during the war. As a result, American submarines could range far and wide against the Japanese economic lifelines.

Operating on single patrol missions or, after 1943, in small 'wolf packs,' the 1500-ton diesel fleet submarines—each with 24 torpedoes, a 20-knot surface and 8.75-knot submerged speed, and a cruising range of 10,000 miles—stalked their prey. The newer boats had radar that permitted them to attack at night on the surface, or they could fire their deadly ordnance from periscope depth. By late 1943 the toll of Japanese merchant shipping began to rise and the Japanese were ill-equipped to contain the destruction. Vice Admiral Charles A Lockwood, commander of the Pacific Fleet's submarines, turned them loose on the ships carrying oil from the Dutch East Indies and Borneo in 1944; soon tankers were being sunk faster than they could be replaced, their valuable crude oil lost to the Japanese war cause. In one month alone, October 1944, one-third of all Japanese tankers afloat were sunk.

Below: **The USS *Barb* leaves Mare Island on her last war patrol in July 1945.**

Right: **Ships of Task Force 58, the main carrier force, at anchor in the South Pacific early in 1944.**
Below right: **The devastating effects of heavy naval bombardment seen on Kwajalein immediately after its capture.**

During the Pacific war, 288 American submarines—with crews of 80 officers and men each—sank 276 warships and over four million tons of Japanese merchant shipping, some vessels approaching or topping 100,000 tons to their credit. In addition, mines planted by submarines, surface vessels or aircraft sank another two million tons. The price paid was only 59 American submarines.

By 1945 the Japanese war machine was wobbling under the blows of American submarine warfare against its lines of supply. Whether or not this unrestricted submarine warfare was the most important factor in Japan's defeat, as some experts claim, there is no doubt that the crews of the 'silent service,' co-operating with their naval surface and air comrades, were disabling the Japanese effort in the later months of the war.

Final Assaults

By the summer of 1944 the US Navy was approaching full strength. It had over 1100 combatant ships including 23 battleships, 22 carriers, 63 'jeep carriers,' 52 cruisers, over 700 destroyers and destroyer-escorts, over 34,000 planes and 59,000 pilots, over 200 subs and almost 40,000 landing craft. Personnel stood at approximately 3,500,000 men and women. In the Pacific the pincers of the Allied grand strategy were moving ever more rapidly toward the Philippines, as MacArthur moved up from New Guinea to take Morotai in the East Indies and the Central Pacific Forces prepared to move in from the Marianas in support of this drive; the Atlantic Fleet, having helped put down the German submarine menace, was assisting the final drive on Nazi Germany.

On 20 October 1944 MacArthur's army landed on the southwest coast of the island of Leyte to surprisingly little resistance. As promised two and a half years earlier, he had returned to the Philippines. At this, the Japanese activated their complicated Sho-Go (Victory) Plan to isolate the landing force on Leyte Gulf and destroy the defending American Seventh Fleet under Vice-Admiral Thomas C Kinkaid. One Japanese fleet of five battleships under Vice-Admiral Takeo Kurita was to cut through the Sibuyan Sea in the center of the archipelago from the west, pass through San Bernardino Strait and assault Kincaid from the north. A second fleet of battleships under Vice-Admiral Shoji Nishimura was to join Vice-Admiral Kiyohide Shima's three carriers and two destroyers to traverse the Mindanao Sea further south, enter Leyte Gulf through Surigao Strait and thus catch Kincaid in a trap between the two fleets. Meanwhile, a fleet of four carriers under Admiral Jisaburo Ozawa would approach from the home islands to the north to lure Halsey's Third Fleet away from Leyte Gulf. The resulting battle—actually four separate actions—is know as the Battle for Leyte Gulf of 23–26 October 1944: in many respects it was the greatest naval battle ever fought.

The Japanese Southern Force under Nishimura made its way through the Mindanao Sea, with Shima trailing behind, heading for Surigao Strait and Kinkaid's southern flank. Kinkaid ordered Rear Admiral Jesse B Oldendorf, with six old battleships salvaged from the Pearl Harbor attack, to stop him. As the Japanese units approached shortly after midnight on 24 October, the battlewagons and their escorts were waiting in Surigao Strait. American destroyers and PT boats launched torpedo boats against Nishimura's force while the battleships' 14- and 16-inch radar-directed guns blasted away. The Japanese lost two battleships and two destroyers and failed to force the Straits. Admiral Shima's fleet arrived hours later and joined Nishimura's retreating ships without firing a shot.

In the meantime Kurita's Center Force was moving through the Sibuyan Sea south of Luzon as the northern wing of the entrapment plan, but Halsey, taking the Japanese bait, moved north to meet Ozawa's Northern Force of carriers (not knowing the Japanese were almost without aircraft due to losses in the Battle of the Philippine Sea). Halsey believed that Kinkaid was covering San Bernardino Strait, the eastern exit from the Sibuyan Sea. Kinkaid, believing Halsey had left a task force at the Strait, was not covering it either: it was wide open.

On through the Sibuyan Sea came Kurita.

Right: **The fast minelayer USS *Shannon* moves through a Pacific fleet anchorage on the eve of the landings on Okinawa.**
Main picture: **Bombarding targets on the Japanese mainland in July 1945.**
Bottom left: **The carrier *Bunker Hill* after being hit by kamikazes off Okinawa on 11 May 1945. Aircraft carriers were particularly vulnerable because of their aviation fuel stores.**
Bottom right: ***LST.829* heads for the shore during the Okinawa landings.**

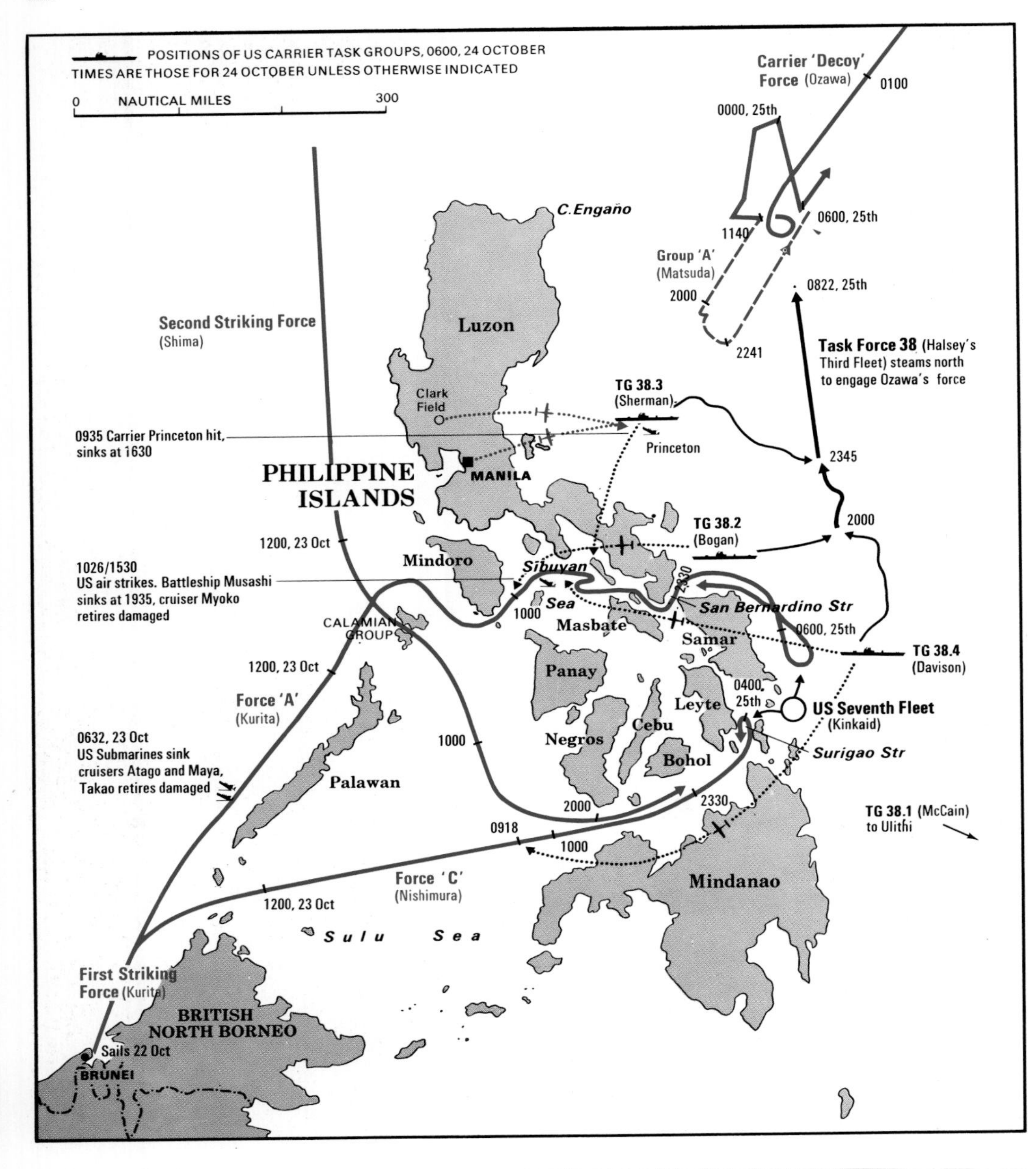

He was attacked by American planes on 24 October and lost the battleship *Musashi* in this second action. But he kept coming despite his losses, sailing through the open San Bernardino Strait under cover of darkness and turning south toward Leyte Gulf. As he rounded the island of Samar with his four battleships, seven cruisers and 11 destroyers and prepared to attack Kinkaid's unsuspecting fleet, he was finally spotted at sunrise on 25 October by a small 'jeep carrier' group and its escorts. They sounded the alarm and tore into Kurita's force with their puny weapons. Fortunately, Kurita thought he was fighting Halsey's main force and stopped to do battle rather than rushing through to hit Kinkaid. Kinkaid threw everything available into the desperate fight to stop Kurita off Samar, while beseeching Halsey to return to help him. In furious fighting in which two jeep carriers were lost, Kurita was stopped and retreated back through San Bernardino Strait.

Halsey, meanwhile, was far to the north chasing Ozawa's decoy force off Cape Engaño. Although Halsey's planes put down the four carriers in handy fashion, he continued chasing the surviving vessels north. Kinkaid was still calling frantically for help in his desperate situation off Samar. Halsey finally broke off the chase and turned south, but too late to catch Kurita as he made his escape back through San Bernardino Strait.

When the Battle for Leyte Gulf was over, the Japanese had lost three battleships, four carriers, nine cruisers and ten destroyers. The Imperial Japanese Navy was virtually finished as a fighting force. The road to Tokyo was open. But the cost of victory for the Americans would still be high because, ominously, the Japanese in the Battle for Leyte Gulf had used kamikaze attacks for the first time. Kamikaze—'Divine Wind'—pilots mostly had little training in flight. Their only mission was to dive their planes onto enemy ships in heroic suicidal attacks. Many American sailors would die in the last year of the Pacific war before the dreaded kamikaze raids ended with Japan's surrender.

Now that the Philippines were accessible and the Japanese fleet was staggering, there was a need for forward bases for landings on Japan itself and air bases to give fighter protection to the B-29s flying from the Marianas. The first to fall to American assault was tiny Iwo Jima in the Bonin Islands, almost midway between Saipan and Tokyo. The island had been bombed methodically from carrier- and land-based planes from the Marianas since June 1944; the invasion took place on 19 February 1945 after fierce naval shelling and bombing by B-29s. The little island of only eight square miles, defended by 20,000 Japanese, was assaulted by an

Top left: **Map of the Battle of Leyte Gulf.**
Left: **Unloading equipment from an LST at Middleburg Is, New Guinea, in Aug 1944.**

880-ship armada and 220,000 men. Because the Japanese were so well dug-in and fought tenaciously, it took five weeks and Marine casualties of 5500 killed and almost 14,000 wounded before the island fell; the Navy lost 90 men before the bloody fighting ended. Long-range bombers could now fly to Japan with continuous fighter-plane cover.

Okinawa was next. This island, only 350 miles from Japan, would be the staging area for the great assault on the Japanese home islands. It had to be taken. The Americans—aided by the Royal Navy—assembled a mammoth force of 1200 ships and 181,000 assault troops to do the job. After the usual fierce bombardments, 50,000 soldiers and Marines landed on Easter Sunday, 1 April 1945, to face 110,000 well-entrenched Japanese troops. Here the full fury of the kamikaze suicide planes fell on the American fleet. Hundreds dove through the skies at the lumbering transport and supply ships and at the combat vessels. Before Okinawa was secured on 21 June, 34 ships had been sunk, 368 more had been damaged. Over 12,000 Americans had died and 35,000 had been wounded (including almost 10,000 sailors killed, missing or injured) in securing the island. It had been a horrendously costly victory, and the Navy dreaded what would come when they turned to the next task—attacking the Japanese home islands. American commanders estimated that the invasion scheduled for late 1945

Right: Firefighters on the USS _Intrepid_ after a kamikaze hit, 25 November 1944.
Below: The Japanese _Ise_ or _Hyuga_ under attack off Cape Engaño, 25 October 1944. Both had been converted to carrier/battleship with a small flight deck aft.

Above: LSM.311 **and other landing ships approach the beach at Leyte on 20 Oct 1944.**

or early 1946 would require the largest amphibious force ever assembled, even larger than the one that had landed at Normandy the year before. Approximately five million men would be needed, of whom about one million would be lost. It would be the largest invasion in history across the largest expanse of water, resulting in record casualties. By July 1945 the Navy had set about its most challenging task with grim determination by carrying out carrier task-force raids on Japanese airfields and industries in conjunction with British carriers and US Army Air Force B-29 raids from Saipan. Meanwhile, Okinawa was being prepared as a great airbase and staging area for the invasion.

Then on 6 August the *Enola Gay* dropped an atomic bomb with the explosive force of 20,000 tons of TNT on Hiroshima. Three days later the Army Air Force dropped a second atomic bomb of similar destructive power on Nagasaki. On 14 August 1945 the Navy's war—the nation's war—in the Pacific came to an end. Significantly, the formal Japanese surrender document was signed on the deck of a US Navy battleship; the *Missouri*, in Tokyo Bay on 2 September 1945. The curtain was rung down on the Navy's greatest challenge and most memorable years of sacrifice and glory.

Above: A destroyer lays a smoke screen during the Leyte landings.
Below: Pilots of the USS *Hornet* rushing to their planes for a mission in the China Sea in February 1945.

CARRYING THE WAR TO HITLER

While the US Navy was fighting its way across the Pacific in the months after Pearl Harbor, it also had responsibilities in another whole theater of action—the Atlantic Ocean. Now, if never before, the United States had to accept its role as a continental island-nation in the midst of the world's two great oceans. And now, if never before, a potential world power was going to have its naval forces tested by two highly dedicated and heavily armed enemies on opposite shores. How the US Navy met the challenge of the Japanese across the Pacific has been recounted; how it met the challenge of the Germans in the Atlantic must now be considered. In the first months of World War II, as we have seen, the USA was not involved—at least formally—and the action was largely in the Atlantic Ocean and between the British and the Germans. But the results of those engagements must be explained if the role of the US Navy in the war in Europe and on the Atlantic is to be understood. For, to anticipate, that role is so unexpected that what we shall see is a US Navy that hardly exchanges a shot with a major German ship, but that nevertheless ends up playing a crucial role in defeating the Germans.

When World War II broke out on 1 September 1939, the German Navy was not prepared for the battles it would be called upon to fight. In 1938 Grand Admiral Erich Raeder, head of the navy, had presented Hitler with two overall plans for naval development. One called for the production of naval weapons of war to be used against commerce—weapons like

Above: Type VII U-boats like *U-101* formed the backbone of the German submarine force.
Above left: Admiral Raeder led the German Navy in the early years of the war until Dönitz took over at the start of 1943.
Below: U-203 sets out on patrol from Brest at the start of April 1943, at the height of the Battle of the Atlantic.

Above: **The destroyer *Gleaves* on her way to the Canadian escort base at Argentia.**

submarines, surface raiders and minelayers. If war with Britain was envisioned in the near future, this type of vessel would be needed to destroy her ocean-going commerce, as had been attempted in World War I. The second plan, Plan Z, called for a great surface fleet to match or exceed that of any other nation, especially Great Britain, in open combat. But this would call for a major shipbuilding program and would take up to ten years to complete.

Hitler chose Plan Z. Why he did so remains a mystery. Perhaps he felt that war with Britain could be delayed or even avoided. Whatever his reasoning, Hitler was subsequently stunned by England's declaration of war upon Germany after the invasion of Poland; thus the German Navy was called upon to change its strategic and tactical missions as soon as World War II began.

At the outbreak of the fighting, Germany had a sizable Plan Z surface fleet building—and scheduled for completion by 1945—but not large enough to gain control of the seas and drive off blockaders from the nation's coast. The navy had only five battleships commissioned and two building, eight cruisers, 26 merchant ships usable as armed cruisers and a number of auxiliary vessels. Furthermore, the Germans had only 56 submarines, these under the command of Admiral Karl Dönitz. These were hardly sufficient to close down the waters around Britain and in the North Atlantic. Although caught without adequate numbers of ships and trained men, the German Navy sailed out to do its best in the early months of the war. Its job: destroy British commerce by all possible means. The British, on the other hand, had two counterobjectives: keep the sea lanes open at all cost and blockade the North Sea exits to keep the German fleet bottled up in the Baltic.

Surface Raiding

Merchant vessels approaching the British coast from the British Dominions or from neutral ports became the targets of the German surface fleet. After a brief and ruinous flirtation with single sailings, the British quickly returned to convoying, the stratagem so successful in World War I. But German surface raiders were still a constant danger, even to convoys; this was made obvious by the cruises of the 'pocket battleships' *Deutschland* and *Graf Spee* as they began to attack merchant shipping on the high seas.

During the fall of 1939 the *Graf Spee* was sinking thousands of tons of shipping in the South Atlantic; a sizable British and French contingent was assigned to hunt her down. This force included two carriers and eight cruisers at various times. On 13 December 1939 three British cruisers found the *Graf Spee* outside the River Plate that flows between Uruguay and Argentina on the east coast of South America, they took her on. A spirited duel of big guns punctuated a series of battle maneuvers by each side. As a result, two of the cruisers were badly damaged by the *Graf Spee*'s 11-inch guns; the German battleship also sustained numerous hits. The *Graf Spee* limped away to the safety of the neutral port of Montevideo with two of the British cruisers in pursuit. Despite intense diplomatic pressure from Germany, the government of Uruguay ordered the *Graf Spee* out of its waters within three days. Being short of ammunition, the captain of the *Graf Spee* decided to scuttle his vessel rather than try to fight his way out. The scuttling took place outside the harbor on 17 December 1939, and—with the *Deutschland* returning to German waters—German surface raiding was abandoned for several months.

In the fall of 1940 serious German surface raiding was renewed when the pocket battleship *Scheer* slipped into the North Atlantic to prey on British convoys, followed a month later by the heavy cruiser *Hipper*. Although neither ship was able to effect great damage in the North or South Atlantic, they did remind the British that surface raiding could raise havoc with convoys if not quickly contained.

In the spring of 1941 Admiral Raeder implemented his plan for a great surface-raiding mission that would completely disrupt or even shut down the North Atlantic sea lanes. He would send the giant new battleship *Bismarck*, along with the heavy cruiser *Prinz Eugen*, into the Atlantic. Here they would be joined by the battleships *Scharnhorst* and *Gneisenau* to lay waste the British supply lines. Although the *Scharnhorst* could not be repaired in time for sailing, and the *Gneisenau* was taken out of action by a torpedo from a British plane, Raeder ordered the two remaining ships out to Bergen in occupied Norway. From there they were to break through the Royal Navy's blockade, move north of Iceland and pounce upon convoys in the North Atlantic. The *Scharnhorst* was to join them as soon as possible.

Warned as to what was afoot, and fearful of the destruction that would await their convoys if this German naval squadron were not stopped, the British alerted every ship available in the Home Fleet and North Atlantic to hunt down the *Bismarck* and *Prinz Eugen*. On 23 May the two German raiders were spotted moving down through the Denmark Strait between Greenland and Iceland by two British cruisers, which shadowed them south. The German raiders were met next morning by the battle cruiser *Hood* and the battleship *Prince of Wales*. The *Hood* was sunk in a fiery explosion of her magazines from the long guns of the *Bismarck*, and the *Prince of Wales* suffered crippling damages. Out of the fight, the *Prince of Wales* made her way toward Iceland, while the two British cruisers continued shadowing the *Bismarck* to report her location. Stunned by the loss of the *Hood*, the Admiralty ordered various ships from Gibraltar and two battleships from convoying duty to run down the *Bismarck* and her companion. But the *Prinz Eugen* slipped away to the south, and the *Bismarck* temporarily gave her dogged shadows the slip. By sheer luck, British persistence and radio-direction-finder signals, the trail of the *Bismarck* was picked up again as she headed toward the French coast, and all British forces available were directed toward her probable course.

Right: **Crew of the USS *Kearney* inspect damage caused by a U-boat torpedo on the night of 16–17 October 1941.**

At 10:30 on the morning of 26 May 1941 the great German battleship was spotted 750 miles west of France. Shadowed now by the cruiser *Sheffield*, the *Bismarck* was hit by air attacks from the carrier *Ark Royal* in an effort to slow her down. They jammed her rudders. The British ships caught up with the *Bismarck* that night and launched ineffective torpedo attacks against the crippled giant. But by the next morning the battleships *Rodney* and *King George V* had arrived on the scene; they began to pound away at the damaged battleship. The hapless vessel was finally put down by a torpedo from the cruiser *Dorsetshire*.

However, in a humiliating display of ineptitude, the British allowed the *Scharnhorst*, *Gneisenau* and *Prinz Eugen* to slip out of the port of Brest on the French coast and run for home right through the English Channel without being properly attacked. Although two of the vessels hit mines off the Dutch coast and sustained damage, they made it to port safely, much to the consternation of the British. But even this heroic dash could not convince Hitler or the German Navy that surface-raider warfare was worth the price, though the battlecruiser *Scharnhorst* eventually sallied out in December 1943 to attack an Arctic convoy off the North Cape and was soon sunk by the British battleship *Duke of York* along with her escorting cruisers and destroyers.

The last major German surface combatant, the new battleship *Tirpitz*, was bombed by British carrier planes while under repair in Alten Fjord in the north of Norway on 3 April 1944. Moved to Tromso Fjord further south for more repairs, she was bombed and capsized at her moorings on 12 November 1944.

German surface raiding by major combatant ships had come to an effective end on 27 May 1941 with the death of the *Bismarck*, despite these later forays. For the remainder of the war, and throughout the time America was fighting side by side with her British allies, the German menace took the form of deadly unrestricted submarine warfare. Germany had reverted to her most effective weapon of World War I, but now she proved herself capable of a more widespread and deadly use of the U-boat—the *Unterseeboot*, as the Germans call the submarine. If the United States and Britain could not contain the submarine campaign as they had in World War I, Britain could not survive. If Britain were to capitulate, the European war would undoubtedly be lost. That was the challenge to the United States and to her navy in the Atlantic as the nation joined the Allies in December 1941 and fought desperately until the U-boats were finally matched, then overwhelmed, in the agonizing years that followed.

Battle of the Atlantic, 1939–41

Although Admiral Dönitz as submarine commander had 56 operational U-boats at the beginning of the war—rather than the 300 he considered the minimum necessary—only 22 of them were both ready and suitable for North Atlantic patrols. Accordingly, he was able to keep less than ten submarines on duty during the early months of the war. They attained some successes against ships sailing without convoys, but lost nine of their number in the process before turning to aid in the invasion of Norway in the early months of 1940. The capitulation of Norway, Holland, Belgium and France gave Dönitz the opportunity to rebase his U-boats nearer their patrol areas in the Atlantic. Great heavily fortified submarine pens were created at five locations on the Bay of Biscay on the west coast of France, and secondary bases were constructed in Norway. Dönitz now had bases closer at hand to their targets, resulting in less time in transit and more at destruction.

With more subs available thanks to the French bases in particular, by the summer of 1940 Dönitz was able to send out his boats to hunt the convoys in 'wolf packs.' They successfully bore down on and sank ship after ship in the North Atlantic convoys by having one submarine shadow a convoy until all subs in the area could close in for a co-ordinated kill. The night surface attack was the favored tactic. In reaction to this increasing menace, the British extended their escort patrols farther out to sea; any vessels marginally suitable for convoy duty were added to the fleet and Churchill made his desperate request to Roosevelt for 50 American destroyers. Still the sinkings continued, especially among independent ships. Furthermore, the 600-mile-wide 'Black Pit' in the mid-Atlantic, where long-range air patrols could not reach, remained a favorite haunt of U-boats against both independents and convoys. In rapid succession 17 of 34 merchantmen in convoy SC-7 were sunk in the summer of 1940, followed by 14 of 49 in another convoy (HX-79), by packs of German subs.

For Dönitz's subs on the Northwestern Approaches, this was the 'Happy Time.' A total of 217 merchant vessels of over a million tons was sent to the bottom with the loss of only six U-boats in the summer and fall of 1940. Still, 2000 merchantmen a day were at sea for Britain, and convoys were getting through despite the wolf-packing technique. Dönitz waited during the winter months of 1940–41 until better weather and more boats should signal a new and stronger effort in the North Atlantic. Here, he believed, the war would be won or lost. As spring 1941 approached, however, Dönitz found that his enemies had improved their antisubmarine warfare (ASW) activities and had thereby made raiding on the Northwestern Approaches increasingly costly. Accordingly, he shifted the U-boats' area of operations farther to the west beyond the range of coastal-based patrol planes. Dönitz would now concentrate his submarines in those areas where he could do the most damage while sustaining the fewest casualties. He was determined to carry out a war of attrition on the North Atlantic sea lanes, constantly moving his subs to where they could do maximum damage to the British commercial lifeline.

In the meantime the United States was moving closer to involvement in the North Atlantic war. The 'destroyers for bases' deal of July 1940 had given way to Lend-Lease legislation in March 1941.

This allowed the British to buy war goods on credit. While this was taking place, Roosevelt had also sent military representatives to England for 'exploratory talks' that resulted in co-ordinated plans for American participation in the Atlantic if America entered the war. These talks, in turn, led to others including the 'ABC-1 Staff Agreement' of January 1941, which spelled out what the United States would do short of war and in the event of war. This included both the idea of Germany as the prime enemy if she and Japan were to make war on the United States and on Britain and the pledge that the United States would soon escort convoys in the North Atlantic.

By February 1941 the agreed-upon neutrality patrols were being carried out by the US Atlantic Fleet under Admiral Ernest J King; by July American naval units were escorting convoys from Newfoundland to Iceland. The eastern end of the patrol area was anchored by American airplanes flying from Reykjavik, Iceland. Combined with the fact that the Americans were broadcasting every U-boat sighting on open channels, this convoying, as we have seen, put America into an undeclared naval war. The attack on the US destroyer *Greer* (4 September 1941) 200 miles southwest of Iceland—after the destroyer had shadowed U-652 for three hours—was only the signal that the undeclared war was on. The torpedoing of the destroyer *Kearney* and the sinking of the USS *Reuben James* in October, both on convoy duty, made no appreciable change in the basic situation, but it enabled Roosevelt to place the Germans in a worse light before the American public while refusing to reveal what was really going on in the North Atlantic. But since the Admiralty was now experimenting with escort carriers to cover convoys in the 'Greenland gap,' (an experiment that was costing the Germans many precious U-boats) Dönitz decided in December 1941 to shift his submarine campaigns to North American waters now that America was in the war. The hunting would be good: the Americans would see the battle of the Atlantic at close range for the first time. Operation *Paukenschlag* ('drumroll'), as Admiral Dönitz named it, was about to begin.

Battle of the Atlantic, 1942–45

Having utilized its slender ASW resources in convoy escort missions across the North Atlantic sea lanes, the US Navy was in no position to protect American coastal waters in the early months of the war. Furthermore, in building up the Navy in the late 1930s and early 1940s, efforts had been concentrated largely on building large combat vessels. Escort vessels, particularly the smaller but effective destroyer-escorts, had been neglected on the assumption they could always be hurriedly built if needed. As a result, the east coast shipping lanes were essentially both undefended and indefensible when the German submarines began to lurk in American waters early in 1942.

Although there were never more than a dozen German submarines operating in the Eastern Sea Frontier (the Navy's designation for the Atlantic coast command area) at any time, the damage they did to the unprotected tankers and freighters moving along the coast with raw materials and oil for east-coast industrial centers was astounding. Having no reason to wolfpack, the individual U-boats lay offshore and submerged during the day, then moved in on the merchant vessels on the surface at night, dispatching them with torpedoes or gunfire. The offshore waters from Cape Hatteras to Cape Breton Island in Nova Scotia were their hunting grounds. The Carolina Capes were a favorite haunt. German submarines often found the unarmed merchant vessels running with lights on; frequently they were clearly silhouetted by the lights of eastern seaboard cities. Only in April 1942 were shore lights dimmed, much to the chagrin of port-city merchants and caterers to vacation pleasure-seekers. The toll of sinkings off the East Coast in what the German submarine crews called the 'Second Happy Time' rose rapidly, reaching 87 vessels of 514,366 tons in the first four months of 1942.

The Navy was trying its best to stop the slaughter, but it was woefully lacking in ASW vessels and aircraft. Only about 100 vessels of all descriptions from naval destroyers and Coast Guard cutters all the way down to converted yachts were available to fight the submarine onslaught. Less than 200 army and naval aircraft were also available. Furthermore, the naval commander of the Eastern Sea Frontier originally refused to adopt convoying and attempted to seek out the prowling subs by 'hunter groups.' But the April 1942 total of 23 ships sunk off the East Coast without the destruction of a single U-boat finally led to a change in tactics.

Right: U-boat ace Gunther Prien is congratulated on his return from sinking the British battleship *Royal Oak* in the fleet anchorage at Scapa Flow in 1939.
Below: The heavy cruiser *Prinz Eugen* arrives at Brest in June 1941 after separating from the *Bismarck* soon after the engagement with *Hood* and *Prince of Wales*.

Utilizing 34 small corvettes and trawlers provided by the British and equipped with asdic (the equivalent of sonar) regular convoying and extended air cover during defensible daylight hours, total sinkings were cut drastically along the east coast. The German submarines had little choice other than to 'keep their heads down' in these waters and so were shifted to the Caribbean and Gulf of Mexico by Admiral Dönitz. Here they were enormously successful. In May 1942 alone, 41 ships of 220,000 tons were sunk in the Gulf of Mexico, over half being tankers sunk off the Passes of the Mississippi. When defensive convoys were instituted for these areas as well, the U-boats—still well supplied with fuel and food by 1700-ton supply submarines called 'milk cows,' which allowed them a longer and wider latitude of operations—moved into the southern Caribbean to continue their deadly work against much-needed merchant cargoes in that area. Driven from this hunting ground by naval convoying and air patrols, the German subs moved farther south along the Brazilian coast to pick off ships sailing independently along the coastal or transatlantic routes. By late 1942 this area too was becoming dangerous for submarines, thanks to convoying and effective air patrols, so Dönitz recalled his boats from American waters. The battle of the submarines against their pursuers returned to the mid-Atlantic, where Dönitz hoped to find easier pickings again, for the Black Pit was still beyond the land-based air cover from North American, Icelandic and British air bases. Here the U-boats would concentrate their efforts in early 1943. Since German submarine production had reached 30 boats per month, Dönitz felt he was now ready to take appreciable losses and put down the mid-Atlantic convoys. But Allied naval

Main picture: **An Atlantic convoy pictured from a US battleship early in 1944.**

forces had also increased productivity and technology. Most surface ASW vessels now had radar, and the increased numbers of ships meant that British Antisubmarine Support Groups of six to eight fast destroyers, corvettes and frigates could be formed to seek out submarines and aid convoys under attack. Soon escort carriers would be added to their numbers.

Employing picket lines on both sides of the sea lanes to attack convoys moving through the Black Pit without air support, Dönitz's crews enjoyed considerable early success, sinking 807,000 tons of shipping in November 1942 alone. But as the Atlantic war moved into 1943, the Allies discovered that fewer but larger convoys, aided by Antisubmarine Support Groups utilizing radar and radio detection systems (HF-DF—'huff duff'—high-frequency direction finders) to home in on the broadcasting submarines, plus air cover from escort carriers and long-range aircraft like B-24 Liberators equipped with radar and depth charges, meant safer passages. The turning point in the Battle of the Atlantic came in April 1943 when the 'kill ratio'—between merchants sunk to casualties sustained—simply became too high for the German submarine packs. Losing 41 submarines to the new Allied tactics in 'Black May' 1943, Dönitz ordered his submarines south to attack Central Atlantic convoys. Improved submarine technology, he felt, would soon permit him to return to the North Atlantic to resume his attacks on the Allies' lifelines across those waters.

But in the Central Atlantic hunting grounds southwest of the Azores, German submarines found only frustration in the summer and fall of 1943. for the US Navy—which from 1 April 1943 had responsibility for this area—had developed 'hunter-killer groups' to combat the submarine menace. These groups, made up

Below: **Crewmen loading provisions on** ***PC.556*** **before a patrol in the Atlantic in October 1942.**
Bottom: **A meeting of the US-British Combined Chiefs of Staff in Washington. Admiral King, second from camera on right, represents the US Navy.**

of destroyers, destroyer-escorts and escort carriers, were very effective against both attacks and 'milk cow' submarines. The air power packed by the groups was overwhelming, and U-boat losses mounted rapidly. In three months the Germans lost 15 submarines while sinking only one convoyed merchant vessel.

Meanwhile, U-boats operating in the Bay of Biscay were also coming under sustained and killing pressure thanks to the work of the Royal Air Force Coastal Command and its use of newly perfected ultra-high-frequency radar units and an 80-million-candlepower searchlight used against the subs in night attacks. American aircraft co-operated closely with the British in carrying out this antisubmarine warfare off the coast of France. Altogether 18 German submarines were lost at this time in the Bay of Biscay. The sub pens of western France were now of much less value to the U-boat forces.

During the critical year 1943 the German Navy lost 237 U-boats, and the Battle of the Atlantic was won through Allied co-operation. Although U-boat operations continued through 1944, the combination of antisubmarine support groups, hunter-killer groups, larger convoys under better escort, improved radar and sonar detection systems and above all, virtually round-the-clock air cover from co-ordinated carrier- and land-based planes was simply too much for the beleaguered crews of the German undersea forces. Wherever Dönitz moved his attack submarines, the Allies were there to beat him and cast his vital U-boats into the depths of the Atlantic. By 1945 the German submarines were a no more than occasional menace to the vital Allied convoys.

During the course of the war 1175 U-boats sailed for the Reich. Of these, 781 were lost, 191 to American forces, the remainder to other Allied air and naval forces. German U-boats sank 14,573,000 tons of shipping, only about one-fourth from ships sailing in convoy. On the other hand, over 300,000 voyages were made across the Atlantic by Allied merchant vessels in support of the war. The safe passage of these ships in convoy—increasingly unmolested as the Battle of the Atlantic was won by Allied naval and air power and virtually untouched in the final 18 months of the war—spelled victory for Allied forces in Europe. Dönitz was correct when he said the battle for Europe would be decided in the North Atlantic. With the defeat of his U-boat forces after their easy victories of 1941–42 on these waters, Allied offensives could continue until the final defeat of the Third Reich.

Above: **View of the quarterdeck of the battleship *Massachusetts* during a lull in the battle of Casablanca.**

North African Offensives

Perhaps less dramatic but equally important to the Allied victory in Europe were US Navy efforts in support of mammoth amphibious landings as opening steps to giant land offensives in Africa and Europe. These operations eventually carried the war into Germany itself.

From the very beginning of World War II, American military planners wanted to strike directly at the heart of German mili-

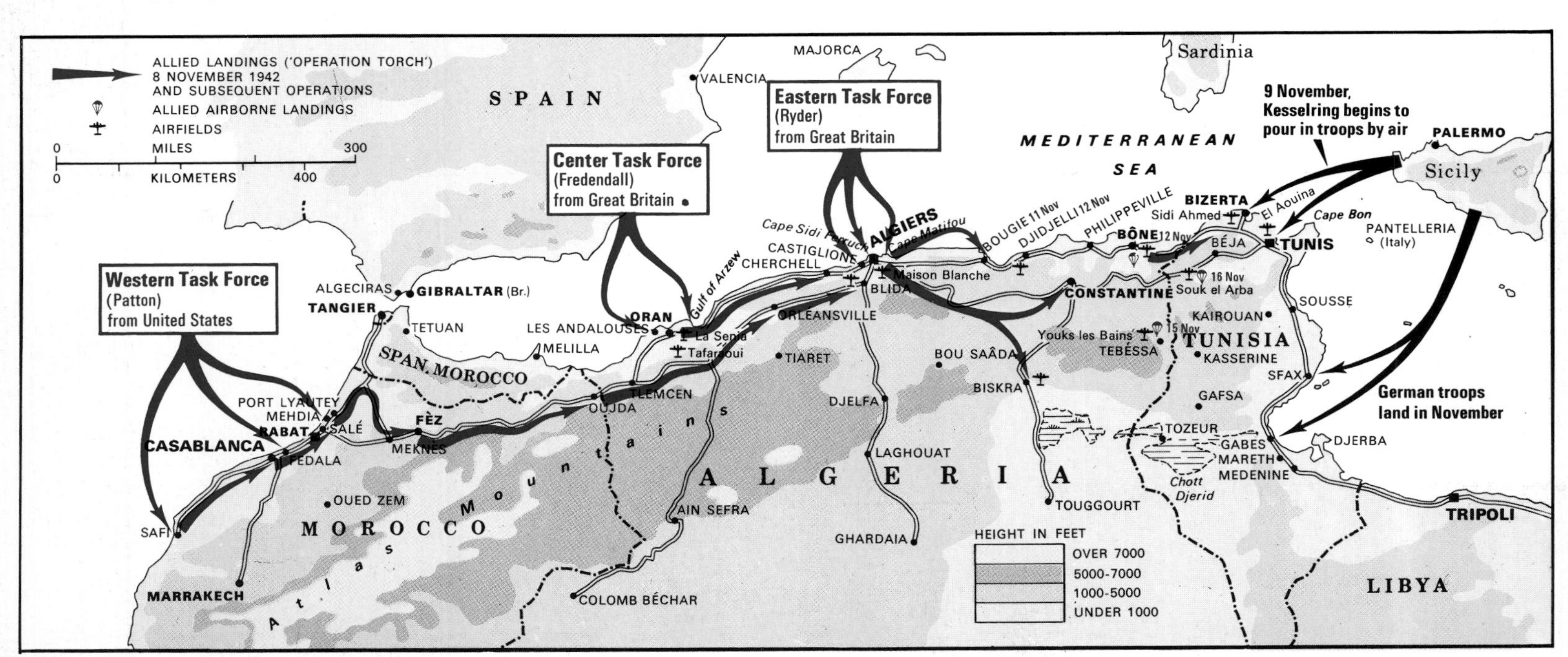

tary power by launching an invasion of Nazi-occupied France. The British, on the other hand, preferred to follow a grand strategy of hitting the Nazi behemoth on the periphery in the Mediterranean and reducing its strength by attrition before launching a mighty invasion in force—either in the 'soft underbelly' of Italy or in France—to drive into Germany itself. The Americans suspected that the British were more interested in saving their Near East empire by waging a peripheral Mediterranean war first, but they could not avoid the hard reality that until Axis military strength was seriously weakened and Allied military strength overwhelming, no invasion of the Continent stood a chance of succeeding. Thus, with the blessing of President Roosevelt and to the relief of Prime Minister Churchill, a decision was made to put off Operation SLEDGEHAMMER (seizing a beachhead in France in 1942) and Operation ROUNDUP (a drive into Germany in 1943) in favor of Operation TORCH (an invasion of North Africa in 1942). This strategy would pressure German forces in the Mediterranean and get the Americans actively into the European war in 1942. The American public was demanding action; as Roosevelt saw it, Operation TORCH was the answer.

Allied planning called for a three-pronged invasion striking simultaneously at Casablanca in French Morocco (outside Gibraltar on the west coast of Africa) and at Oran and Algiers, Algeria, on the Mediterranean. All were major ports and, very importantly, beyond range of the *Luftwaffe* in Sicily. From these points a drive to the east would move into Tunisia. The object was to catch General Erwin Rommel with his Afrika Korps and the Italian Army between the combined British-American forces from Algeria and the British Eighth Army advancing west across North Africa from Egypt. For this invasion, Western Naval Task Force (American Task Force 34), led by Rear Admiral Kent Hewitt, was to sail directly from the United States with 35,000 men to the beachheads in Morocco; the Navy was also assigned the task of covering the landings. Center Naval Task Force

Above: **A damaged and irrepairable F4 Wildcat pushed overside from the *Santee*.**

Below: **The crowded flight deck of the USS *Chenango* on the eve of the Torch landings.**
Bottom left: **Map of the Torch landings.**

Above: **Transports and warships at anchor in the harbor at Mers-el-Kebir near Oran.** ***Bottom right:*** **The crowded deck of an escort carrier, probably the *Santee*, during Operation Torch in November 1942.**

(British) was to sail from Britain with 39,000 American troops to hit Oran. Eastern Naval Task Force (British) was also to sail from Britain with 23,000 British and 10,000 Americans to invade Algiers.

Western Task Force would be under control of the US Navy in the person of Admiral Royal E Ingersoll, Commander in Chief, Atlantic Fleet, until the mid-Atlantic, at which time the entire operation would come under the direction of Lieutenant General Dwight D Eisenhower, Commander in Chief, Allied Forces. Eisenhower would then delegate control to his deputies in each area. This would ensure that in these amphibious operations control of an entire sector in the landings—military and naval, American and British—would be under one man for better coordination and mutual support. The interservice command squabbles that so often characterized Pacific amphibious operations were not to be found in the European theater.

Planning and training for the three amphibious operations went on through 1942, but time was short for learning complicated landing patterns, and the landings might be stoutly resisted. The hope that the Vichy French troops would not fight the invading Allies could not be taken for granted. All three major ports had to be taken to secure solid bases of operations before moving on to the east. Invasion was set for 8 November 1942, the latest date possible before winter weather made beach landings impossible. More time was needed for training the soldiers and sailors in amphibious techniques, but time was not available; the invasion forces were assembled despite the unsatisfactory level of preparation.

The three attack groups of Western Naval Task Force (destined for Mehdia and the airfield at Port Lyautey nearby, 90 miles north of Casablanca; Fedala, 15 miles north of Casablanca; and Safi, 150 miles to the southwest) left Hampton Roads on 23–24 October 1942 and joined a naval covering group of one battleship and two cruisers three days later at sea. The next day, 28 October, a carrier group built around the *Ranger* and four jeep carriers joined the armada. Reaching the African coast on 7 November, the group split up to approach the three target cities the next day.

The landings early in the morning of 8 November were marked by predictable confusion as the undertrained naval crews piloting small plywood 'Higgins boats' and 50-foot steel LCMs (Landing Craft, Mechanized) tried to put men and equipment on the beaches in the dark. Subsequent invasions would use LSTs (Landing Ships, Tank) and other specialized vessels to get the Army's men and equipment off expeditiously, but the forces in Morocco had no such luxury and paid for it in confusion and casualties. Beach landings had to be made in order to swing around behind the cities to take them from the rear.

Despite the fact that the Vichy French did, indeed, resist strenuously, and despite the confusion in landing both men and equipment, the Fedala, Mehdia and Safi landings were successful. Much of the credit must go to the offshore naval covering units for effective support of the soldiers on the beaches. US Navy gunfire silenced batteries along the Fedala shore; put the great French battleship *Jean Bart*, firing her 15-inch guns from Casablanca harbor, out of commission; reduced the batteries at El Hank west of Casablanca and at Fedala; and stopped one French counterattack at Safi and another at Mehdia. The naval attack and covering groups also had to beat off attacks by one French cruiser, seven destroyers and eight submarines against the invasion fleet. All French vessels except one were severely damaged in the confused melee; the Americans lost no ships. On 10 November the damaged *Jean Bart* was sunk by dive bombers from the *Ranger*; next day the French forces in Morocco surrendered. The Casablanca landings had proved a useful baptism of fire for the American forces. Certainly a great many of the mistakes made here were not repeated in later assaults.

The landings at Oran and Algiers also revealed the paramount importance of amphibious co-ordination and close naval support throughout the entire landing and securing phases of the operations, although the fighting here was less hectic than in Morocco. The French Admiral Francois Darlan, Commander in Chief of the Armed Forces of Vichy France, ordered a cease-fire for all French troops in Africa on 10 November, convinced of the wisdom of such a move by an American diplomat, Consul-General Robert Murphy. Operation TORCH was over, and American and British troops now moved on toward Tunisia to drive the Germans and Italians out of North Africa. It took six months of hard fighting to overcome the last Axis resistance on 13 May 1943, but the first giant—if indirect—step had been taken toward the German heartland.

The Invasion of Sicily

While the North African campaign was still in full swing, Roosevelt, Churchill and their chiefs of staff met at the Casablanca Conference (14–25 January 1943) to work out future strategy for the European war. The Americans still wanted a cross-Channel invasion of France in mid-1943, but the British argued that the Allies would have only 25 divisions available by then to face a 44-division German resistance. Therefore, the British said, the peripheral strategy should continue with an assault on either Sicily or Sardinia to erode German resistance and simultaneously aid Russia by pinning down more German troops in Western Europe. A successful seizure of Sicily in particular might well knock Italy out of the war and bring in Turkey on the Allied side. Although not fully convinced of the wisdom of such a strategy, the Americans agreed—but only if more men and supplies were diverted to the Pacific campaigns. Thus a bargain was struck, and Operation HUSKY, the invasion of Sicily 90 miles across the Sicilian Channel from Tunisia, was agreed upon as the next major operation for 1943.

Although Allied commanders were hampered in meeting to discuss strategy for HUSKY by the North African campaign in full swing, plans were finally worked out. The narrow Strait of Messina between Sicily and Italy was the ideal location for a landing—seizing the city of Messina on the west coast of the Straits would seal off all Italian and German troops on the island before they could be evacuated. But this was rejected because of doubt that Allied planes could cover a landing in that area. Accordingly, it was decided that British forces would land on the southeast coast of Sicily on the Gulf of Noto below the important port of Syracuse to seize that crucial city. They would then move north along the coast to capture Messina.

American troops, meanwhile, were to attack along a 37-mile beachhead on the southern coast of Sicily, taking the towns of Licata, Gela and Scoglitti along the Gulf of Gela. For these massive operations over 470,000 troops were assigned, more than the number used at Normandy a year later. After seizing their beachheads, American forces were to move west and north to take the western end of the island and its capital, the north-coast port of Palermo. They would then move east to Messina as the left wing of a giant pincer to meet with the British at Messina and seal off the island. Invasion was set for 10 July 1943.

Although US Navy planners were unhappy about supporting an invasion force over such a wide area, they were cheered by the arrival of many new craft: LSTs (Landing Ships, Tank), LCTs (Landing Craft, Tank), LCIs (Landing Craft, Infantry), LCVPs (Landing Craft, Vehicles and Personnel), LCMs (Landing Craft, Mechanized) and hundreds of newly developed DUKWS (called 'ducks'—not an acronym, but the first four letters of the serial numbers on these amphibious cargo trucks from General Motors). The new vessels, able to unload men and equipment on the beaches, or run up on to the beaches with supplies in the case of the DUKWS, might allow them to seize and hold their beaches. On the other hand, naval planners were very annoyed by the night-time invasion plan that would preclude supporting bombardment. They were also disturbed about the Army Air Force's decision not to give close tactical air support to the troops in favor of 'sealing off the beachhead' by bombing behind the landing areas to prevent reinforcement. The Army shared the Navy's skepticism of such a use of air power—close air support having proved so critical in the Morocco landings—but both services were overridden. Air Force pilots were specifically forbidden to answer naval or land-force requests for support unless approved by Air Force headquarters in North Africa. Even air support from Allied carriers was denied.

On 8 July 1943 the two great amphibious armadas left from various North African ports for their assigned invasion points on Sicily. A total of almost 1400 ships and over 1800 landing aircraft were involved. Facing the 470,000-man invading force were 240,000 Italian and German troops, far from a comfortable margin for the Allied invaders. The Allies would be aided by the fact that the 180,000 Italian defenders had little stomach for a serious defense.

H-Hour, 2:45 am on 10 July, found the American vessels rolling in a heavy swell; misery and confusion were rampant in the assault boats, but the landings proceeded on schedule. Resistance on the Gulf of Gela beachhead was fierce but short-lived, as American troops overran pill-

boxes and gun emplacements with the help of naval units offshore, who were finally allowed to fire when it was obvious that surprise was over. When 'false beaches,' or sandbars, offshore and the target beaches themselves hampered unloading, the DUKWs proved a godsend for the invasion forces. Nothing stopped their crews from delivering their three-ton loads of vital equipment and ordnance.

The Navy scored its most successful contribution to the Sicilian campaign—and taught the Army a valuable lesson in close naval support——when German tanks counterattacked the beachhead at Gela on the morning of 11 July. Lieutenant General George Patton, in charge of the Army's forces, agreed to let the Navy try to handle the problem. Aided by seaplane spotting, the cruiser USS *Boise* and two destroyers opened up with a hailstorm of six-inch shells and obliterated the enemy tanks in short order. Even Patton was impressed.

The British also had a hard time landing because of rough seas in the Gulf of Noto, but faced little resistance onshore: by nightfall of D-Day they had taken the valuable port city of Syracuse. The race to Messina and the capture of the Axis forces was now on. Patton's Seventh Army moved up the southwest coast and took Port Empidocle on 16 July, then raced 100 miles north to capture Palermo on 22 July. By 23 July Patton was moving east along the northern shore of Sicily accompanied by several US Navy light cruisers and destroyers to provide fire support. The Navy also tried to entrap enemy forces by making three amphibious landings ahead of the Seventh Army's advance; these failed in their objective for various reasons, but did expedite the rapid withdrawal of enemy forces.

Meanwhile, General Bernard Montgomery's British Eighth Army got bogged down on its northern thrust. Held off by crack Axis troops, they could make little progress. By 3 August German and Italian forces were withdrawing, and when Patton beat Montgomery into Messina on 17 August—to the delight of the former and the consternation of the latter—45,000 German and over 60,000 Italian troops had already been evacuated across the three-mile Strait of Messina to fight again on the Italian peninsula. Despite this failure, the swift subjugation of Sicily, combined with a massive Allied air raid on Rome, convinced King Victor Emmanuel III to depose Benito Mussolini as *Duce* and take him into 'protective custody.' Hitler, knowing that the new government under Marshal Pietro Badoglio would not seriously pursue the war on the mainland, ordered additional troops into Italy and soon replaced Italian troops in France, Yugoslavia and Greece with his own. Operation HUSKY had been a phenomenal success. Allied communications in the Mediterranean were now secure, Italy was about to fall out of the war and Hitler's forces were spread ever thinner over his shrinking empire. In Churchill's memorable phrase, the Allies were 'closing the ring.'

The Invasion of Italy

The decision to invade Italy (Operation AVALANCHE) after securing Sicily had been made even before Allied forces launched HUSKY. American planners had preferred a cross-Channel invasion of France, but British arguments—that an invasion of the Italian mainland would definitely drive that country out of the war and force Hitler into spreading his forces even thinner—had won the day. Churchill and Roosevelt had agreed—that was all-important in these cases—and Italy was placed next on the agenda, but the Americans insisted on using no additional troops and naval units besides those already in the Mediterranean to carry out the operation. They also insisted on beginning to build up troops and supplies in Britain for the invasion of France. This was granted, and D-Day for the long-awaited invasion of France was set for 1 May 1944. But first came the invasion and conquest of Italy, which proved to be a formidable and supremely frustrating task.

As final plans were worked out, Italy

Below: **Landing operations at Salerno. A landing craft from the USS *James O'Hare* unloads despite incoming German artillery fire.**

would be invaded at two points. General Montgomery's Eighth Army would cross the Strait of Messina on 3 September 1943 and invade at Reggio on the toe of the 'boot.' The main attack, by American and British forces, would come on 9 September at the Gulf of Salerno, a quarter of the way up the boot, from which a drive would be made for Naples, Italy's best port, just 35 miles north. American forces, now called the Fifth Army, were under Lieutenant General Mark W Clark. Negotiations were also under way with Marshal Badoglio to pull Italy out of the war at the same time as the Salerno landings, with the Italian troops switching sides; quick action by Hitler prevented this, as most Italian units were soon disarmed. Only a few Italian naval and airforce units joined the Allied forces.

But the Germans, expecting Italy to be the next target, had reinforced the *Wehrmacht* there. Field Marshal Albert Kesselring, in command of German forces in the south of Italy, did not get all the troops he requested from Hitler, but still had enough strength to more than contest the Allied landings at Salerno. The beaches were mined and wired, the Gulf of Salerno was mined and gun positions bristled in the hills above the beaches.

The Allied amphibious forces, under overall command of Admiral Hewitt, were divided into a British force of two divisions to land on the north beach and drive left toward Naples, with an American force of like size to land to the south and move right to meet Montgomery's forces coming up from Reggio, plus two divisions in reserve. A naval landing force of 26 transports, 120 LSTs and 90 LCTs would carry them ashore, backed by a support force including three American cruisers, a British carrier group and a British covering group. H-Hour was again before sunrise, at 3:30 am; much to Admiral Hewitt's amazement, the amphibious landings were again to be without previous naval bombardment. Army arguments for surprise prevailed, and the German divisions waiting behind the Salerno beaches were not shelled; in the American sector there was not even naval gunfire as the troops crossed the beaches. According to plan, the assault forces deployed from North African and Sicilian ports on 3–6 September. Even the news of Italy's capitulation on 8 September, the day before the invasion, did little to soften the trials of those soldiers and sailors assigned to the assault on the Italian mainland.

Fighting on the two designated beaches was fierce and waged at point-blank range, although the British forces to the north received the help of naval gunfire as the US Navy's amphibious group commander ordered destroyers and rocket-launching craft to open fire after German artillery opened up. The beachheads in Allied hands at the end of the day had been preserved by American and British naval gunfire that knocked out German batteries, machine gun nests, infantry and tanks. Fighting off both conventional and new, devastating glide bombs delivered by the *Luftwaffe*, the naval forces held their ground for three crucial days while the beachhead was reinforced and widened. Unlike Sicily, this time there were carrier-based planes for tactical support of ground troops. The climax of the battle came on 13–14 September when a major German counterattack with tanks failed. Credit must go to effective naval gunnery support, dogged resistance by the foot soldiers and effective air support. Kesselring's tanks and infantry were pounded by naval artillery until 16 September, when he ordered his troops back to a defensive position behind the Volturno River. At the cost of 13,000 dead, missing and wounded, the Salerno beachheads were taken. Naples, Italy's most valuable port, fell to the allies on 1 October 1943.

Yet despite the conquest of Naples and Italy's capitulation (much of the Italian fleet was now interned at Malta), the battle for Italy was far from over. Topography favored the German defenders, and as they backed off from the Volturno River line to a more permanent barrier 40 miles north of Naples, the Winter Line, the whole Allied land offensive slowed to a crawl. Seeking to break the developing stalemate, an amphibious operation against Anzio—to end-run the German line—was planned. But only one division could be assigned to the assault on this port city 37

Above: **The Italian submarine *Nichelio* surrenders to the Allied forces during the Salerno operation.**
Right: **Sunrise over Salerno Bay. Two USN tugs are among the nearest ships.**

miles south of Rome: beaching and landing craft were being transferred to Britain, so the Fifth and Eighth Armies had to move effectively to support it from their positions south of the Winter Line or the whole mission would surely fail. Postponed in November when these two armies could not move because of resistance and rain, the project was revived with a 22 January 1944 invasion day. By this time a two-division force had been scraped together for the landings and sufficient LSTs, LCIs and LCTs had been assembled. From H-Hour at 2:00 am throughout the day, the landings went remarkably well despite the lack of naval bombardment. By evening 36,000 troops were ashore, and in the next few days tons of tanks, guns and supplies followed.

But Kesselring was determined to throw the Allied invaders into the sea. He counterattacked with fury. Army units and naval gunfire held him off, and the beachhead was saved, thanks largely also to the Navy's new scheme of loading trucks and DUKWs in Naples and ferrying them on LSTs directly to Anzio and the beachhead. For weeks the Navy's ferry service ran the gauntlet into Anzio to keep the offensive alive. Yet not until the rains had stopped in mid-May 1944 and the Allies had 27 divisions built up in Italy were they able to force the Germans back from their defensive lines. Only on 4 June 1944, two days before the Normandy invasion, did Allied troops enter Rome. The whole Italian campaign had proved to be a long, bloody virtual stalemate. Yet it drew off German strength by tying down 25 divisions of the *Wehrmacht* and ultimately helped lead to Germany's defeat. Frustrating as they had been, however, the Salerno and Anzio landings had further educated Allied naval, ground and air forces in the intricacies of effective amphibious landings against a determined enemy with maneuverability and effective firepower. The landings in France in 1944 represented the finished product of two years of costly interservice schooling in modern warfare: armies, navies and air forces had to work as one.

The Landings in France

Planning for the long awaited cross-Channel invasion of France had been going on since early 1943. When General Eisenhower was given command of Operation OVERLORD in December 1943, it was to be the definitive operation to take Germany out of the war. After the first assaults by five divisions, 50 divisions were to pour into Europe to destroy the Nazi war machine once and for all. It followed, therefore, that the initial landings on French soil had to be carried out with overwhelming force and intricate precision to attain both immediate and ultimate objectives. It was in view of these considerations that Operation ANVIL (the projected assault on southern France in

Above right: **DUKWs landing supplies at Anzio come under German artillery fire.**
Right: **The cruiser USS *Biloxi* during her shakedown cruise in October 1943.**
Below: **The escort carrier *Kasaan Bay* seen framed by the signal flags of her sister-ship the *Tulagi* off southern France, during Operation Anvil, 15 August 1944.**

the Toulon-Marseille area)—later renamed Operation DRAGOON—was postponed. Eisenhower originally envisioned this invasion as a major diversion, but landing craft for OVERLORD were in such short supply that the two operations could not be carried out simultaneously. DRAGOON was finally launched two months after OVERLORD, on 15 August 1944.

After much study, the landing site chosen for OVERLORD was a stretch of the Normandy coast east of the Cherbourg Peninsula. It was directly south across the English Channel from Portsmouth and the Isle of Wight in southern England. Although the area beyond the beaches, the *bocage* country of earthen walls and thick hedgerows of trees, would present some problems, Normandy gave ready access for cutting off the Cherbourg Peninsula to the west and the port of Cherbourg itself; troops could also move east from the Normandy beaches toward Le Havre and up the coast to take other key ports.

Plans for NEPTUNE-OVERLORD D-Day (NEPTUNE designating the naval part of the operation) called for three paratroop divisions to be dropped during the night before the invasion: one British division to seize the Orne River crossings and the Caen canal, the American 82nd and 101st Airborne Divisions to seize the causeways leading from the beaches to lands beyond and to capture various bridges on the Cherbourg Peninsula. The American First Army on the morning of the first day would seize Utah and Omaha Beaches to the west, and the British Second Army would take Gold, Juno and Sword Beaches on their left.

Naval support, predominantly British, would include pounding the German defenses before and during the invasion—naval gunfire was now finally accepted by the Army as crucial—and carrying the landing forces to the beach, then reinforcing them steadily thereafter with trips across the Channel. NEPTUNE would be an immense undertaking. Anglo-American naval units were also to keep German naval forces away and sweep the mines from the invasion channels to the beaches. For this great combined naval operation, over 2700 vessels from battlewagons to landing craft were available, the vessels to be armed, loaded and assembled all along the southern coast of England and at points as far away as the Thames Estuary on the east and Belfast, Northern Ireland, on the west. All had to converge via precise timetables if the invasion were to succeed.

D-Day was originally scheduled for 1 May 1944, but was delayed a month until 5 June for more training of the landing crews. H-Hour was from 6:30 to 7:55 in the morning depending on tidal conditions on the beaches. At the last minute, weather conditions dictated a 24-hour delay, but on 6 June 1944 the long-awaited invasion began precisely on schedule.

On 31 May, 54 old ships had left Scotland to be sunk off the invasion beaches to form a breakwater. They had been followed by 150 minesweepers that would advance to clear the Channel for the invasion forces. By 3 June the fire-support ships were underway, and the troop convoys with almost 200,000 men aboard began to form in the Channel south of the Isle of Wight.

Above: **Coast Guard landing craft head for Normandy, June 1944.**
Right: **The pre-landing bombardment, D-Day.**
Below: **A small part of the Allied invasion fleet lying off the English coast before setting out for France.**

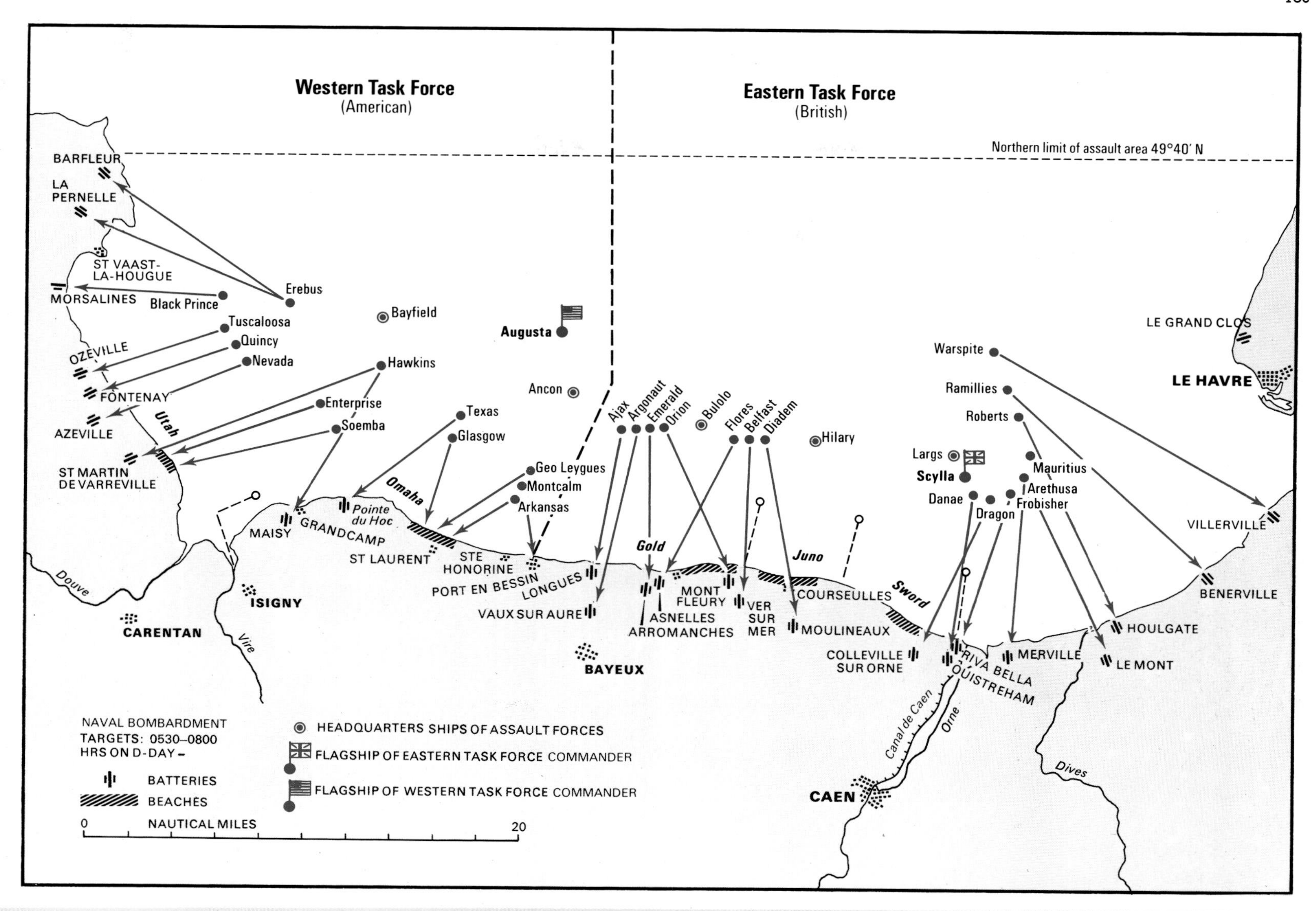
Western Task Force
(American)
Eastern Task Force
(British)
Northern limit of assault area 49°40′ N
BARFLEUR
LA PERNELLE
ST VAAST-LA-HOUGUE
MORSALINES
OZEVILLE
FONTENAY
AZEVILLE
ST MARTIN DE VARREVILLE
Erebus
Black Prince
Tuscaloosa
Quincy
Nevada
Hawkins
Enterprise
Soemba
Bayfield
Augusta
Ancon
Texas
Glasgow
Geo Leygues
Montcalm
Arkansas
Utah
Omaha
Pointe du Hoc
MAISY
GRANDCAMP
ST LAURENT
STE HONORINE
PORT EN BESSIN
LONGUES
VAUX SUR AURE
ISIGNY
CARENTAN
Douve
Vire
BAYEUX
Ajax
Argonaut
Emerald
Orion
Bulolo
Flores
Belfast
Diadem
Hilary
Gold
Juno
Sword
MONT FLEURY
ASNELLES
ARROMANCHES
VER SUR MER
COURSEULLES
MOULINEAUX
Largs
Scylla
Danae
Dragon
Warspite
Ramillies
Roberts
Mauritius
Arethusa
Frobisher
COLLEVILLE SUR ORNE
RIVA BELLA
OUISTREHAM
MERVILLE
HOULGATE
LE MONT
BENERVILLE
VILLERVILLE
LE GRAND CLOS
LE HAVRE
Canal de Caen
Orne
Dives
CAEN
NAVAL BOMBARDMENT TARGETS: 0530–0800 HRS ON D-DAY –
BATTERIES
BEACHES
HEADQUARTERS SHIPS OF ASSAULT FORCES
FLAGSHIP OF EASTERN TASK FORCE COMMANDER
FLAGSHIP OF WESTERN TASK FORCE COMMANDER
0
NAUTICAL MILES
20

LSTs landing cargo over the Normandy beaches in the first days of the invasion.

US 262
US 310

***Above:* Landing operations at Omaha beach showing the technique of unloading from grounded LSTs.**

Despite the 24-hour weather delay, the mighty combined armadas formed up on schedule and moved across the Channel the night of 5–6 June . By 3:00 am on D-Day the fire-support ships were in place. The invasion of France was about to begin, not in the Pas-de-Calais area to the north as the Germans expected but in Normandy. Here the final fate of Germany would be decided.

The British and American paratroopers were dropped on schedule at 1:30 and 4:00 am, while out in the Channel troops began to pour into the landing craft. Between them and the beaches were the naval support vessels, the US battleships *Texas*, *Arkansas* and *Nevada*, plus three US heavy cruisers, two British battleships, five cruisers and 22 destroyers, all lined up to rake the German emplacements behind the American beaches with their murderous fire. British vessels were covering their target beaches to the east. Gunboats and LCTs were to accompany the landing craft and cover the beaches with fire support as the troops made their way ashore through the surf. By 6:00 the naval bombardment was underway.

Covered by this withering fire and many tons of bombs from hundreds of heavy bombers, the troops waded ashore right on schedule at 6:30 in the morning. Utah Beach proved to be relatively easy for the invading forces, but Omaha Beach was heavily fortified and strenuously defended. Tanks dropped by LCTs ahead of the infantry either sank despite their flotation belts, or were knocked out by heavy shelling. The troops on the LCVPs that followed were also shelled unmercifully and the DUKWs accompanying the waves of infantry with artillery were almost all wiped out. But naval gun power saved the day for the thousands of infantrymen hugging the sands of Omaha Beach as their bombardments, directed by spotters in Spitfires flying from England, decimated German emplacements and prevented reinforcements from moving up to push the Allied forces off the beachheads. Sometimes moving as close as 1000 yards from shore to blast away at targets called in by ground spotters, or targets of opportunity, 12 American and British destroyers tore holes in the defensive lines and allowed the ground troops to advance.

By nightfall 34,000 troops were in the beachhead at Omaha; 21,300 were on Utah. The American beachheads were secure, and for days thereafter thousands of tons of equipment and supplies passed over the beaches from the naval armadas running back and forth to England. The British beaches were easier to assault, but here too naval bombardment before and during the landings ensured eventual success. But if vast quantities of men and equipment did not continue to flow into the invasion area, the whole operation would be stymied, for Hitler now belatedly decided that the Normandy landings were not a mere diversion and began to pour crack troops into the area to push the Allies out.

However, the Americans and their British allies were prepared to reinforce the cross-Channel landings in a new and effective way. Even before the first day's action had ended, the old merchant ships ('Gooseberries'), having been towed across the Channel, were being sunk to form artificial breakwaters parallel to the beaches. 'Phoenixes,' enormous concrete box-like caissons, and 'Bombardons,' huge steel floats used to form floating breakwaters, had accompanied them in their slow towed procession from the English coast. Collectively these devices formed 'Mulberries,' artificial harbors off Omaha and Gold beaches, within which Allied ships could safely unload the tons of supplies needed by the invading forces. By 17 June these supplies were flowing ashore to support the expanding offensive; although the worst storm in 50 years destroyed the Mulberry off Omaha Beach two days later, the precious supplies continued to move ashore across Gold Beach.

Furthermore, the navies had discovered while awaiting the construction of the Mulberries that LSTs could be beached at high tide and then unloaded as the tide receded, so off-loading proceeded apace both before and after the storm of 19 June, and the operation was saved. In the first 30 days, the navies carried 929,000 men, 177,000 vehicles and almost 590,000 tons of supplies to the beachheads at Normandy. The breakout from the beachheads and the Cherbourg Peninsula was now possible. During these same crucial early days the US Navy with three battleships, two heavy cruisers (plus two British cruisers) and 11 destroyers had destroyed the heavy coastal batteries at Cherbourg on 25 June and, with the advancing Army units, had compelled the surrender of the city the next day.

The American armies moved west to cut off the Cherbourg Peninsula and south across the French countryside, turning east after 7 August at Avranches to begin forcing the Germans back toward the Rhine and their own borders. Meanwhile, British forces to the east along the Channel beat off a German counterattack, and as one army moved south to link up with the Americans, another advanced northeast toward Le Havre. By late August 1,500,000 Allied troops had broken out and were moving toward Paris and the Rhine. They were knocking on Hitler's door.

Once OVERLORD had been safely launched and secured, landing craft and naval units headed for the Mediterranean to assist in Operation DRAGOON. D-Day was set for 15 August 1944. American and French forces would make the landings between Toulon and Cannes, 50 miles to the northeast. From there the soldiers would move inland to capture the great harbor at Marseilles to the west, then drive up the Rhone Valley to Dijon to meet General Patton's Third Army for the drive into Germany.

Above: **General Eisenhower and Secretary of the Navy Forrestal following a conference in France in August 1944.**

The invasion went more easily than expected. Preceded by extensive aerial bombing and landings behind the beaches by 5000 British and American paratroopers, the main assault groups went ashore at 8:00 in the morning. Before the troops touched shore to meet limited resistance, a full two hours of naval and aerial bombardment had preceded them. The bombardment was deadly and effective: destroyers and LCIs drenched the beaches with fire to knock out any remaining emplacements just before the troops moved ashore. The naval bombarding forces were aided by the planes of seven British and two US escort carriers that spotted for them and also attacked German reinforcements behind the lines. Air supremacy was almost complete, as it had been at Normandy.

The capture of the ports of Toulon and Marseilles required naval bombardment in support of land and air forces assaulting the cities, but by 28 August both had capitulated and the French-American forces were moving northward up the Rhone. By 11 September contact had been made with Patton's Third Army, and German troops in southwest France were sealed off. The two Allied army units joined up to march in tandem toward the German homeland.

Operations OVERLORD and DRAGOON had been phenomenal successes. The Germans were now being hounded from the west and southwest by the American, British and French Armies. To the east and southeast the Russian offensives were also picking up speed. It was now just a matter of time before the Third Reich fell to the Allies. The German's last-ditch attempt to split the Allied forces in mid-December in the Battle of the Bulge temporarily threw the Allied offensive into retreat and confusion in the Ardennes region at the French-Belgium border, but the great German war machine had been fatally crippled by this time. It finally collapsed on 7 May 1945, when a surrender document was signed in Eisenhower's headquarters at Reims by Field Marshal Jodl. The next day, 8 May 1945 at 11:01 pm, the war ended in Europe.

As in the Pacific campaigns, entering their final stages as American forces moved inexorably toward the Japanese home islands, the US Navy had played a major role in securing the peace of the world. From the U-boat wars to the landings at Morocco, Algiers, Sicily, Italy and France, the Navy had served with distinction and pride. As the world began to breathe the clear air of peacetime once again, the Navy looked to its new duties on a now radically changed world scene.

Below: **The USS *Tide* sinking off Omaha after hitting a mine, 7 June 1944.**

U. S. S. MIDWAY
Queen of the Seven Seas
COMMEMORATIVE WAR BONDS
SOLD HERE

Launching of the large carrier *Midway* in March 1945, too late for service in World War II.

PART III

NEW NAVAL MISSIONS

THE COLD WAR AND THE CHANGING NAVY

In the summer of 1945, when victory in Europe was newly won and American military forces were fully geared up for the final assault on Japan, the Navy had almost 3,400,000 officers and men on duty. There were approximately 1200 major ships and 40,000 aircraft of all types in its inventory. Five years later active duty personnel had shrunk to 375,000: 90 percent of the Navy's World War II personnel had been discharged to civilian life. Major combatant vessels numbered fewer than 250, aircraft only 4300. The greatest naval force in history has been slashed to prewar levels, while responsibilities had continued, even increased, in many areas of the world. Additionally, during these five crucial postwar years the Navy had been forced to battle for its very existence as an American fighting force. All signs pointed toward rough seas in maintaining its position as the nation's first line of defense.

Demobilization and Air Attacks

At the end of World War II the American people, in an atmosphere of victory and euphoria, seemed to conclude that a strong military was no longer necessary. Forgetting the lessons of their own history, that peace can be maintained and national interests ensured only through adequate military—and especially naval—strength, they demanded that the government 'bring the boys home' as fast as possible so the nation could return to peaceful pursuits now that overseas threats had been eliminated.

Accordingly, the Navy's first job after hostilities ended in August 1945 was 'Operation Magic Carpet,' utilizing all vessels available—including even carriers and battleships—to ferry the fighting men home. In one year alone, the Navy carried over 2,000,000 men and women back to the United States; in the Far East it transported 400,000 Chinese, Japanese and Korean soldiers back to their homelands. The boys were coming home, peace was in the air and demobilization proceeded apace. In addition to cuts in ships and personnel, the Navy also saw its operating budget drop from $45 billion in 1946 to $14.5 billion in 1947, then to $11.5 billion in 1948. Construction contracts were cancelled on almost 10,000 ships and small craft. Some 2000 other vessels were retired from active service and 'mothballed' in various anchorages along the coasts. Even more were simply declared surplus and sold off for scrap. The Navy had not undergone such a drastic cut in ships, personnel and budget since the end of the Civil War.

An even greater threat to a viable naval defense force was posed by the new atomic bomb and the devotees of air power, who felt their day had finally come. There was widespread public acceptance of the idea that the atomic bomb had made all other weapons obsolete, and that sufficient air power to deliver the deadly bomb against any aggressor was all that was necessary to ensure peace. Air enthusiasts promulgated the theory that strategic bombing had really won the war: if this were true, it followed that the Navy and its fast carrier task forces—as well as the Army and the Marine Corps—were now superfluous. Since the Air Force alone could deliver 'the bomb' (then weighing five tons), air power must grow while the other services were phased down or out, victims of their own vulnerability in the face of new technology. Air Force generals publicly asked why any navy at all was needed.

The Navy's admirals fought back with cold hard facts and technological counterattack. Demobilization, attacks from air enthusiasts and the advent of atomic power would not spell the demise of the Navy if its leaders could prevent it. And world events moved toward confirming the Navy's view that a strong sea force was critical to the nation's security.

The Cold War Begins

Despite fervent hopes in the West that Russia's co-operation with the Allies during World War II would effect a change in her government's attitudes and goals espoused since the revolution of 1917, Kremlin leaders still dreamed of a Communist-dominated world. War-devastated Europe and the Far East offered splendid opportunities to take significant steps in that direction. So did anticolonial nationalistic ambitions of peoples in the Near East, Southeast Asia and Africa. These aspirations could be utilized to further Soviet ambitions, particularly when Western Europe lay prostrated by its wartime efforts.

Any lingering Western complacency in the face of Russian expansion was shaken when a 1948 coup in Czechoslovakia drew that country into the Soviet orbit. Furthermore, in June 1948 the Soviets clamped a blockade on the city of Berlin—contrary to all agreements among the Allies—to display their intention of complete control over the future of Germany. If the Allied occupying powers—Great Britain, France and the United States—could be forced from the divided capital city, it would be a clear sign that Russia was the dominant power in all of the former Reich.

Faced with a decision to withdraw or

Below: **A feature of the design of the *Midway* was the siting of the guns below the flight deck to avoid blast damage to the aircraft.**

remain in Berlin, the Allies carried out an 11-month airlift of supplies into the city. This kept the population alive and Allied claims to joint governing powers intact. By the time the Soviets backed down and lifted the blockade in May 1949—the Western powers meanwhile having created the Federal Government of Germany at Bonn as a sign that Western Germany was a viable and permanent entity outside the Russian-dominated East Germany orbit and control—ten million tons of supplies had been airlifted into the beleaguered city. US Navy and Air Force planes carried 70 percent of these vital supplies; British planes accounted for the rest. It had been a grueling test of will that the Allies had won, and a valuable lesson in Soviet intentions.

While these challenges to US and Western goals and determination were primarily within the purview of the Army and Air Force, checking Communist expansion in the Mediterranean Basin fell largely to the Navy. As early as April 1946 the Navy had shown the flag at Istanbul, the capital of Turkey, in the form of the battleship *Missouri*, which visited the strategic city ostensibly to return the body of the Turkish ambassador (who had died in Washington), but in reality to demonstrate America's interest in Communist activities in the area. Russia had demanded from the Turkish Government a share of control over the historic and strategic

Above: **The submarine *Cusk*, *circa* 1948, fitted with a hangar and launch ramp for the Loon cruise missile.**

Straits and Dardanelles. The *Missouri* was there to show that the United States backed the Turkish Government in its refusal to acquiesce in such an arrangement. The message was received in the Kremlin.

Following a visit by the carrier *Franklin D Roosevelt* to Greece that fall to demonstrate American support of the Greeks in their fight against a Communist-led insurgency, the Navy announced that deployments could henceforth be expected in the Mediterranean. The Navy was returning to the *Mare Nostrum* as an instrument of diplomacy after a century of absence. This US naval presence became more pronounced in 1947, when the insurgents threatened to overthrow the Greek government and thereby other pro-Western governments in the area, including Turkey with its hold on the historic waterway from the Black Sea. Refusing to allow this, or to allow the eastern Mediterranean to fall into Soviet hands, President Harry S Truman announced the 'Truman Doctrine': the United States would help free peoples everywhere resist threats by totalitarian governments, whether openly or through armed minorities within a government. Since Greece was then in a civil war against Communist rebels supplied by the Communist Government in Yugoslavia (at that time a Soviet puppet state), there was no doubt that America was serving notice that Greece and Turkey would not be allowed to fall under Soviet domination. Subsequently supplies and military advisers were sent to Greece, and the US Navy continued to patrol the eastern Mediterranean.

With the assignment of an American carrier to the Mediterranean on a permanent basis late in 1947, bolstered the next year by additional vessels, the Sixth Fleet was born and the American presence in the Mediterranean became a military and diplomatic fact of life thereafter. In effect, the American Navy took over the task of guarding the southern flank of the gradually emerging Western defense line designed to resist Soviet attempts to expand either toward Western Europe or into the Mediterranean Basin. When NATO was created two years later, the US Navy continued this function for the Western alliance, a duty it maintains to this day.

All these actions in Europe and the Mediterranean resulted in a gradual awakening of the American people to the consequences of Russian 'expansionism of opportunity.' Clearly, different options of effective reaction had to be fashioned to meet the challenge. Both economic aid and formal military alliances emerged in what came to be called the Cold War.

Economic aid took the form of the Marshall Plan of June 1947. The plan flowed from a suggestion by Secretary of State George C Marshall that economic assistance be offered to European countries to get them back on their feet after the wartime destruction, thereby lessening the threat of radical reactions against their governments. While this US aid was offered to all countries in Europe in need of economic reconstruction, the Soviet Union refused the offer of help and prevented its puppet states from accepting it too, binding them, instead, to the Molotov Plan administered by Russia. By 1954 the European Recovery Program (the embodiment of the Marshall Plan) had spent over $34 billion on nonmilitary aid (and over $14 billion in military aid) and was a phenomenal success, helping to rebuild the shattered economies of the Western European nations and keeping many of them, particularly Italy, from falling under Communist control.

Military aid took the form of the North Atlantic Treaty Organization (NATO), created in 1949 with 11 Western European nations joining the United States in a mutual defense pact, obviously against Soviet aggression. The North Atlantic Treaty Pact, the first peacetime military alliance the United States had ever entered into, allowed any or all nations to come to the aid of any member state if that state became the victim of aggression. To this day NATO defense forces, heavily supported by the United States, have continued to play a stellar role in providing a shield against outside aggression for the people of Western Europe. Without US naval power to project American determination to Europe's shores, NATO would be a shell without substance.

With world events, and particularly Soviet aggressive moves in Europe and in the Mediterranean, propelling the United States into a role as defender of the peace and security of the West, the US Navy, with its potential for controlled and flexible response, had demonstrated its value in a convulsive post-World War II situation. Yet the Navy constantly had to beat off flank attacks by its sister services in order to exist as a separate and effective arm of America's national defense structure.

Unification Attacks and the 'Revolt of the Admirals'

Unification of the armed services for better co-ordination and economy had been discussed for decades. Over four dozen bills supporting unification had been proposed from the 1920s to the end of World War II. But as the war came to an end with the Army Air Force claiming major credit for defeating enemy forces by strategic bombing—and smarting under its control by the Army—the issue became more pronounced. The Air Force wanted unification as a means of gaining independence from the Army; it also wanted unification to strip the Navy of its air arm. The Army, on the other hand, supported unification not only to let the air forces go, but also to take over the Navy's amphibious Marine Corps. The Navy, stripped of its air function (representing 30 percent of its men and materiel) and of the Marines, would be left with only surface combatant, submarine, convoy-escort and surface-support services. The Navy did not oppose unification as such, but it did resist losing its air arm and its Marines. It argued that it could not

Opposite: The _Forrestal_ at sea in 1959. _Below:_ An F2H Banshee comes in for a hard landing on the _Midway_ in 1953.

carry out its traditional and necessary functions of control of the seas and projection of power without its air and amphibious arms. Nor could the other two services carry out these functions either, leaving the military forces severely limited in anything less than an all-out atomic war.

Unification came about in the National Security Act of 1947, which provided for a National Military Establishment of three departments, Army, Navy and Air Force; a civilian secretary of defense to oversee all three services and sit in the cabinet as principal adviser to the President in all defense and national security matters; three civilian secretaries of the Army, Navy and Air Force; and a Joint Chiefs of Staff to co-ordinate military strategy and logistics. The Navy's continued existence as a multifaceted fighting force was assured under this legislation, which specifically provided for continuation of the Navy's air arm and the Marine Corps. The Navy could live with this arrangement, especially as the first secretary of defense was James V Forrestal, a financier who had come to Washington as naval undersecretary and had become secretary of the navy in 1944 upon the death of Frank Knox. Things proceeded rather well among the unified services for two years under Forrestal's leadership, although the generals and admirals fought one another continually for a fair share of the declining defense allocations of a parsimonious Congress. The act was amended in 1949 to change the NME to the Department of Defense and to provide a chairman for the Joint Chiefs of Staff.

The Navy had thus parried one serious threat against it in the early stages of unification, but threats to its existence were to continue, as it found out only two years later. In 1949 Forrestal suffered a nervous breakdown from overwork and was forced to resign. President Truman appointed as his replacement a West Virginia lawyer-politician active in veterans' affairs, Louis A Johnson. Johnson's appointment came primarily as a reward for his activities as a fund-raiser during Truman's 1948 presidential campaign. The secretary of the navy at the time was John L Sullivan, who had taken the post in 1947. Sullivan shared the admirals' profound distrust of the Air Force's reliance upon massive retaliation in the form of the B-36 bomber with an atomic payload as the primary answer to America's defense needs. And Sullivan was fully committed to naval air power for both strategic and tactical purposes. He approved the building of a 60,000-ton supercarrier to implement the Navy's plans for multiple missions built around newly developed jet fighters. On 18 April 1949 the keel for the supercarrier, to be named the *United States*, was laid with due ceremony at Newport News Shipbuilding in Virginia. The modern naval air age was about to begin. But the Navy never figured on the pro-Air Force Louis Johnson, who had every intention of merging naval aviation with the Air Force and putting the Marines into the Army to save money, even if he had to 'crack heads' to do so. Johnson was determined to have 'real unification' and save over a billion dollars in the process, a fine claim for one who aspired to higher office.

Five days after the laying of the keel for the *United States*, the tactless Johnson, backed with a two-to-one vote in the JCS, summarily cancelled the contract on the carrier. John L Sullivan was out of town and had not been consulted. With this act, the issue of unification was rejoined. Sullivan was furious and resigned forthwith, blasting Johnson for his pro-Air Force and pro-Army prejudices. Johnson followed up the carrier cancellation by revealing that plans were underway to transfer Marine air units to the Air Force. Soon thereafter, the secretary of the army told a Senate committee that the Marines should be part of the Army.

The Navy was resolved to fight to the death over these issues; it got its chance to voice its concerns when the House

Left: **Crewmen of the carriers *Saratoga* (top) and *Independence* commemorate the establishment of US Navy aviation.**
Below: **A typical task group of the late 1950s based around the USS *Valley Forge*.**

Armed Services Committee launched an investigation of Johnson's connection with the procurement of the B-36; Johnson had been a director of the company that received the B-36 contracts. The committee, headed by Georgia Congressman Carl Vinson, cleared Johnson of any wrongdoing, but opened the hearings to extended comment on the whole question of the role of each of the armed services with their respective missions in the nation's defense posture. Navy leaders took advantage of this opportunity to make their case—and vent their frustrations.

Although Francis P Matthews, a banker and businessman from Nebraska and Truman's new secretary of the navy (although he had absolutely no background in naval affairs), backed secretary of defense Johnson during the Vinson hearings, the admirals came out swinging. Vice-Admiral Arthur Radford, Commander in Chief, Pacific Fleet, called the B-36 a 'billion-dollar blunder.' Naval witnesses argued time and again against a single weapon and delivery system and pointed out that unification would not work without allowing each service to proceed with weapons development and testing according to its needs. In this 'revolt of the admirals,' both active duty officers and retired line admirals like King, Nimitz, Spruance and Halsey argued for balanced forces and centered their criticisms on reliance on the B-36 as the heart of America's strategic defense posture. With a maximum speed of only 375 miles per hour and a ceiling of 40,000 feet, they argued, the B-36 was extremely vulnerable to the new Russian MiG-15 jet fighter. The Air Force argued strenuously for the efficiency of the B-36 strategy, and General Omar N Bradley, chairman of the joint chiefs of staff, even asserted that the Marines should be absorbed by the Army since large-scale amphibious operations would never again occur in warfare. For siding with his naval colleagues in the fight, Admiral Louis E Denfield was fired by Matthews as Chief of Naval Operations.

But the Navy was helped by the essential logic of its arguments, and by the fact that during the course of the hearings the Soviet Union exploded an atomic device. The American atomic monopoly was gone, and use of the A-bomb against Russia or its satellites could bring atomic retaliation. The name of the game had been changed dramatically, and the Vinson Committee's report of March 1950 reflected both the Navy's well-argued case for its multi-reaction capabilities and the new atomic realities that opened the door to conflicts of less-than-atomic proportions. The report noted the Navy's needs for means of flexible response and recommended that

Above: **Terrier surface-to-air missiles ready to launch on the *Josephus Daniels*.**

a supercarrier be built when funds became available. It also charged the Air Force with being unbalanced in favor of strategic, as opposed to tactical, power. Finally, it declared that Louis Johnson had violated the law by canceling the *United States* contract.

The Navy stood vindicated: its right to exist as part of a balanced defense force was never again challenged. More importantly, by its fight it had awakened the Congress and the nation to the realities of modern military power and the need for a flexible response at sub-atomic levels. The proper functions of the Army, the Navy and the Air Force were now in a better perspective. Even the generals and admirals understood one another better. The 'revolt of the admirals' had worked out for the best, but Congressional support for more adequate funds for the military services whereby they could respond to all types of threats to the peace were slow in coming. Only when North Korea invaded South Korea on 25 June 1950 and propelled the United States into limited warfare did it become obvious that American forces were simply not prepared for conventional warfare challenges, and that the Navy's demands for flexible response had been right on target.

War in Korea, 1950–53

The conflict in Korea rose out of World War II, after which the Russians accepted the surrender of Japanese troops in Korea north of the 38th parallel; the United States accepted their surrender south of that line. Free elections to determine the fate of the peninsula fell through when the Soviets refused to go along with the United Nations supervision of the process in the north. Thus evolved a *de facto* situation wherein two governments came into being—one in the north supported by the Russians and one in the south supported by the United States—with both claiming sovereignty over the entire country.

This stalemate was broken on 25 June 1950, when 110,000 North Koreans with over 1000 artillery pieces, more than 100 Soviet-built tanks and 100 tactical aircraft swept across the 38th parallel into South Korea. It is clear that both the Soviet Union and China had given the green light to the North Korean Government, perhaps to test American determination to back up her words with action, or perhaps because on three occasions since 1947 high American officials had declared Korea to be outside the American defense perimeter. As the well-trained troops swept south against an increasingly demoralized and hapless South Korean Army, American determination to resist Communist expansion was put to the test. The capital city of Seoul, on the western coast just below the 38th parallel, was quickly overrun, and it appeared that the country would be conquered with breakneck speed.

Reacting swiftly to the invasion, the United States took the matter to the United Nations Security Council: on 26 June (in the absence of the Soviets, who were boycotting the organization) that body condemned the invasion and the next day directed member states to furnish assistance to the Republic of Korea in repelling the attack. By this time President Truman had already acted, ordering General Douglas MacArthur in Japan to take over all American forces to direct the defense of South Korea. As he said, 'We've got to stop the sons of bitches no matter what.' The President also ordered the US Seventh Fleet into the Formosa Strait to prevent the Chinese Communists from attacking the Nationalists, or vice versa, during the Korean confusion; either act would have expanded the conflict into World War III. But Truman's determination to halt the aggression by military means rested with US military forces that had been hard hit by budget-pruning for five years.

With the United States taking the lead in the defense of South Korea (to be joined by forces from Britain, Greece, Turkey and 16 other nations) and furnishing the bulk of land, naval and air forces, supplies

Right: **The battleship *Iowa* off the Korean coast in May 1952.**
Bottom: **Map of the Inchon landings.**

and money, the fate of South Korea obviously depended on American military strength and how soon it could be assembled. MacArthur's Army units stationed in Japan were at only 50 percent of combat readiness, the Fleet Marine Force was down to only 24,000 men, the Air Force F-80 jets were based in Japan and could remain over any Korean target for 15 minutes at the most and the Seventh Fleet had only one large *Essex*-class carrier, two cruisers, 12 destroyers and a few minesweepers and auxiliary craft in the area. The British had one carrier available to aid the American naval efforts.

Despite the small arsenal available for the job, the Navy went to work. While the Army and Marines poured men and supplies into the defense perimeter established around Pusan on the southern tip of the Korean Peninsula, the Navy began gunfire missions in support of the land forces—there was little to fear from North Korean naval efforts, which involved only four dozen small and insignificant craft—and air strikes were launched from the carriers. On 5 July American naval forces received orders to establish a blockade of the entire Korean coastline to prevent reinforcement by sea of the North Korean forces. Thus the pattern for the Navy was set in the first days of the war. It was to furnish surface gunfire support for land units; transport Army, Marine and Air Force personnel and equipment to the fighting areas; and furnish tactical air support to the land forces by cutting North Korean supply lines from the north.

The Air Force found itself hamstrung to a large extent because there was little occasion for strategic bombing in this type of war and because its fighters, based in Japan, did not have the range to attack targets in Korea effectively. Carrier-based Navy planes, either jets or piston-driven, had no such problem and played a stellar role—along with the bombarding cruisers and destroyers hitting shore batteries, enemy convoys and bridges, and the land forces fighting a desperate defensive battle around Pusan—in bringing the North Korean offensive to a halt. The

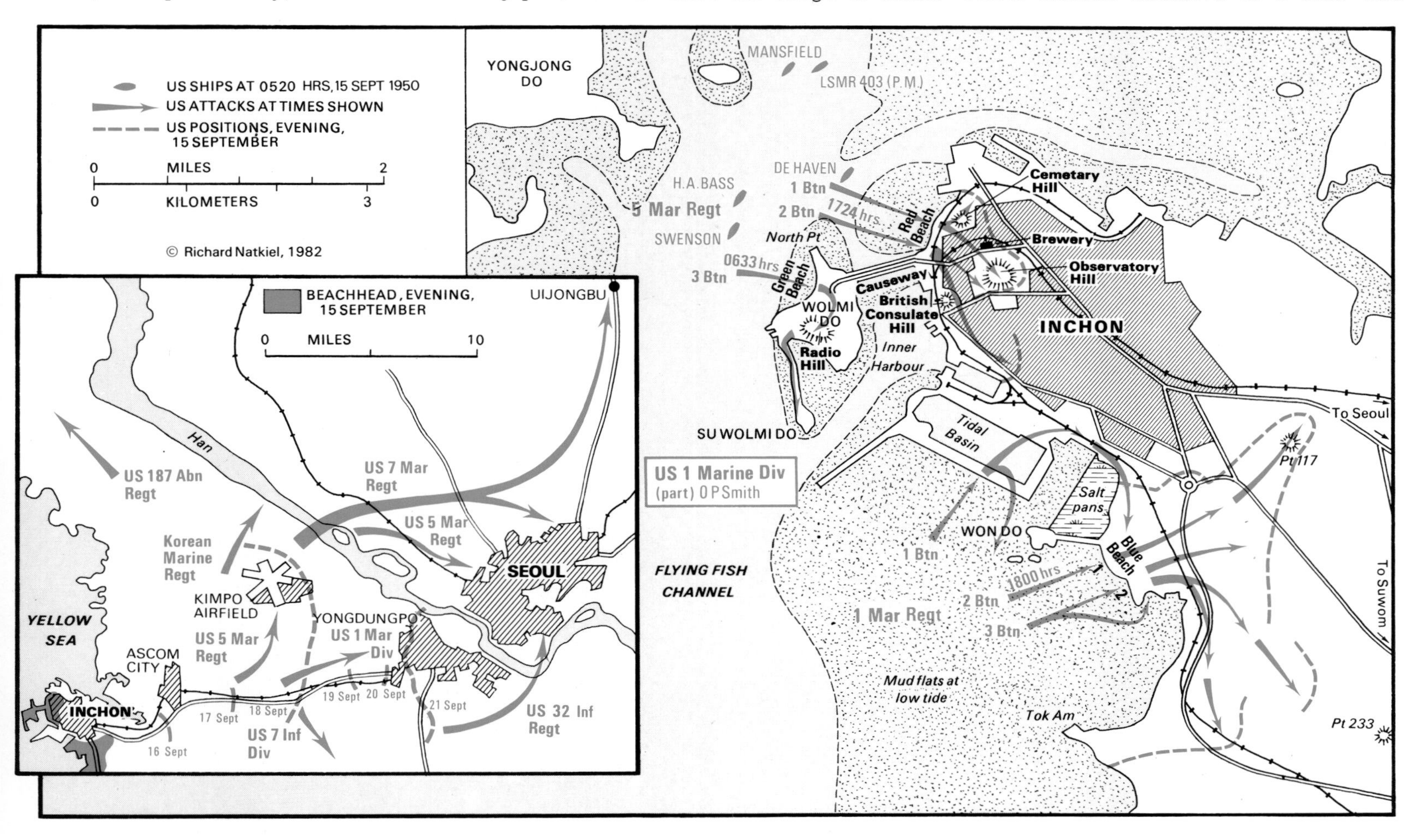

Above: **The *New Jersey* off Korea in May 1951. All four *Iowa* class ships served during the Korean War.**

carrier-based planes also scored a coup by knocking out most of the North Korean Air Force on the ground in an effective bomb-and-rocket attack on the main North Korean air base near Pyongyang. Any lingering doubts about the Navy's capability of providing effective support in a limited war below the atomic threshold, and of taking the war to the enemy, vanished in the opening weeks of the Korean conflict.

Even at this, the Navy's greatest role in Korea was still to come. Since the situation had stabilized around Pusan by the end of the summer of 1950, General MacArthur decided that the time had come to strike a decisive blow against the enemy. He planned to do so in classic style, with a giant attack on the enemy flank to isolate the North Korean forces by cutting them off from reinforcements. The site chosen for the vast amphibious landing on the enemy's flank was Inchon, a port city on the western shore of Korea near the capital of Seoul. Strategic Kimpo Airbase was nearby. The Marines would land at Inchon and push inland, while the Eighth Army would break out at Pusan, catching the North Koreans in MacArthur's vise. The landing was scheduled for 15 September 1950.

But carrying out an amphibious landing at Inchon would be a terrific gamble—some military officers estimated its chances of success at 5000 to 1—because of the 29-to-36-foot tides found there and because the assaulting Marines would be forced to land not on a beach but against a giant sea wall, well defended by enemy forces. The tremendous tides also meant that dangerous currents in the harbor would be a problem and, given the tidal depths, landings could be made only a few days each month and only for a few hours on those days, assuming the naval amphibious landings units could successfully navigate the tortuous channels within the harbor with their ever-threatening mud flats that could ground a vessel without warning. The odds-makers were not far off in their estimates of success, given the complexity of the operation, but the decision to proceed had been made by MacArthur, the commander, and the Navy prepared for the landing.

Softening up of enemy positions in the Inchon area began on 10 September, as planes from the fleet began hitting the island fortress of Wolmi-do within Inchon Harbor. American and British cruisers and destroyers added their guns to the bombardment by hitting gun emplacements in the harbor area. In the grey dawn of 15 September, the 230-vessel invasion fleet appeared off Inchon, a fleet scraped together from the entire Pacific command. Wolmi-do and its garrison of 400 men was the first target. After more pounding by naval guns and aircraft, the Marines moved ashore at 6:30 in the morning and by 8:00 had taken the fortress. The city of Inchon was next; after preliminary softening up, the Marines hit the target with its perilous sea wall that evening. Despite heavy enemy fire, they climbed up and over the walls and moved on the city and Kimpo Airfield. Aided by close naval support, including air strikes, they had taken the city by midnight. Kimpo fell shortly thereafter, and the rail line to Seoul was cut. Sea and air control had aided the Marines in bringing about one of the most successful amphibious landings in American history. Only 22 men were killed, fewer than 200 wounded.

With American units closing in on the capital of Seoul, and the Eighth Army under Lieutenant General Walton H Walker moving north (supported by naval gunfire directed at the east coast road), the

Below: **The *Iowa* during the Korean War. Note the helicopter on the quarterdeck.**

North Korean Army beat a hasty retreat. In an attempt to catch them, MacArthur decided on another amphibious landing—this time at Wonsan, a port city on the eastern coast of Korea north of the 38th parallel. This operation was delayed for eight crucial days because the harbor was strewn with 3000 mines, and the Navy had only a handful of minesweepers available. By the time the task was completed, the ROK (Republic of Korea) armies had encircled the city, forcing the defenders to flee to the north.

During these military actions, three important decisions had been made by President Truman. First, he announced on 27 July that the use of atomic bombs would not be permitted in the war. This was a clear sign to all—especially China—that he would not escalate the war to new heights: it would be fought only along conventional lines. Second, on 12 September he relieved Secretary of Defense Johnson of office for supporting a preventive war against the Soviets. Johnson was replaced by General George C Marshall, who brought higher morale and greater efficiency and co-operation to the department of defense. Third, having decided to attempt political unification of the Korean Peninsula, on 27 September he authorized MacArthur to operate north of the 38th parallel (an order approved by the UN), but specifically forbade the general to cross into Manchuria or to allow any air or naval action north of the Yalu River.

Truman backed up his orders not to provoke Chinese or Russian intervention by attacks on Manchuria via a meeting with MacArthur on Wake Island in October. MacArthur assured the President that neither the Chinese nor the Russians would cross the border, despite the fact that Chou En-lai, the foreign minister of China, had already warned that the Chinese would enter if Americans crossed the 38th parallel. MacArthur was wrong. On 27 October 1950 thousands of Chinese 'volunteers' began crossing the border into North Korea. Within a month the American Army and Marine forces were forced into controlled retreat. The Eighth Army fell back across the 38th parallel, leaving men of the First Marine Division with the task of fighting their way out of the Chosin Reservoir on the east coast and making their way through eight Chinese armies to the port of Hungnam 35 miles away. Thanks to close air support from naval fliers who harassed the Chinese at every turn, the Marines made their way into Hungnam, where every vessel available had been dispatched to ferry them out. Setting up a curtain of fire around the town with naval guns and firepower, the relief force under Rear Admiral James H Doyle was able to evacuate over 100,000 American and ROK troops and 91,000 civilians from Hungnam by Christmas Eve. They were carried to safety at Pusan.

From this point on, the conflict settled into a war of attrition with the battle line just north of the 38th parallel. Before long it was a stalemate, and peace talks began in July 1951, but not before General MacArthur had been ingloriously fired by President Truman for advocating—publicly—the use of atomic weapons in Manchuria and the utilization of Chiang Kai-shek's 500,000 troops in Korea or

Below: **A Navy Corsair about to make a rocket attack on a North Korean bridge in September 1951.**

Main picture: The *Essex* class carrier *Leyte* seen in the mid-1950s.
Below: An A-4 Skyhawk being prepared for launch from the USS *America*.
Below left: The *Missouri* blasts enemy positions at Chonjin, 21 October 1951. The *Missouri* was the only US battleship in commission at the start of the Korean War.

against China itself. The nation was as split over the Truman-MacArthur controversy as it was over the war itself, which ultimately cost the United States 142,091 casualties—killed, wounded, captured or missing.

Once peace talks began, the fighting gradually died away except for a few months when negotiations broke down and the battles were resumed. General Matthew B Ridgway, MacArthur's successor, had no intention of expanding the scope of the war, and Vice-Admiral C Turner Joy, heading the UN delegation, assumed the unenviable job of carrying out negotiations with the communist delegation, the enemy knowing full well that any significant enlargement of the war by the United States was politically impossible. The stalemate was finally ended with the signing of a formal truce on 27 July 1953, placing the truce line almost where the border had been before the fighting began 37 months before.

It had been a frustrating war for a rather bewildered American public, but the communists had been stopped cold in their first attempt to enlarge by force. Truman, however, by refusing to use America's greatest strategic striking power, had sent a message to would-be aggressors that they could escape responsibility for their warmongering by using proxies without fear of American retaliation. This unintended message of America's willingness to use only limited means in limited wars was not lost on either China or Russia, as the next two decades would show.

As the Navy surveyed its part in the conflict, it could not but be proud. It had done its job on limited resources, and done it well. The war had also revealed that the Navy did, indeed, need greater financial support to provide the ships, weapons and personnel to carry out its multiresponse mission. In Korea it had proved that it could do the jobs assigned—shore bombardments, close air support, transportation and supply of ground troops, amphibious landings—as no other service could. To talk of the Navy as being obsolete was now patently ridiculous. The Army knew it; the Air Force knew it; and the American public knew it. The Navy's new wartime mission was its old mission updated.

Upholding American Commitments in the 1950s

During the remaining years of the 1950s, the Navy was called upon to uphold American and noncommunist world rights in the Far East, in the Mediterranean and in the North Atlantic. It did this without firing a shot. The imposing Seventh Fleet in the Far East, the Sixth Fleet in the Mediterranean and the vessels assigned to NATO for European duty stood at the ready to deter Communist aggression and localize conflicts wherever they occurred. Not only were American commitments maintained within the NATO alliance, the nation also made an agreement with the Philippines (which gained its independence on 4 July 1946) whereby 23 military and naval bases, including Subic Bay, would be maintained on a 99-year-lease basis by the United States in the archipelago, thus ensuring an ongoing American presence in the Far East. The United States signed a mutual defense pact with Australia and New Zealand called ANZUS in 1951. Furthermore, in 1954 the United States joined Britain, France, Australia, New Zealand, the Philippines, Thailand, and Pakistan in the South East Asia Treaty Organization (SEATO) which, while not a defense alliance—since it provided only for consultation in the face of aggression—served to keep the United States in naval alliance with the other member countries. In each case it was expected that the Navy would be called upon to bear a heavy burden in supporting America's friends in the face of communist aggression.

Left: **The carrier *Kitty Hawk* refuels her escorting destroyers *McKean* (right) and *Harry Hubbard* during exercises in October 1962.**

The nation and the Navy also became actively involved to the point of intervention in many areas of the world. In 1954 the Navy prepared to intervene by carrier strike force to aid the French army of 12,000 surrounded at the fortress of Dien Bien Phu in Vietnam by 50,000 communist forces, but the decision was made at higher levels to forego unilateral intervention.

Later in the year and into 1955, after the abortive Geneva Conference resulted only in a division of Vietnam along the 17th parallel, the Navy carried out Operation 'Passage to Freedom' by using its vessels to relocate 800,000 people from North Vietnam in the south and to remove tons of military equipment to South Vietnam from the north. Then in 1958 the Chinese Communists began a military buildup across from the Nationalist-controlled islands of Quemoy and Matsu, only four miles off the Chinese coast. The communists saw the islands as stepping stones to the conquest of Taiwan; the Nationalists saw them as springboards to their return to the mainland. When bombing of the islands by the communists began on 23 August 1958, the Seventh Fleet was called upon to aid the 100,000 Nationalist defenders on the islands without getting into a shooting war with the communists. The Navy helped convoy supplies to the islands from Taiwan by carrying amphibious tractors close to shore, from which point they could make their way in. The Navy also flew sorties from its five carriers in the air space over Taiwan, thus freeing the Nationalist air forces to deal with the communists' Russian-built MiGs. The crisis soon died as China turned to attack Tibet and the frontiers of India.

The Navy was also called upon to act in the Mediterranean in 1958. The Middle East was quickly becoming a hotspot, with the Americans in full support of Israel against her Arab neighbors and the Soviets trying to break out into the eastern Mediterranean by supporting nationalist and anti-Western colonial movements throughout the area. At stake, too, was the

Below: **Terrier missile fired from the carrier *Constellation* during her shakedown cruise in 1962.**

rich supply of oil which the Western nations had developed in the area and which the Soviets were seeking to deny to the oil-starved Free World countries. On 14 July 1958 an armed revolt ended the pro-Western government in Iraq. The President of Lebanon, Camille Chamoun, believed the coup had been staged with the help of Egyptian president Gamal Abdel Nasser (closely tied to Russia) and, fearing the same might happen in his country, asked the United States for military aid. In line with the 'Eisenhower Doctrine' of 1956—which said that the United States would aid any Middle Eastern Government threatened by communism if aid was asked for—the Sixth Fleet was ordered into the area. It was an imposing sight, with its three carriers plus escorting cruisers and destroyers and amphibious ships loaded with Marines as it approached the Lebanese shore on 15 July. By afternoon the Marines were landing on the beaches near Beirut under cover of Navy jets overhead. Eventually 14,000 Marines moved into Lebanon and remained there until the situation stabilized and the threat of a coup passed. Although there was no resistance to the landings—indeed, the Marines were greeted only by scantily clad sunbathers and ice-cream vendors—the Navy demonstrated clearly that it could move quickly and effectively to trouble spots on incredibly short notice. Thanks to this swift response, the Russian pledges of assistance to the Egyptians were revealed as hollow promises. The lesson was not lost on a disappointed Nasser. Nor was it lost on the Soviets, who decided that a multiple-response fleet in the Mediterranean was indispensable to success in that area.

Thus during the Eisenhower years the Navy was able to play an effective role in countering the Soviet military threat in line with the President's basic desire to protect the Free World within the framework of necessary national economic stability and balanced budgets. Money was tight, but all three services were allowed to move forward in research and development of the weapons systems they needed in the event of either nuclear or sub-nuclear confrontations. The US Navy stayed on station as in the past, although now it was increasingly armed with weapons of the atomic age.

Birth of the Nuclear Navy

Atomic research had not stopped with the development of the atomic bomb, but had proceeded apace from that point. If the development of atomic power for warfare by the United States had needed any impetus, it was supplied when the Soviets exploded an atomic device of their own in 1949. In 1952 the USA demonstrated the first hydrogen bomb. Then in 1954 the Russians exploded a hydrogen bomb, prompting President Eisenhower to demand military armaments that would deter attack by the Soviets. The race for nuclear superiority in weaponry was on.

The Navy had been working on atomic power for vessels since the late 1940s, particularly on an atomic-powered submarine. Such a submarine could remain submerged as long as necessary, because it drew its steam power from a nuclear reactor that required no oxygen and gave off no exhaust. The need to surface periodically had always been the greatest tactical weakness of submarines. Remaining submerged for days or weeks on end, an atomic submarine would be virtually impervious to attack. The trick was to produce an atomic reactor suitable for the limited space available in a sub. The man who spearheaded the Navy's project for atomic-powered submarines was Hyman G Rickover.

Rickover was the Navy's leading expert on nuclear propulsion and chief of the Nuclear Propulsion Division of the Bureau of Ships. At the same time he was head of the Naval Reactors Branch of the Atomic Energy Commission. In this dual military-civilian capacity, he could both demand that each agency fulfill his goals and coordinate the research of both organizations. Always crusty and demanding (to the point of frequent insufferability, according to many who had to deal with him) he constantly prodded his researchers on and saw his dream come true with the launching of the atomic submarine *Nautilus* at Groton, Connecticut, in 1954. The black-hulled boat, with a sleek 'sail' replacing the old conning tower, was taken out for trials in January 1955 and passed with flying colors. It was a proud day for this son of a Polish immigrant, who had graduated from Annapolis in 1922 and begun his brilliant career in marine engineering shortly thereafter. Now he had placed the United States in the lead in the atomic sub

race. Rickover must have drawn satisfaction, too, from the fact that he had been passed over for promotion to rear admiral and had faced mandatory retirement in 1953, only to be saved by a spirited outcry from the public and Congress. Whatever the merits of Rickover's personality and his way of doing business, there was no doubting his accomplishments. He was leading the Navy into the atomic age.

Work on nuclear-powered submarines and their technology continued at a brisk pace in the years that followed. In 1958 the *Nautilus* proved her ability to stay submerged for long periods of time while navigating with pinpoint accuracy, when she sailed from the Pacific to the Atlantic under the polar ice cap. Later that year the *Skate* rose from the sea to surface at the North Pole. Perhaps the most dramatic demonstration of the atomic submarine's ability to remain submerged and navigate accurately came two years later, when the *Triton* made a complete circumnavigation of the globe underwater, cover-

Left: The USS _Grayback_ enters San Diego harbor carrying a 400-mile range Regulus I cruise missile.
Below: The USS _Ethan Allen_, name ship of the second US Navy class of nuclear-powered, ballistic-missile submarines.

25

9

Left: The nuclear-powered *Bainbridge* at sea in 1979.
Below: The *Long Beach* showing the square-sided superstructure that was for many years a recognition feature of this nuclear-powered cruiser. The installation of new radars in the early 1980s has changed this profile however.

GJ
GL
14892
AF
8413
8396
8402
8398
NAVY
NAVY
NAVY
NAVY
NAVY
101
106
105
112
111

Above: The *Lafayette* class ballistic-missile submarine USS *Nathan Hale* (SSBN.623).
Left: F-4 Phantom II aircraft at the forward end of the *Enterprise*'s massive flight deck in April 1962.

ing the 36,000 miles in 83 days, her inertial navigation system making the feat possible.

Nor did the Navy pass up the chance to develop atomic-powered surface vessels in these years. In 1957 the keel was laid for the *Long Beach*, a cruiser with a nuclear propulsion plant buried in her sleek hull. The 17,000-ton vessel was not only the first nuclear surface ship in the Navy's inventory when she joined the fleet in 1961, but also the first cruiser built for the service since World War II. Her main batteries consisted of guided missiles rather than guns. She was followed into the surface fleet by the giant atomic-powered carrier *Enterprise*, whose keel was laid in 1958 and who joined the fleet in 1962. This 1123-foot giant of almost 90,000 tons was powered by eight reactors and could steam at 30 knots and go two years without refueling. Her angled flight deck (an innovation copied from the British) had four powerful steam catapults that allowed her to launch a plane ever 30 seconds. The *Enterprise* added a new and powerful dimension to the Navy's arsenal and dictated that other ships in carrier task forces of the future would have to match her in speed and mobility. Together they would be armadas of the 1960s and beyond. Having also launched the guided-missile frigate *Bainbridge* with nuclear power generation, the Navy had demonstrated by the early 1960s that nuclear power had come to stay on the oceans, and that the US Navy would command the lead in new firepower and technology.

But the secret of the tremendous potential of these new naval craft lay in the simultaneous development of the guided missile. Not satisfied with having nuclear submarines equipped with short range Regulus missiles (which required them to surface in order to fire their ordnance), Admiral Arleigh A Burke, Chief of Naval Operations from 1955 until 1961—and the chief figure in the 'revolt of the admirals' less than a decade before—pushed for guided missile research and development that would allow missile firing from beneath the sea. Success was attained in 1960 when the submarine *George Washington*, in a test off the Florida coast, fired the first Polaris missile from a submerged position. From this point on, the matching of atomic submarine propulsion with accurate long-range ballistic missiles gave the Navy one of the most advanced and secure weapons systems in the world. Other and more powerful submarines, surface vessels and ballistic missiles would follow, but the pattern had been set in these years of trial and rearmament for the Navy.

In 1956 President Eisenhower had set the tone and direction of defensive weaponry when he outlined the weapons of the future, weapons to deter aggression in either nuclear or sub-nuclear confrontations. He had argued for balanced forces consisting basically of strategic air power, guided missiles, supercarriers, atomic submarines capable of launching missiles with atomic warheads, plus a sizeable army, a capable Marine force for land operations and a strengthened Air Force tactical capability. With these coming into place in the Navy and its sister services by the end of the 1950s, it was clear that the questions of national defense reorganization and of the types of weapons that were necessary to maintain an adequate military readiness in all situations had been answered by conflict, compromise and the grim realities of world events. The greatest teacher had been the Korean War. The greatest gainer had been the American people and their friends around the world who, feeling a sense of direction and purpose, had shouldered the burden of the defense of the non-communist world as part of their historical legacy. But the calm assurance of the 1950s gave way to the turbulent 1960s and 1970s, and with them came new problems for the nation—and for the armed services that protected American interests.

Aircraft maintenance in the cavernous hangar of the USS *Enterprise* in 1964.

CONFLAG
STA No 4
AE
AE
7745
9543
3307

DECADES OF TURMOIL

'Let every nation know, whether it wishes us well or ill, that we shall pay any price, bear any burden, meet any hardship, support any friend, oppose any foe to assure the survival and the success of liberty.' With these soul-stirring words of his inaugural address, John F Kennedy made his debut as President of the United States in 1961. The former World War II naval officer and Congressman and Senator from Massachusetts had beaten out Vice-President Richard M Nixon by a whisker in the 1960 presidential elections and now came to the nation's helm. To the Navy and the entire defense establishment, the implications of the new President's words were clear: America, having rediscovered its world mission and its resolve, was about to take the offensive for liberty. Yet time would show that this was a false start. Not until almost twenty years of trial and confusion, both internal and external, had passed would the nation appear to rediscover its sense of direction. The 1960s and 1970s would prove to be decades of internal confusion and of commitments without conviction: and the Navy and its sister services would undergo further purgatories before America began to awaken to the realities of worldwide responsibilities in the late twentieth century.

The McNamara 'Revolution' and Caribbean Crisis

Robert S McNamara, Kennedy's choice for secretary of defense, had compiled an outstanding record as a brilliant systems analyst and organizer from his early student days at Berkeley and Harvard to his stint as president of Ford Motor Company after World War II. The aggressive McNamara was the embodiment of the new style of industrial manager who based his decisions on systems and cost analysis. As a leader in scientific management, he attracted a legion of young, dynamic men of the same mold who followed him to Washington to flesh out his personal staff, which soon expanded to 1600 persons. With the young president's support, McNamara's drive to introduce modern principles of management to the Pentagon met little resistance from above, but plenty of resistance from below.

To the Navy, McNamara's 'whiz kids' (plus the burgeoning professional staffs

Right: **Soviet-made *Komar* class missile patrol boats photographed in Cuba on 3 November 1962.**
Below right: **Missile equipment being removed from Cuba, 6 November 1962.**
Below: **Suspicious crates opened by the crew of a Soviet freighter to expose comparatively innocuous bomber aircraft, not missiles.**

KRONSTADT PC
4 KOMAR PGMG
6 MISSILE TRANSPORTERS
TRUCK
TRUCK CRANE
TRUCK

of permanent Congressional committees) represented a clear danger to the services —and thereby to the nation—by operating on two false premises: first, that management by civilians in areas of professional military expertise and judgment would result in essentially sound military decisions. Military critics argued that theoretically sound managerial decisions could well be poor military decisions, especially with over-direction taking away the proper sphere of judgment from experienced leaders and competent field commanders on the spot. The second false premise was that military decisions are essentially quantifiable. Military leaders preferred to rely on previous performance and prudential judgment of the situation in view of overall strategies. To quantify the unquantifiable (whether in weapons procurement, strategic or tactical options, or personnel decisions) was both foolhardy and usually counterproductive. Many, if not most, of the crucial problems faced by the armed services, they argued, did not yield to systems analysis.

But these objections did not deter the defense secretary and his assistants. If the admirals (or generals) could not produce quantifiable proof that a proposed weapons system or tactical analysis would or would not work (at least on paper), or that a particular type of ship or plane was or was not cost-effective because of its particular role in wartime deployments or diplomatic situations, the assumption was made at Defense that the military leaders could not know what they were talking about. Admirals and generals would function only to offer suggestions to their civilian superiors. Time would prove that the admirals and generals stood on solid ground in their resistance to excessive civilian control and systems analysis processes, but many tragedies would occur before the service leaders would regain attention as professionals in their own right.

During President Eisenhower's time a plan had been hatched for the United States to support anti-Fidel Castro Cubans in attempting an invasion of the island to overthrow the Caribbean dictator, who had come to power in 1959. By late 1960, 'Operation Pluto' had been formulated by the Central Intelligence Agency. Free Cuban airplanes would carry out pre-invasion air strikes against Castro's 30-plane air force, and a 1500-man invasion force, trained covertly in Guatemala, would land at Bahia de Cochinos (The Bay of Pigs) on the southern coast of Cuba. This invasion, according to CIA operatives, would set off an anti-Castro uprising, and the capital of Havana would soon fall to the invaders. At this point all planning was tentative and subject to cancellation by the White House.

By 1961 final planning for the invasion was well under way, without the Navy having been informed that this combat operation had been approved in the highest government circles and that they were to support it to assure its success. The Navy received virtually no critical information on the invasion plans, the military being told simply to 'Stay the hell out of it.'

The invasion attempt on 17 April 1961 was a notorious fiasco. United States naval units were sent to the area to assist the civilian-directed operation, but Kennedy then refused to authorize US naval aircraft standing by on the deck of the carrier *Essex* to give critical air cover as the invasion proceeded on 17 April. Survivors of the invasion forces were soon trapped on the swampy terrain at the Bay of Pigs landing site and within three days had been rounded up and thrown into prison camps by the Castro forces. (They were ransomed by the United States in December 1962 for $53 million in food and medicine.) American prestige was damaged both in Latin America and throughout the world. More importantly, the aborted invasion attempt pushed Castro even closer to viewing the Soviet Union as his protector. Soon thereafter the Soviets were permitted to begin installing nuclear ballistic missiles on Cuban soil.

Although Operation Pluto proved conclusively that military operations should be planned by military professionals, not civilian amateurs, and that no commitment should be made unless the country was willing to follow through with sufficient force to accomplish the objective, the embarrassing lesson was apparently lost

Right: The Soviet freighter _Metallurg Anasov_ with missiles and related equipment on deck after leaving Cuba on November 1962.
Below: The similarly laden _Komsomol_ pictured in the Mediterranean.

on civilian White House advisors, although perhaps not on President Kennedy who, when the next Cuban problem intruded itself, worked closely with the Navy and other services to effect a solution.

During the summer of 1962 it became obvious to US intelligence forces that something ominous was happening in Cuba. Dozens of Russian ships had arrived bringing men, fighter planes and surface-to-air missiles to the island. Inquiries to the Soviet Union brought assurances that the weapons were only defensive in nature, but refugees from Cuba insisted that something very menacing was taking place. Finally, on 14 October, a high-flying U-2 American reconnaissance plane took photographs that revealed clearly the rapid preparation of long-range missile sites—one type of missile being readied was capable of a 1000-mile range, and another had a 2000-mile range. America at this time enjoyed a clear superiority in ballistic missiles, with 130 ICBMs (intercontinental ballistic missiles), 144 Polaris missiles in Navy subs and about 1500 strategic bombers. But in one bold stroke Soviet Premier Nikita Khrushchev could neutralize that lead by placing the entire United States within two-to-three minute warning range of Soviet missiles. Eighty million Americans could be killed in a single pre-emptive strike.

After examining the options—a 'surgical' air strike on the missile sites, a blockade of Cuba, or an invasion of the island—Kennedy decided that a blockade, or 'quarantine' as he called it, was the proper response. He asked Admiral George W Anderson, Jr, CNO, if the Navy could do the job: Anderson responded, 'The Navy will not let you down.' While the government informed the United Nations, the Organization of American States and the nation's major allies what was in the offing, the Air Force put four tactical aircraft squadrons and its ICBM crews on alert. The Army began moving thousands of troops to embarkation points in Georgia and Florida; the Navy alerted its Polaris crews and formed 180 ships, including eight carriers, into Task Force 136 to carry out the blockade. In all, some 480 ships eventually took part in the operation, and almost 400,000 military personnel went on alert.

With the military at the ready, and with Air Force B-52s in the air, Kennedy went before the nation via television on the evening of 22 October 1962 to inform the American people and all nations that the Soviet Union had placed offensive missiles in Cuba and that the island would be quarantined until they were removed. To give the Russians time to think it over and back down, Kennedy announced that the naval blockade would begin $1\frac{1}{2}$ days hence, on 24 October at 9:00 in the morning, EST.

Tension mounted steadily as two dozen ships from Russia neared the announced quarantine line northeast of Cuba (first established at 800 miles from the island, then reduced to 500 miles when it was realized that some Russians ships underway would reach the deeper line before 24 October). As work continued on the missile sites, Kennedy informed Khrushchev on 23 October that he had OAS support and that Soviet ships would not be fired upon for the purpose of sinking them, but would be disabled. Furthermore, he said, the US Navy would force Soviet submarines to the surface or depth charge them. The Navy put the quarantine into effect as scheduled on 24 October, stopping and boarding all Soviet-chartered ships approaching the island; those without offensive weaponry were allowed through. Most turned back. No Soviet ship with offensive weapons crossed the line, and six subs were forced to the surface after they had been picked up and warned by signal to surface and identify themselves or be depth charged. Finally, on 28 October Krushchev announced that he would remove the missiles under UN supervision if Kennedy would pledge not to invade Cuba (at that moment 30,000 Marines were poised offshore for invasion). Although Castro remained in power after the Cuban confrontation, the Russians had clearly backed down. The missile crisis was over, although American forces would stay on alert for another three weeks, and the US Navy would monitor removal of the missiles from Cuba.

The crisis had been the supreme example of flexible response by a balanced naval force. The Navy, co-operating with the Air Force and Army, had again proved its versatility. Nuclear war had been avoided because other options had been available. The Navy had not let the President—or the nation—down, as Admiral Anderson had promised; it had performed its duty in exemplary fashion.

Into the Quagmire of Vietnam

American involvement in South Vietnam began as far back as the closing months of World War II, when American military-intelligence agents moved into the country to encourage uprisings against the occupying Japanese and worked briefly with the communist guerrilla leader Ho Chi Minh. As the French tried to re-establish control over their colony at the end of the war by putting down Ho's guerrilla forces who threatened to take it over, the US made the fateful decision in 1950, under President Truman, to extend economic and military aid to the French—probably in reaction to the 'loss' of China to the communists the year before. By 1954 communist forces under Ho had won a resounding victory over the French fortress at Dien Bien Phu (the United States refusing to carry out last-minute bombings, or to commit American ground forces to aid in the defense in the absence of clear support from other allies of the French): the French were forced to close their war at the bargaining table. The Geneva Conference of that year divided the beleaguered country into North Vietnam and South Vietnam, and the French began to leave.

In response to the perceived danger of spreading communism, the United States formed the South East Asia Treaty Organization (SEATO) early the next year, allying itself, Australia, France, New Zealand, Pakistan, the Philippines, Thailand and Great Britain. Also in 1954 the United States enthusiastically endorsed Ngo Dinh Diem as Prime Minister of South Vietnam. Diem, a highly regarded anticommunist patriotic leader for many years, was overwhelmingly elected President the following year but soon proved to be authoritarian in his governing style. Still, he seemed the best man for US support in

Below: A US Navy _Swift_ boat engages a shore target in South Vietnam. The _Swift_-type patrol boats were armed with 0.5-inch machine guns and an 81mm mortar.

Above: A US Navy assault support patrol boat operating in the Mekong Delta in November 1967. In the background a Chinook transport helicopter.
Below: The carrier *Franklin Roosevelt* pictured in the Gulf of Tonkin in 1966.

the difficult situation wherein Ho and North Vietnam refused to accept the concept of a divided Vietnam and waged incessant guerrilla warfare against the government of South Vietnam.

American advisers continued to visit South Vietnam in search of a means of winning counterinsurgency victories, but their job was made more difficult by Diem's refusal to make the reforms that would win him wider popular support in his clash with the North Vietnamese forces, and by Ho's claims to be the real leader of all of the Vietnamese people. In 1961 Vice-President Lyndon B Johnson visited the South Vietnamese leader and returned to tell President Kennedy that more economic aid should be extended, but that military intervention on a large scale should not be tried. He added, however, that the United States had to stand by its friends and assist South Vietnam in its struggle against communism. Kennedy, fearing a communist victory, decided to increase the number of American advisers in South Vietnam from a total of 1000 to 16,000 over a two-year period.

By the end of 1962, almost 10,000 advisers were in Vietnam, but the war against the North Vietnamese insurgents was still going badly. Convinced that the basic problem was the uncooperative government of Ngo Dinh Diem (who surrounded himself with family members in power positions, including especially Ngo Dinh Nhu, his brother, and his brother's wife, the diminutive but fiery Madame Nhu), the White House, the State Department and the Central Intelligence Agency endorsed a coup by South Vietnam's military against Diem. Kennedy, perhaps naively, assumed that the worst fate awaiting Diem would be exile. Instead, the military leaders arrested Diem and Nhu early in the morning of 2 November 1963, as they were praying in a church, and assassinated both in cold blood in the rear of an armored personnel carrier. The US had now taken a major and bloody step into responsibility for the war halfway around the world. Ironically, Kennedy himself would

fall to an assassin's bullet before the month was out.

Before the end of this fateful month, 23,000 Americans had been assigned to Vietnam; two-thirds of them were military, but fewer than 800 were naval personnel. American presence and responsibility were growing; soon it would escalate rapidly as a decision was evolving to accept a face-off between communism and democracy in this far-off divided land. The key step was the Tonkin Gulf Resolution, passed by Congress on 7 August 1964 by virtually unanimous votes.

The occasion was an attack three days earlier by North Vietnamese torpedo boats on American destroyers patroling international waters in the Gulf of Tonkin. Ordering retaliatory air strikes against the torpedo boat bases (64 sorties were launched from American aircraft carriers), Johnson asked Congress for authority to 'take all necessary steps, including the use of armed forces' to prevent further North Vietnamese aggression. The resulting resolution opened the door to further escalation of American support to the government of South Vietnam. By July 1965 the President had committed 100,000 combat troops; by the end of 1965 the number had climbed to 250,000; by 1968 the total commitment stood at 550,000 men, including 38,000 naval personnel. America was in a full land war in Asia against guerrilla forces from the north. The Army and the Marines took the brunt of the fighting, but the Navy played a major role in the conflict for a full decade.

Above: **USN inshore patrol boat *PCF.38* during Operation Slingshot, Vietnam, February 1969.**
Left: **The *New Jersey* bombards a target near Tuyhoa in March 1969 during her last spell on the gun line in Vietnam in March 1969.**

Naval support for the war effort centered on the planes of Task Force 77, lying 100 miles offshore on 'Yankee Station' in the Gulf of Tonkin. From this point the Navy flyers flew combat support missions for the Army and Marine Corps. The planes also bombed Hanoi industrial plants, as well as tactical military targets along the guerrillas' supply lines including railroads, bridges and truck convoys. To the consternation of the pilots and their commanding officers, the planes were forbidden to hit certain areas designated 'sanctuaries,' including the important port of Haiphong where large supplies of arms and equipment were unloaded from Soviet and satellite vessels. Nor was this crucial harbor ever mined until May 1972, just before the close of the war, even though the operation could have been accom-

Below: ***PCF.43*** **at high speed on an inland river in Vietnam in February 1969.**

plished with ease from the air. Haiphong was 'off limits' to bombing because of White House fears that a Russian vessel might be hit, setting off an incident with the Soviets.

In addition to using air power, the Navy also brought the battleship *New Jersey* into the war zone, utilizing her nine 16-inch guns against shore targets. Minesweepers, patrol boats and Coast Guard cutters were deployed along the extensive coastline to interdict junks and other vessels carrying supplies to the Viet Cong forces. Meanwhile, shallow-draft converted landing craft outfitted with machine-guns, 20- and 40-mm cannon, and 81mm mortars—in a throwback to Civil War tactics—patroled the Mekong Delta and the waters near Saigon to interdict supplies and, working with the US Army, to carry out raids on the enemy forces. Other shallow-draft vessels patroled the rivers of the Mekong Delta on similar missions. America's 'brown-water navy' served with as much distinction as their 'blue-water' comrades in the troublesome war that was Vietnam.

Yet the basic frustrations suffered by the naval—and other service—forces in this 'no win' war were the result not of military decisions, but of civilian decisions imposed upon the military who had to do the fighting. In the 1950s, in addition to the concept of 'flexible response' by which military reaction was matched to the challenge at hand, another doctrine had emerged—that of 'strategic gradualism,' which argued that response should be escalated in stages with pauses between each escalation. Eventually, according to the theory developed by the academicians responsible for the idea, the enemy would realize he could not win without the danger of ever-greater escalation and would come to the conference table. This theory, which in effect denied the principle of the vigorous offensive to compel the enemy to do your will, was not accepted by the military leaders. They saw it as giving the enemy the opportunity to prepare his defenses for the next escalation. And, as Paul B Ryan has argued effectively in his *First Line of Defense*, 'If it potentially lowered the level at which diplomacy would give way to shooting, it also opened the door to a progressive stepping up of the use of force.'

Unfortunately, President Johnson, savoring historical recognition as the founder of the Great Society and therefore desiring to limit the war and its consequent costs, embraced the theory despite the advice of his military leaders. With Robert McNamara at his side to quantify the escalations and tactics used, Johnson moved into civilian control of the war in a manner unprecedented in American history. So closely did Johnson and McNamara control the fighting that the President is reported to have said that the American military 'could not even bomb an outhouse without my approval.' Civilian interference also saw such phenomena as Air Force B-52s used for tactical air support while the Navy's carrier planes carried out strategic bombing of enemy targets. Added to these problems was the fact that Johnson, believing the war must be fought and won in South Vietnam only—despite the fact that Laos and Cambodia were being used as staging areas, and that the obvious source of aggression was inside North Vietnam—prohibiting bombing the two neighboring, supposedly 'neutral,' countries and in 1968 forbade any bombing inside North Vietnam.

Above: **The ammunition ship *Mount Katmai* transfers supplies to the *New Jersey*.**
Right: **Spectacular full broadside from the *New Jersey* against a target in Vietnam.**

Above: **The last act of the Vietnam War. Refugees come aboard the USS *Hancock* during the humiliating evacuation before the fall of Saigon to the Communists in 1975.**

As American casualty lists climbed and the cost of the war reached $30 billion per year by 1968, forceful opposition began to break out at home, and Johnson announced he would not run for re-election. Hubert H Humphrey got the Democratic nomination, but he lost to Richard M Nixon for the Republicans. From this point on, the American commitment in Vietnam was de-escalated as Nixon sought to 'Vietnamize' the war. In 1970 Nixon sent troops into Cambodia and Laos to neutralize the communist sanctuaries there—despite unfavorable reaction at home—and by 1971 he had cut troop and naval strength in Vietnam by half. In 1972 he kept to the troop withdrawal schedule, despite a heavy Communist offensive, by increasing the number of naval planes on 'Yankee Station' and by authorizing the bombing of North Vietnam. This was soon followed by orders to mine the harbor of Haiphong and six other ports and to hit power plants in the Haiphong area. Meanwhile, he also arranged a detente with Russia and China, and in January 1973 announced the end of the war. In 1975 the whole of South Vietnam fell to the Communists, for good or ill, a controversial chapter in American history came to an end.

During the course of this long and frustrating war, the Navy and her sister services distinguished themselves in the most trying circumstances ever encounter-

ed by American military forces at war. Without public support or understanding, and hobbled by well-meaning but ineffective civilian controls, the services were nevertheless blamed for the whole debacle. Yet as Clausewitz had pointed out long before, once a nation decides on war it must set its goals in the conflict and then let the military carry out the war in the most effective way. If a nation is unwilling or unable either to define its goals in warfare or to allow the military to carry out these goals, it should never engage in war. The problem in Vietnam lay not in the military, but in the nation and the government that it was attempting to serve.

Duties Elsewhere—Plus Z-grams

While the Navy was carrying out its assigned duties in Vietnam waters—losing 83 pilots and crewmen killed and at least 200 others missing in action, and suffering the loss of 300 planes and over 1000 damaged—it also continued to carry out its responsibilities elsewhere in the world, although stretched increasingly thin by the Far Eastern conflict. In 1965 President Johnson ordered a Navy amphibious task force to the Dominican Republic to prevent a Castro-type takeover of the provisional government installed there after the murder of the dictator Raphael Trujillo (the ostensible reason was to assure the safety of American lives and property in that troubled land).

In June 1967 the problems of civilian versus military control of vessels were highlighted when an American intelligence-gathering ship, the USS *Liberty*, was bombed and strafed in broad daylight by Israeli planes during the Six-Day War fifteen miles off the coast of Egypt. Israel claimed it was all a case of mistaken identity as her pilots assumed the ship was Egyptian—despite her markings and the fact she was clearly flying the American flag. Thirty-four men died and about 170 were wounded in the incident. American naval vessels had been ordered to stay

100 miles from the coast the day before, but the *Liberty* was under the direct control of the Joint Reconnaissance Center in Washington, not the Navy. The *Liberty* had been sent at least five messages from nonnaval sources to pull back from the coast, but apparently never received any of them and remained hovering in the danger zone. Had the ship been under the command of the Sixth Fleet, it would have been pulled back and the incident and loss of lives would never had occurred. The Navy pointed this out to McNamara, who apparently missed the point completely. Divided command structure had claimed 34 victims.

The same type of incident occurred only seven months later, on 23 January 1968, when another intelligence-gathering ship, the lightly armed USS *Pueblo*, was captured by North Korean vessels off the coast of that nation after a less than all-out defense by its crew. The 83-man crew and all its secret equipment fell to the captors, and the officers and crew spent a year in a North Korean prison before being released. Investigation of the incident revealed that the ship was under a score of federal civilian agencies plus the Navy, and that with no one taking charge of her destination or mission she had sailed into waters too distant for US naval forces to come to her rescue. Divided command structure had claimed its second ship and crew, this amid the turmoil of the Vietnam war already becoming untenable for much the same reasons. When the *Mayaguez* was seized off Cambodia in 1975, the American reaction would be swift and decisive: perhaps something was learned from the *Liberty* and *Pueblo* incidents.

The elevation of Richard M Nixon to the presidency in 1969 brought some lessening of American commitments around the world, but little aid to the Navy greatly

Main picture: **The first Trident submarine, the USS *Ohio*, at speed on the surface.**
Bottom: **Scene inside the missile compartment of the *Ohio*. Each missile carries up to eight independently targetable warheads.**

RHODE ISLAND
SSBN
DYNAMICS
BOAT DIVISION

Launch of the *Los Angeles* class nuclear-powered attack submarine USS *Portsmouth*. The *Los Angeles* class is the latest type of attack submarine to be built for the US Navy and production is continuing. In the background the partially-complete Trident submarine *Rhode Island*.

Above: **The nuclear-powered *Truxtun* was initially described as a frigate but was redesignated as a cruiser (CGN) in 1975.**

weakened by the protracted Vietnam conflict. The Navy was critically short on replacement vessels and necessary hardware. On the one hand, the new administration announced the Nixon Doctrine in July 1969: henceforth the US would keep its treaty commitments by providing a nuclear shield from all-out aggression and supplying aid to its allies, but it would not bear the burden of fighting for any nation in a limited war. On the other hand, the Navy (now relying on a basic strategy of nuclear submarines and an all-purpose defense fleet as part of the Nixon Doctrine) would have to carry out its missions with a smaller force. The impact of this new austerity became clear in August 1969, when the Navy was forced to decommission 100 vessels and discharge over 70,000 men.

While undergoing these cutbacks, the Navy was also forced to adjust to the policy moves inaugurated by its newly appointed chief of operations, Admiral Elmo R Zumwalt, Jr. 'Bud' Zumwalt was chosen over the heads of a number of more senior officers; at 49 he was the youngest officer ever to hold that position. The new secretary of defense, Melvin Laird, had met the admiral while Zumwalt was serving as commander of naval forces in Vietnam and had been greatly impressed by the dynamic young officer. Standing with Laird and Zumwalt was Rhode Island politician John H Chaffee, the new Secretary of the Navy, who apparently agreed with the projected policy changes of his new Chief of Naval Operations and gave him free rein to put them into practice, despite objections from senior admirals.

Believing that the Navy should adopt more forward-looking social attitudes in tune with the times, and make naval life more attractive to its men and women by eliminating 'Mickey Mouse' regulations, Zumwalt soon inaugurated a stream of new directives to the service (non-affectionately dubbed 'Z-grams'). Beards were allowed, as were 'non-regulation' haircuts; civilian clothes were permitted on liberty; committees were established aboard ships to discuss human relations problems; and a more relaxed attitude toward traditional discipline became manifest. In line with affirmative action and equal opportunity standards in the civilian community, efforts were made to bring more minority and underprivileged youths into the service (the Navy, like the other services, had become racially integrated after World War II). When this goal was not met quickly, enlistment standards were lowered, thus bringing into uniform many young men who had less than adequate backgrounds for an increasingly technological Navy. When these minorities could not qualify for technical training specialities and were shunted into low-skill jobs, they interpreted it as demeaning, racially inspired and a breach of promises made to them.

Matters came to an unfortunate head in 1972, when four racially inspired riots took place aboard naval vessels, and there was widespread evidence of additional disobedience, riot and even mutiny in the fleet. Once the glare of publicity surrounding the incidents had subsided, and the consequent Congressional investigation had concluded, the new secretary of the navy, John Warner (who had replaced Chafee earlier in the year), along with Zumwalt, reimposed higher enlistment standards and purged the Navy of its marginal performers, who were at the heart of the problem, through early discharge. But many senior admirals felt that substantial damage had been done by utilizing the Navy as a laboratory-cum-showplace for 'enlightened social policies' and that the service would suffer the effects of Zumwalt's policies for years. Few doubted the wisdom of Zumwalt's instituting longer homeporting and similar measures, but many questioned whether the flood of Z-grams pushing for too much too fast had ultimately served the Navy well at a crucial time in its existence.

Despite these internal adjustments, the Navy continued to do its duty, sometimes under rather strained conditions with Washington ever coaching from the sidelines. In the fall of 1973 the Arab forces of Syria and Egypt, attempting to regain lands lost to Israel in the Six-Day War of 1967, attacked the Israelis with Soviet-supplied armor and artillery. Fearing that Israel would be conquered, President Nixon ordered an airlift of American equipment to the tiny nation, but found to his consternation that many allies, fearing retaliation by the various Arab oil-producing states if they interfered, refused to help the US aid Israel and denied rights to land and refuel airlift cargo planes on their soil.

At the same time the airlift was assembled, the Sixth Fleet was sent into the eastern Mediterranean, but White House directives (probably issued by Secretary of State Henry Kissinger, as the Nixon Administration was reeling from the effects of Vice-President Spiro Agnew's resignation under fire) severely limited the fleet commander's maneuvers. When the chairman of the Joints Chiefs requested permission to move the fleet closer to the war zone so as to evacuate Americans in the embattled area if necessary, he was

Right: **The ammunition ship *Kaleakala* under way off the coast of Oahu.**
Below: **The nuclear cruisers *Arkansas* (nearest), *Mississippi* and *Texas* during exercises in the Caribbean in 1981.**

E25
2
4

40

65

Above: **The deck of the *Enterprise* is crowded with some of the carrier's 80-plus aircraft as she heads for San Diego in 1983.**
Above right: **Radar operator in the Combat Information Center on the *Enterprise*.**
Left: **The hydrofoil submarine-chaser *High Point* fires a Harpoon missile.**

persistently refused by the White House. Only when it appeared that the Soviet Union might send troops to Suez to extricate Egyptian army units from encirclement was the Sixth Fleet hurriedly augmented by a carrier task-force group and a destroyer task-force group—a belated attempt to increase American naval strength in the troubled area to equal the recently reinforced Russian fleet. When the conflict ended a month later in a shaky truce and the fleets dispersed, it was obvious that while the Sixth Fleet had demonstrated the Navy's ability to carry out a flexible response by a force in place without firing a shot, it was also clear that the Russians had successfully challenged American dominance in the Mediterrnean. Stability had been reintroduced into the volatile area thanks to American naval presence, but whether this presence would remain viable in these waters in the face of a continuing Soviet naval buildup was another question. For their part, the Arab nations repaid the United States for its help to Israel by a five-month oil embargo that graphically illustrated the dependence of the Western nations and Japan on the oil resources of this crucial area of the globe.

The Onset of Détente

In the midst of these controversies of the early 1970s a decided change in American foreign policy was taking place. This new policy, while ostensibly pointing to a less confrontational posture between the United States and Russia, also resulted in far less clarity in American foreign-policy goals. This confusion in goals, in turn, made the tasks of the Navy and also of its sister services even more difficult in the years which lay ahead.

In an effort to ease budget-breaking nuclear rivalry for both countries, the US turned away from its two-decade policy of containment of communist expansion in favor of a policy of détente, or relaxation of tensions between the two powers. This, it was hoped, would lead to more understanding between the two nations and a relaxation of the mutual distrust that stood in the way of world peace and security. In 1972 President Nixon journeyed to Moscow, where he signed the first Strategic Arms Limitation Treaty (SALT I) as an initial step toward curbing nuclear rivalry.

Yet the concept of détente in no way hindered the Soviets from aiding and sponsoring revolutionary regimes in Africa and the Middle East. Actually, the Soviet Navy continued to display an ever-widening presence in those areas and on the sea lanes of the world. Meanwhile, the US Navy was expected to continue its worldwide vigilance with more sophisticated weaponry on budgets deliberately restrained, not only for domestic priorities but to illustrate America's good intentions. It was an anomalous situation in which the Navy and the nation found itself: the era of détente was to introduce relaxed tensions and increased good will at the same time the Soviets were taking measures to increase tension in key areas of the world and thus destroy good will.

In August 1974 Richard Nixon resigned the presidency, turning over the office to

Below: **The guided-missile frigates *Jack Williams* (nearest), *Antrim* and *Oliver Hazard Perry* with the Atlantic Fleet in 1982.**

Above: **The USS *Leahy*, name ship of a class of nine cruisers, built in the early 1960s and still in service.**

Gerald R Ford, the popular House Minority Leader selected as Vice-President the year before on Spiro Agnew's resignation.

President Ford—and the entire nation—underwent the anguish of seeing thousands of refugees from South Vietnam flee their homeland (along with the US embassy staff) as Saigon and the entire country of South Vietnam fell to the North Vietnamese Communist forces in March 1975. Americans noted with pride that the Seventh Fleet rescued hundreds of these refugees from death or imprisonment in the wake of the communist takeover, but the riveting scenes of the terror-stricken flight of America's erstwhile allies was a memory that would not go away.

President Ford did, however, win abundant if temporary praise six weeks after the inglorious fall of Vietnam in the *Mayaguez* incident of May 1975. The *Mayaguez* was a US container vessel seized sixty miles off the coast of Cambodia in the Gulf of Siam by Cambodian Communists. Its crew of 39 was interred. The US Government tried to gain the ship's release through China and the United Nations; when this failed, Ford ordered a Marine-Navy combat unit with Air Force helicopter aid to regain the ship and free her crew. When the lost ship was sighted at Tang Island, 34 miles off the mainland, a Marine assault team was carried to the site by a destroyer escort. They boarded the ship, only to find it abandoned. Meanwhile, planes from the *Coral Sea* blasted Cambodian positions ashore and sank three gunboats. A Marine assault team was landed at Tang Island at the same time. Finding none of the crew, but soon engaged in a brisk exchange of fire with the Cambodians, the Marines were helicoptered out under naval protective fire. The crew, meanwhile, had been picked up from a fishing boat off Tang Island, so the *Mayaguez* incident ended as an American victory of sorts, although 41 American servicemen died in the episode.

The Carter Years

Despite this show of determination and force, and despite his obvious attempts to give the nation a sense of direction and healing, Ford lost the presidency to Governor James E Carter of Georgia in 1976. For the Navy, having an Annapolis graduate at the helm of the ship of state gave reason for optimism that the needs of the service might at last be met, or at least understood. But it was not to be, and the Navy found the years from 1976 to 1979 as confused and confusing as any it had lived through since 1960.

As a candidate, Carter had pledged to cut the defense budget by $5 billion. When he became president, he slashed Ford's shipbuilding program from 157 to 67 ships. Considering that the defense budget had been steadily declining—from $115.7 billion in 1970 to $104.4 billion in 1972, to $100.8 billion in 1974—and raised only to $104.7 billion in 1976, it was obvious that the recent modest gains made by the services were about to be reversed. At the same time the nondefense budget had grown from about $80 billion in 1950 to over $150 billion in 1960, then to about $250 billion in 1970, and finally to almost $350 billion in 1975. By 1980 the defense budget would stand at about $145 billion, while the nondefense budget had skyrocketed to over $400 billion. In 1960 defense represented 49 percent of the federal budget; by 1980 it had fallen to only 23 percent. Yet it was the defense budget that received almost all the blame for the tremendous budget deficits and accompanying inflationary pressures. During these same years, it is interesting to note, the Navy's share of the Department of Defense budget remained at almost the same figure and in constant dollars actually declined slightly.

What made the situation more perilous for the Navy—and the nation—was the fact that the Soviet Union had awakened to its need for sea power and was building its navy with mounting vigor. By 1973 Soviet expenses for defense purposes actually exceeded those of the United States; by 1980 its defense budget stood at

Left: **The carrier *Constellation* and the support ship *Niagara Falls*.**
Below: **The experimental amphibious assault landing craft JEFF-B. Hovercraft have, as yet, seen little service with the military.**

the equivalent of 175 billion American dollars. While President Carter and his party colleagues in Congress were canceling nuclear carrier construction in 1978, delaying cruise missile construction, closing down the B-1 bomber program and agreeing to restrict the range of cruise missiles in the SALT II talks, the Soviet Union continued to build its military forces to and beyond American levels in almost all areas.

At the end of World War II the Soviet Navy was a weak coastal-defense force, which it remained until the 1960s. However, during this period of naval quiescence, Nikita Krushchev in 1953 appointed as commander-in-chief of the Soviet Navy Admiral Sergei G Gorshkov, who would hold this position into the 1980s. For the next ten years this 'Mahan of the Russian Navy' argued that a naval buildup was indispensable if the Soviet Union was to defend itself and project its power around the globe. Concrete results had been attained by 1961, when the Soviets had commissioned their first nuclear submarine and installed air-to-surface missiles on their long-range patrol bombers to guard their shores.

While this essentially defensive power was satisfactory, the importance of a credible offensive and sub-surface fleet, and the consequences of their lack, were dramatically illustrated in the Suez crisis of 1956 and the Cuban missile crisis of 1961. The Russian embarrassment in the Middle East and her backdown in Cuba were due to American preponderance in surface vessels. Not only could the US Navy surface fleet interdict vessels, it was covered by mighty air power supplied by the carriers. As Gorshkov explained in *The Sea Power of the State* some years later, Russia had effective nuclear-missile submarines but needed attack submarines, powerful missile-carrying surface ships, carriers and long-range missile-bearing planes to protect the missile subs against ASW agents of any type. The targets of the better-protected Soviet nuclear-missile submarines would be land targets or bases, destruction of which would deny enemy ships and planes their logistical bases and thereby render them helpless. (By 1978 the Soviet Navy would have 58 nuclear-missile submarines, up from 0 in 1960; the United States, in contrast, would have only 41 in 1978, up from two. By 1979 the Soviets had 142 nuclear-powered subs; the United States had 109, 23 percent fewer).

At the same time he was obtaining his new vessels, Gorshkov also obtained long-range ballistic missiles for his submarines. With a 4200-mile range by the mid '70s his boats could lurk in home waters like the Barents Sea without ever having to expose themselves to detection or destruction on the sea lanes of the world. With such weapons as ballistic-missile submarines protected by surface fleet vessels and attack submarines (which could fire long-range missiles at enemy fleets or battle groups), and Backfire long-range reconnaissance bombers equipped with air-to-surface missiles, Gorshkov by the late 1970s had a major striking force capable of victory in an all-out nuclear confrontation, a force also capable of lesser responses according to the circumstances. The Soviet Navy had come a long way since the humiliations of the late 1950s and early 1960s.

While the Soviet fleet was growing in

Above: Loading a Phalanx multibarrel antiaircraft gun.

Right: The ammunition ship *Mount Baker* and the *Nimitz*. US carriers cannot accommodate all their aircraft in the hangar, some must be kept parked on deck.

Below: A torpedo-armed SH-60B SeaHawk antisubmarine helicopter, the latest US Navy shipboard ASW helicopter.

size and capability, the US Navy was shrinking from over 900 ships in 1970 to approximately 460 ships in 1978. American tonnage in carriers slipped from 2 million in 1964 to 1.4 million in 1978; surface vessels took the greatest drop, from 2.3 million tons to 1 million tons, in those same years. Submarines slipped slightly in tonnage, as did amphibious vessels. From a total tonnage of 6 million in 1964, the Navy could claim only 3.9 million tons in 1978. The Soviet Union had climbed from 1.7 million to 2.3 million tons, leaving the American fleet only 41 percent larger than the Soviet fleet (down from 72 percent larger in 1964). But when America's tonnage preponderance in aircraft car-

Right: **A Sea King antisubmarine helicopter lowers its dipping sonar during an antisubmarine-warfare exercise in 1982.**

Above: **The attack submarine *Phoenix* is launched from General Dynamics yard at Groton, CT, in 1980. Three Trident submarines can also be seen under construction.**

riers (1.4 million tons) was subtracted, the Soviet fleet was almost the same size as the American. And it must be noted that the Soviet fleet far outstripped the American in all types of submarines. By 1978, it seemed clear, the United States no longer had a two-ocean navy; with luck, it had a one-and-a-half-ocean navy, and no one could predict the outcome in case of a Soviet-American clash.

Part of the Navy's difficulty in the 1970s lay, however, within itself. During this trying decade it was constantly accused of waste in ship and weaponry procurement, of 'going first class' at the taxpayers' expense. Cost overruns and expensive delays in delivery were charges frequently leveled against the Navy, whose blame of civilian contractors as the culprits impressed few. The shipbuilders and contractors, in turn, blamed the higher costs on the Navy for changing specifications over and over again during construction. Wherever the truth lay in these charges and countercharges, the Navy suffered severely through bad publicity.

Nor was the Navy helped by criticism that it was a divided service, with the aviation admirals dominating their surface and submarine counterparts and clinging to the carrier task force strategy, come what may. Disunity also seemed the order of the day, as the public witnessed disagreements between certain admirals and Admiral Hyman Rickover, who even at the age of eighty could not be retired because of Congressional support. Rickover's charges in the media spotlight inclined the public to believe that high-ranking admirals were not being honest; he excoriated waste and inefficiency in every area of naval procurement and implied that the admirals were covering up. Such suspicions were made more plausible by the charge that senior military officers retired to well-paying jobs with defense contractors and thereby created a secret network of collusion, widely believed to exist since President Eisenhower's 1950s charges of a military-industrial complex. Eisenhower was actually referring to problems generated by increasing investment of the national economy in defense production, thereby endangering the national economy, but the existence of a 'conspiracy' had been an article of faith for antimilitary opinion-makers for two decades.

Part of the problem lay, too, in the fact that most Americans simply did not understand the role of the Navy—and its sister services—in the post-World War II situation. The nation had been on a warlike standing—with its attendant budgets—almost continuously since 1941. The Navy

could make a case for more ships, men and weaponry to protect the sea lanes, project American force where necessary and aid allies throughout the world, but who was listening? The Navy might well work out plausible scenarios as to what could happen in any of a dozen hotspots at any time when it would be called upon to respond quickly and powerfully, but such reasoning was beyond the concerns of most Americans (and not a few Congressmen and media representatives). The deterrent potential of a Trident submarine that could carry 24 ballistic missiles and operate anywhere in the oceans seemed less compelling than the fact that the 560-foot boat carried a price tag of $1 billion. Continued faith in the spirit and wisdom of détente, and negative fallout from the debacle of Vietnam, combined to propel the Navy into the last years of the 1970s on a wave of criticism, with nothing but flak bursts on the horizon. Then, almost overnight, the nation awakened to a fundamental reassessment.

Above: **The *Kitty Hawk* class carrier *John F Kennedy* with F-14, A-6 and A-7 aircraft among those on deck.**

By 1979 world events had begun to show the American people that neglect of their Navy had made them very vulnerable. The United States, they began to realize, was forced to import over three million barrels of oil from the Middle East each day, one-third of which had to pass through the Hormuz Strait from the Persian Gulf to the Arabian Sea. Furthermore, the Soviets seemed to be moving into the area, while American naval defense forces in the Indian Ocean were minimal at best. In response, the Navy offered to form a Fifth Fleet in the Indian Ocean, since this vital body of water could not be protected by the Seventh Fleet stationed in the Far East. This vulnerability in the Middle East

Below: **The *Pegasus* class hydrofoil *Taurus* on trial at Elliot Bay, Washington. She is armed with Harpoon missiles.**

and Persian Gulf became a major concern in 1978–79, when Iran fell into revolution and under the control of the fanatical religious leader the Ayatollah Khomeini. In November 1979 Americans watched newsreel coverage of the storming of the US embassy and the capture of 66 fellow citizens. That same month a mob burned the US embassy at Islamabad, Pakistan. This was followed the next month by a Soviet invasion of Afghanistan. In every case the US was in no position to retaliate effectively.

The invasion of Afghanistan was an attempt to stem a nationalist revolt against a docile communist regime in the capital of Kabul: the Russians were taking no chances on losing this subject state, but the invasion, with the other events breaking upon American complacency, had effects felt throughout the nation. President Carter, sincere in his humanitarian idealism, now recognized that human rights can never be protected without means of punishing or discouraging the aggressor. By 1980 the dovelike Congress, which had for years turned a deaf ear to the Navy's warnings about the consequence of weakness, was becoming more hawkish in mood. Requests for nuclear aircraft carriers, long-range attack planes, antisubmarine warfare systems for planes, submarines and surface ships, and better pay and benefits for naval officers and crews for greater retention rates in technical specialities, now received a favorable hearing. The military budget began to rise to meet the Services' needs. All this was carried out against the background of Carter's State of the Union message of January 1980, in which he announced the 'Carter Doctrine'. henceforth the Persian Gulf region was considered germane to the vital interests of the United States, and any attempt by any power to gain control of it by force would be repelled. Although the President asked America's allies to share the burden of defending the Persian Gulf region, it was clear that the US Navy would be the chosen instrument for implementing that doctrine in the volatile Middle East: it would have to be strengthened to do the job.

Above: The guided missile destroyer USS *Cochrane* (*Charles Adams* class).
Left: Stern view of the *Leahy* showing her after missile launcher and two radar trackers.

The altered mood in Congress and in the White House reflected a new commitment and the realization that, despite the spirit of détente and American efforts to influence Soviet action by restraint of its warmaking capabilities, Soviet ambitions had not changed. Whether this new attitude of firmness on the part of the American public with its concomitant support of the military—including especially the Navy with its mammoth job of protecting American interests around the globe through capacity for instant readiness and reaction—would continue through the 1980s and beyond could not be gauged, but clearly a change of heart and mind appeared to be taking place. The 'new cold war' was on. The election to the presidency of Ronald Reagan over Jimmy Carter in November 1980 seemed to confirm a reversal of opinion.

The Present and Future of the Navy

In 1978 the Navy had released an assessment of its needs for the foreseeable future. Entitled 'Sea Plan 2000,' the plan spelled out the Navy's tasks in the years ahead: to maintain stability by forward deployment

Above: **The battleship *New Jersey* and the frigate *Meyer Kord* shortly after the *New Jersey* recommissioned in 1983.**

of carrier battle groups in the Atlantic and Pacific, Northeast and Southeast Asia, the Mediterranean and the Indian Ocean; to contain crises by US superiority at sea by either the use of force or a show of force; and to deter major war by supporting allies on the flanks of the Soviet Union and by maintaining the ability to threaten Soviet forces. These would be accomplished by more and better ships coupled with technological improvements in antimissile and antisubmarine-warfare defense systems. The Navy proposed three options to the nation. Option 1 called for a 1 percent per year real naval growth rate to 439 ships by the year 2000 (a minimal level); Option 2 called for a 3 percent per year growth rate to 535 ships (a moderate level); and Option 3 proposed a 4 percent per year growth rate to 585 ships (the optimum defense level). Sea Plan 2000, calling for a balanced fleet of conventional and atomic weaponry, argued essentially that national defense capabilities had to square with national goals, and that choosing the first option would mean a pullback in US commitments; the second option meant that the US could probably match the Soviets in naval strength; the third option was the best guarantee of the protection of American interests.

While Sea Plan 2000 represented alternatives in a measured, nonalarmist manner and undoubtedly impressed many members of Congress, talk of a SALT II agreement and public apathy precluded any widespread appreciation of the Navy's argument—until the events of 1979 brought about a new consciousness of the effects of allowing America's military and naval strength to erode.

Thus the early years of Ronald Reagan's presidency saw the beginning of an American naval renaissance. The President himself set the tone when he said, 'Freedom to use the seas is our nation's lifeblood. For that reason, our Navy is designed to keep the sea lanes open worldwide . . . [and] we must be able in time of emergency to venture into harm's way and to win.' Reagan's support of a reborn and powerful navy of 600 warships —'a 600-ship Navy' became a popular rallying cry for enthusiasts—was not without an ironic twist, since the President had no naval background. His predecessors from 1961 to 1981—five presidents—were all ex-naval officers—including an Annapolis graduate—and none of them gave comparable support to their former service branch and its unique and critical missions.

Reagan's arguments for a larger and more effective navy as crucial to the national interest were bolstered by the effectiveness of Great Britain's 1982 defense of her claims to the Falkland Islands against counterclaims and occupation by Argentine military forces. Although Britain lost six ships to Argentine jets and missiles (which revealed her reliance on short-range aircraft and lack of long-range surveillance forces to protect her main

Below: **The nuclear-powered guided-missile cruiser *Arkansas*.**

727
NAVY
0007
501

Two of the US Navy's most important current aircraft.
Main picture: An F/A-18 Hornet in flight over Lake Tahoe. The F/A-18 is scheduled to replace both the A-7 and the F-4 in US Navy carrier air groups.
Top left: An E-2C Hawkeye of Carrier Airborne Early Warning Squadron 122 in flight. Each carrier normally embarks some four of these aircraft.

fleet components), the islands were reclaimed in a spectacular demonstration of the mobile, multipurpose forces that only a navy could supply and especially of how submarine power could neutralize a surface fleet. The lesson was not lost on knowledgeable observers.

In September 1982 1200 US Marines were sent into Lebanon as part of a multinational peacekeeping force, as that harried Middle Eastern nation saw renewed conflict between internal and external forces trying to claim it for their own ends. When the Marine contingent came under fire from the militia factions commanding the hills beyond Beirut International Airport in 1983, it was the big guns from the recommissioned battleship *New Jersey* that gave them relief, even as a sizable US fleet stood offshore to reinforce and protect them. The naval forces remained on station after the Marines were withdrawn from Beirut early in 1984.

With greater public and political backing evident, the Navy moved into the mid-1980s with a revitalized building program including two additional 91,000-ton *Nimitz*-class nuclear carriers capable of simultaneous air action against air, land, surface and subsurface enemies; the potential of 15 battle groups built around 15 deployable carriers; almost 100 fast attack submarines in service or building of the *Los Angeles*-class nuclear-powered variety (to be used against either enemy submarines or surface vessels); a fleet of over 39 operational ballistic-missile submarines, including the new *Trident* boats

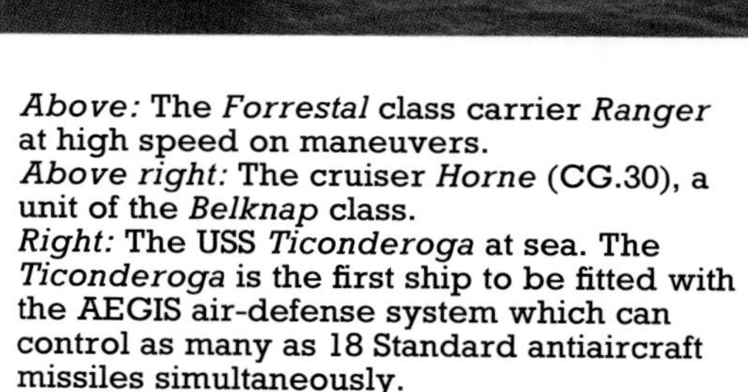

Above: **The *Forrestal* class carrier *Ranger* at high speed on maneuvers.**
Above right: **The cruiser *Horne* (CG.30), a unit of the *Belknap* class.**
Right: **The USS *Ticonderoga* at sea. The *Ticonderoga* is the first ship to be fitted with the AEGIS air-defense system which can control as many as 18 Standard antiaircraft missiles simultaneously.**

with Trident I and II missiles, armed also with deadly Mark 48 torpedoes for self-defense; and one reactivated and rearmed battleship in commission (the *New Jersey*), another on its way (the *Iowa*), and two more scheduled for recommissioning in 1984 and 1985. In addition, *Spruance*- and *Kidd*-class destroyers, *Perry*-class frigates, and Aegis cruisers were joining the fleet, which by 1983 had 490 ships and 76 under construction.

These new and modernized vessels were armed with highly effective A-6E Intruder and A-7E Corsair attack bombers; F-14 Tomcat fighters armed with Phoenix missiles effective at ranges of up to 100 miles; and new F/A-18 Hornet fighter and attack aircraft, Harpoon air- or surface-to-surface missiles, Tomahawk tactical antiship and land attack missiles, acoustic-homing ASW torpedoes, attack and ASW shipborne helicopters like the SH-3 Sea King, and the latest and most effective computerized radar guidance systems available for these weapons. Furthermore, the Aegis cruiser/SM2 weapons system which joined the fleet with the commissioning of the *Ticonderoga* in 1983 offered superb defensive capabilities

47

Right: An S-3A Viking makes the 200,000th carrier landing for the type, aboard the USS *Kitty Hawk*.
Second right: An A-7E Corsair light attack aircraft in flight over the carrier *America*. The A-7 can carry up to eight tons of ordnance.
Main picture: An A-6E medium attack aircraft. Each carrier normally embarks a single squadron of this type which has proved so successful that it is still in production 20 years after it entered service with the USN.

10
VA-82 MARAUDERS
NAVY
AMERICA

02
AG
158533
NAVY
VA 65

Right: The *Spruance* class destroyer *Elliot* at sea in 1978. By early 1984 there were 31 *Spruance* class ships in service with the Navy.
Main picture: An F-14A Tomcat of VF.2 in flight. Each carrier normally operates 24 Tomcats in the fighter role with an additional small detachment assigned to reconnaissance.
Bottom: Two Tomcats ready for launch on the forward catapults of the nuclear carrier *Nimitz*.

to fleets against co-ordinated high-density air attacks and Soviet antiship cruise missiles, thus protecting the heart of any carrier battle group. By 1988 almost 1900 new and effective aircraft would be added to the fleet, looking to 14 fully equipped and modernized carrier wings by that time. And all these ships and weapons were being acquired under a new direct-contract approach that forced contractors to assume more of the burden for cost overruns, thus eliminating many of the publicity problems so burdensome in the troubled two decades before.

Backed by a rediscovered national sense of direction and commitment, and by a political system responding to that force, the Navy was in full renaissance by the mid-1980s. In the words of Admiral Thomas B Haywood, Chief of Naval Operations: 'We are a Navy on the move, with a full head of steam. We are a Navy with confidence. We are a Navy determined to be the finest professional force at sea, today and in the future.' The US Navy would, as always, do its duty.

NEW CHALLENGES, NEW RESPONSES

The first four years of the Reagan administration were years of resurgence for the Navy, not only in its budget, ships and hardware but also in its sense of self-confidence. The popular president was clearly aware of the importance of a strong naval force in a still-dangerous world, and in his secretary of the navy, John Lehman, he had an articulate and persuasive advocate for naval power to the Congress. Building a '600-ship navy' seemed a realizable and popular goal. But Ronald Reagan's second term in office saw the Navy's fond dreams disappointed. Thanks both to domestic and foreign events, the buildup of the Navy that had marked Reagan's first term in office was replaced by a contraction in his second, even though the Navy's obligations had in no way diminished and may even have grown.

1985: Year of Change

The year 1985 was pivotal for the Navy and America's other three armed forces. In that year Mikhail Gorbachev came to power in the Soviet Union and began his historic drive for fundamental change in his nation through both *perestroika* (restructuring of the Soviet system) and *glasnost* (openness to public debate). Doubtless the new Soviet president was in part moved by necessity, for his nation's economy was in shambles after 70 years of inefficient centralized control. But whatever Gorbachev's motives may have been, and however he imagined the course that domestic reform might take, he soon found that the desire for wholesale reform was so strong among the people of the various republics making up the USSR, to say nothing of the satellite states, that control of events both within and without became increasingly difficult. Within six years secessionist movements had broken out in the Baltic states; the Russian Republic and other constituent Soviet states were demanding more autonomy; the eastern European satellite nations were declaring their independence of Soviet overlordship; the hated Berlin Wall had been torn down and Germany had been reunited; and the Warsaw Pact, the core of the Soviet land defense system, had been formally dissolved.

Now the nations that had worked so diligently to contain Soviet expansionism for 45 years had to decide how to react to these events. How were they to adapt their national

The World-War-II battleship USS *Missouri* was recommissioned in May 1986. She was armed with Tomahawk and Harpoon missiles.

Top left: Soviet leader Mikhail Gorbachev. who came into power in 1985.
Above and left: Among the most powerfully symbolic gestures made by Gorbachev in his effort to end the Cold War was the tearing down of the hated Berlin Wall, an action that was greeted ecstatically by Berliners when it was begun in November 1989.

defense postures to the new Soviet reality – whatever it might prove to be? America's strategists, including the Navy's, were forced to rethink their assumptions after 1985. Events worldwide, however, suggest that the need for a global strategy remained.

That same year also saw the beginning of a fundamental restructuring of all the US military services in an effort to eliminate once and for all the lack of inter-service coordination that had so often plagued American military operations in the past. Criticism of America's command structure had been considerable during the Vietnam war, and it became a focus of renewed attention after the debacle of the Iranian hostage rescue attempt in 1980. The clamor intensified two years later when the abortive and tragic intervention in Lebanon ended in the bombing deaths of 241 Marines, and it rose to a crescendo with the American invasion of Grenada in 1983, a small-scale operation that revealed, despite all the talk about cooperation and coordination between the services in combined operations, that the reality was far different.

Operation URGENT FURY, the invasion of Grenada to free the tiny Caribbean island from left-wing radicals, to put an end to Soviet and Cuban influence and presence there and to assure the safety of some 600 American students and tourists, began on 25 October 1983 and ended three days later. The invasion was planned as primarily an Army and Marine Corps operation, backed by tactical air cover from the *Independence*

carrier group and by naval gunnery and logistical support. But in the event, inter-service coordination proved lamentable. No service commander present had overall tactical authority, and lack of integrated radio communications precluded the ground forces from being able to call in naval gunfire. The publicity given the obvious foul-ups on Grenada gave the final push to reorganizing the American military.

In 1985 the Packard Commission (chaired by David Packard, former deputy secretary of defense) was created to assess the organization of the Department of Defense. Its conclusions matched those of the Senate Armed Services Committee: DOD had to be reorganized, and unified multi-service commands had to be created. When, that same year, Senators Barry Goldwater (R-AZ) and Sam Nunn (D-GA), the leaders of the Senate Armed Services Committee, threw their support behind a DOD staff report authorizing DOD reorganization, the die was cast. Eight unified commands (the European, Pacific, Atlantic, Southern, Central, Space, Special Operations and Transportation Commands) and two specified commands (the Strategic Air Command and Forces Command) were subsequently created or completed. Henceforth, unified commanders would control all service activities in their areas of operation, a reform that bore fruit dramatically in the Gulf War when General H Norman Schwarzkopf of Central Command directed the warmaking activities of all the services in the five-month conflict with Iraq.

A follow-on reorganizational change that affected all the services and their strategic and tactical roles was made the next year when Congress passed the Goldwater-Nichols Defense Reorganization Act of 1986. This legislation gave the chairman of the Joint Chiefs of Staff the final decision-making power over all the US military and made him the president's principal military advisor. Henceforth, decisions at the JCS level would be made by one man, not by committee consensus. Furthermore, the Joint Staff was now to work for the chairman alone, not for the JCS as a body. (Service on the Joint Staff was also made a prerequisite for flag rank in all the services.) At the same time, the commanders of the unified and specified commands were given complete authority over all operations, training and logistics within their commands, the individual service commanders thus losing their operational authority. These reforms signaled that henceforth interservice and intraservice cooperation and coordination would be the rule, not the exception.

Nineteen eighty-five may have introduced changes that would ultimately benefit the Navy, but at the time, the year seemed to offer the service scant good news. Certainly the Walker spy case was not good news.

The leader in the Walker espionage ring was John A Walker, Jr, a naval warrant officer and cryptologist with top secret clearance, who began spying for the Soviet Union in the mid-1960s. He was aided by Jerry A Whitworth, a radioman and satellite communications expert who had retired from the Navy in 1983. Also implicated were Arthur J Walker, John's brother and a retired lieutenant com-

Above: A big US Air Force C-141 Starlifter removes evacuees from Grenada in 1983 (in the foreground, an Army CH-47 helicopter). The Grenada operation underscored the need for better interservice coordination.

Below: Navyman John A Walker, Jr (left) is taken to his trial for espionage in 1985.

mander, and Michael L Walker, John's son, who stole secret documents from the Oceana Naval Air Station in Virginia and from the carrier *Nimitz*.

Tried for espionage in Norfolk, the four received long prison sentences in November 1985, but naval and intelligence officials are still trying to assess the damage inflicted on the Navy's code systems and underwater warfare capabilities by the Walker spy ring. Critics pointed out that the Navy's internal anti-espionage safeguards had obviously broken down in this case and wondered how national security might be further compromised when some 900,000 naval personnel had access to classified materials, 139,000 of them to top secret documents. The shadow of the Walker case hung over the Navy long after prison doors had swung shut on the foursome involved.

The other bad news in 1985 involved naval appropriations. The Balanced Budget and Emergency Control Act of 1985, the Gramm-Rudman-Hollings Act (or 'Gramm-Rudman'), arose from wildly escalating federal budget deficits during President Reagan's first term in office. Urged by David A Stockman, his budget director, to spur economic growth and take the nation out of increasing deficits by cutting taxes that stifled incentive while also cutting federal spending, Reagan embraced the first economic principle without attending sufficiently to the second. Reagan, to be sure, received enthusiastic assistance in keeping federal expenses high from the Democratically-controlled Congress, which not only increased defense spending at an average rate of 8.9 percent per year for four years but increased non-defense spending at a much higher rate. Thus, even though tax revenues went up as the result of economic expansion, the federal debt continued to grow alarmingly. Clearly, something had to give.

The result was Gramm-Rudman, which aimed to reduce the annual federal deficits from $171.9 billion to 0 in four years. According to the law, if the federal budgets did not hit their descending target amounts each year, automatic cuts in spending would have to take place.

Two things, however, doomed Gramm-Rudman's laudable goals. First, the legislation exempted monies for Social Security, veterans' compensation and benefits, interest on the national debt and Medicare from the automatic cut provisions. Since this amounted to about half the budget, the other half would have to take double cuts to meet the legislation's goals. Thus a 10 percent automatic cut would mean in actuality a 20 percent cut for defense or any other non-protected expenditure, surely a draconian and unworkable measure. Second, the Supreme Court the next year 'de-fanged' Gramm-Rudman by invalidating the automatic triggering provision of the law that mandated across-the-board cuts, thereby leaving the Congress free to spend as before.

The Gramm-Rudman-Hollings Act thus turned out to be a law without effect, and the budget deficit continued to climb higher and higher, reaching almost $3 trillion in 1990. The debates engendered by Gramm-Rudman did, however, provide a forum for those Congressmen and special interest groups opposed to spending for defense. They launched a concerted campaign for balancing the budget by reducing spending for the military – even though the savings thus realized would in fact be small and would in any case be spent on domestic projects, *ie*, not used to balance the budget or be applied to the federal debt. In fact, the defense budget, in growing from $161 billion to $300 billion in the decade, rose from only 23 percent of the federal budget to 26.1 percent. Put another way, it represented an increase from 5.2 percent of the nation's GNP to only 5.7 percent, and it meant no increase whatever in constant dollars. But the campaign to decrease military spending continued, with the Navy, like its sister services, forced constantly to retrench, regardless of the cost to national security.

The Libyan Challenge Met

Whatever its problems with reorganization, spies, and budget-cutting, the Navy in the meantime had to continue to carry out its duties on the waterways of the world. These included the Mediterranean Sea and the persistent problem of terrorism encouraged and supported by Muammar Qaddafi, the unstable and dangerous fundamentalist military dictator of Libya.

Ever since he had come to power in a coup in 1969, Qaddafi had displayed an obsession for lessening Western influence in North Africa and the Middle East, for expanding Libya's role in these regions and for destroying Israel. As a result, US relations with Libya began to deteriorate, especially as evidence mounted that Qaddafi was playing a direct role in organized terrorism not only in North Africa and the Middle East but indeed throughout the world. Definite ties were established between Qaddafi and terrorist

Far left: Michael Walker, part of the John Walker spy ring, goes to jail.
Below: Libya's Muammar Qaddafi.

organizations in no less than 36 countries, including Japan, Ireland, Germany, Italy and Nicaragua.

It was he who provided the money, arms and air transportation for the terrorists who carried out a massacre at the 1972 Olympic Games in Munich, and his support for other terrorist activities continued in the years that followed. In 1981 it was discovered that Qaddafi had even sent an assassination team to the United States to kill President Reagan, Secretary of Defense Caspar Weinberger and other top government leaders.

Then, on 7 October 1985, members of the Palestinian Liberation Organization highjacked the Italian cruise ship *Achille Lauro* and murdered an American passenger in cold blood. When the highjackers were caught (the Boeing 737 carrying them from Egypt to Tunisia being forced to land at an Italian naval air station in Sicily by four Navy F-14 Tomcat fighters from the carrier *Saratoga*), apparent ties to Libya were discovered. This was followed two months later by terrorist attacks on airport lobbies in Rome and Vienna in which 18 persons were killed (including five Americans) and more than 100 were wounded. Qaddafi praised the attacks and gave refuge to Abu Nidal, the mastermind behind them.

Ever since 1973 and the Yom Kippur War, Qaddafi had been arguing that the Gulf of Sidra, south of a line between Tripoli on the west and Benghazi on the east, belonged to Libya alone, with no right of international passage through its waters. This claim was in direct contradiction to all international conventions regarding the use of the world's seas, and the United States, having no intention of honoring such a specious assertion, had deliberately ignored Qaddafi's proclaimed 'line of death' by conducting Sixth Fleet exercises in the Gulf of Sidra in order to prove its right of navigation there. This had led to minor incidents over the years, including an unprovoked air-to-air missile attack by two Libyan Su-22 fighters on US Navy F-14's in August 1981, an engagement that saw the Libyan planes expeditiously destroyed by American Sidewinder air-to-air missiles from the Tomcats. Libyan terrorism and harassment of the Sixth Fleet continued even after this incident – until 1986, when President Reagan decided finally to do something about it.

Early that year Reagan ordered all US citizens to leave Libya and told five US oil companies to begin moving out. He also directed the JCS to prepare military contingency plans to be used against that country and sent a second, then a third, carrier task force into the Mediterranean. Unable to force the US to accede to his demands and unable to confront it successfully with his military hardware, Qaddafi moved in other directions.

In late March 1986 he directed his operatives around the world to begin attacks on American citizens and installations. On 3

April, Syrian terrorists exploded a bomb on a TWA flight from Rome to Athens, killing four Americans. Qaddafi congratulated them and promised further escalation of violence against American citizens. He made good on his promise two days later when a discotheque in West Berlin was bombed, leaving two US soldiers and one Turkish civilian dead and another 229 persons wounded, including 78 Americans. Citing 'incontrovertible evidence' of Libyan complicity in the bombing, Reagan ordered the US military to carry out attacks on terrorist targets in Libya. The resulting raids took place on the night of 14 April 1986.

The US Navy was already in the area in force for Operation ELDORADO CANYON, the previous month having conducted a four-day exercise in the Gulf of Sidra with 30 vessels, including the carriers *Coral Sea*, *Saratoga* and *America*. Missile boat attacks had been leveled at the US warships, and at least two of the Libyan craft had been sunk. Land-based missiles had also been fired at the American fleet, and Libyan jets had tried unsuccessfully to penetrate the American air screen. The US naval forces were therefore primed for immediate action when the word came down to take out a number of terrorist sites in Libya.

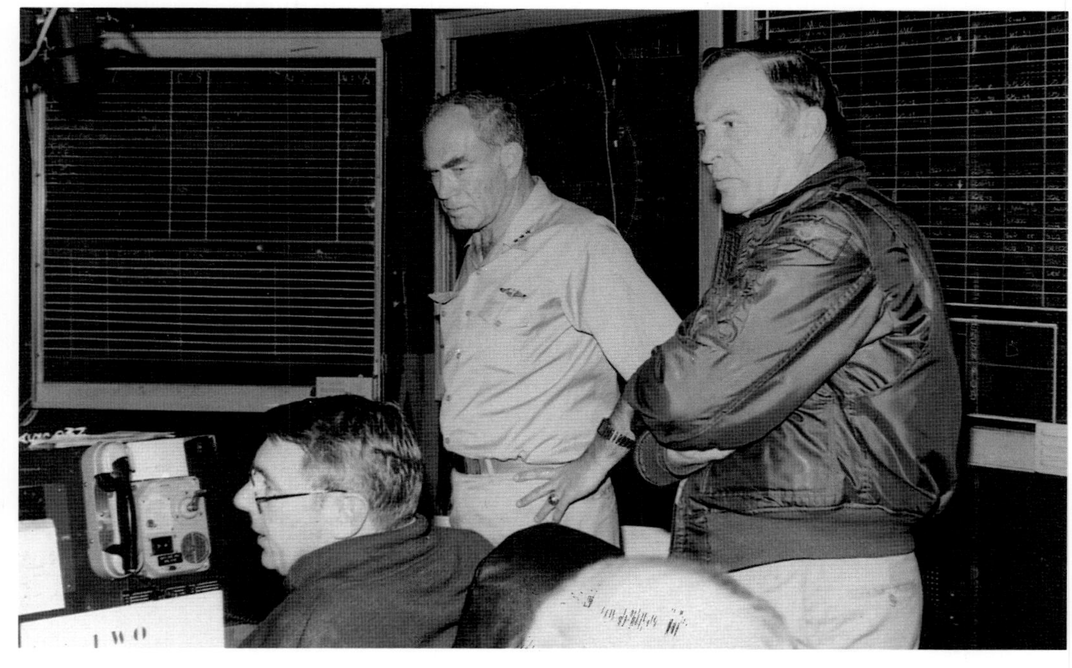

Above: Senior officers on board USS *America* tensely await reports of bombing results during the joint USN-USAF airstrike that was mounted against selected targets in Libya on 14 April 1986.
Opposite:USS *Saratoga* refuels at sea off the Libyan coast in March 1986.

Only those Libyan installations which were clearly terrorist in their activities were targeted: strictly military installations were excluded, and tactical orders made it clear that civilians, as far as possible, were not to be injured in any way. The United States wanted to make it clear to the populace of Libya that Qaddafi's terrorist mechanisms, not the Libyan nation, its army or its people, were the objects of the raids to be made on Tripoli and Benghazi.

Chosen as the instruments for the attacks were Navy and Air Force tactical jets. Tactical aircraft would be able to inflict the most damage on the designated targets with the least amount of collateral damage. Nighttime was chosen for the attacks because the Libyan Air Force pilots had little proficiency at nighttime operations, because civilians would be off the streets of the cities and because Libyan anti-aircraft defenses would be limited to hand-held SAMs that could not be effectively aimed in the dark.

Assigned to carry out the Navy's part in the simultaneous attacks on the five designated targets were versatile A-6E Intruders. The Air Force's variable-sweep 'swing-wing'

The wreckage of Muammar Qaddafi's personal headquarters in Tripoli's Azizyah Barracks after the April 1986 US airstrike.

Libyans inspect the damage wrought on a Benghazi airfield by Navy A-6E Intruders during the April 1986 airstrike.

F-111F attack aircraft, flying out of Great Britain, was the tactical weapon of choice for that service because of its long-range, high-payload, low-level and high on-target precision capabilities. The Air Force was brought in to cooperate with the Navy in carrying out the raids not because the Air Force demanded 'a piece of the action,' as reported by the media, but because the Navy did not have enough tactical aircraft to hit all the necessary targets simultaneously while carrying out its other duties. Its A-7 Corsairs and F/A-18 Hornets would be flying air defense-suppression missions, while its F-14 Tomcats and other F/A-18s would be providing combat air patrol to protect the three-carrier fleet.

In the ensuing five-target, 12-minute, one-pass-over-target raid, six Navy A-6Es from the *America* attacked the Benghazi Military Barracks, an alternaite site for terrorist command and control headquarters, while six more Intruders from the *Coral Sea* hit Benina Airfield outside Benghazi to assure that its MiG fighters would not rise to attack the American forces. On the western side of the Gulf of Sidra at Tripoli three Air Force F-111Fs attacked the Sidi Bilal Terrorist Training Camp, an aquatic commando school outside the city, while three more F-111Fs bombed the Aziziyah Barracks, the command and control center for Qaddafi's worldwide terrorist activities and his headquarters at the time of the attack. Tripoli Military Airfield, home of Qaddafi's terrorist transportation system, was the target of five more F-111Fs. Only one American aircraft was lost in the operation, this an F-111F which disappeared during the flight from England to Libya.

The raids of 14 April 1986 must be scored a success. While Qaddafi escaped with his life from the Aziziyah Barracks, the American air attacks both destroyed important terrorist installations in Libya and, perhaps more important, demonstrated to Qaddafi that he could continue to sponsor overt terrorism only at considerable personal risk. Incidents of terrorism dropped sharply in the aftermath of the combined Navy-Air Force raids on Libya of April 1986.

The lightning air offensive against the Libyan strongman-terrorist also demonstrated that American military forces could work together smoothly and effectively. Cooperation and coordination had been the watchwords of Operation ELDORADO CANYON from initial planning to successful execution. Interservice cooperation may have been imposed officially only in 1985, but the Libyan operation of April 1986 showed that the Navy and the Air Force were already well along the road now mandated for them.

Convoys and Conflict in the Middle East

The Mediterranean was not the only hotspot for the US Navy in the mid-1980s. Simultaneously, it was called to dangerous duty in the Persian Gulf to protect the giant tankers carrying a large portion of the world's oil supply out of the Gulf during the long eight-year war between Iran and Iraq.

The Iran-Iraq War began in September 1980 when Iraqi forces under President Saddam Hussein attacked the neighboring Islamic Republic of Iran, then under the sway of a fanatical Muslim fundamentalist leader, the Ayatollah Khomeini. The Iraqi offensive began with a series of victories, but Iran launched successful counteroffensives, and the conflict settled into a war of attrition. Since 90 percent of Iran's oil exports transited the Persian Gulf (whereas Iraq exported most of its oil through overland pipelines), its Kharg Island loading facility and other ports on the Persian Gulf – plus the ships of nations buying oil from Iran – became prime targets for Iraq's air force. On the other hand, since Iran borders all of the eastern coast of the Gulf, it was in a position to attack vessels trading with Iraq's allies, Saudi Arabia and Kuwait, either by air or by land-based weaponry. Thus all ships trading with either of the belligerents or with Iraq's allies were in danger of being attacked and sunk.

President Reagan, determined that American-flagged vessels should not be successfully attacked while in the international waters of the Persian Gulf and that the critical narrow Strait of Hormuz at the lower end of the Gulf should not be closed, ordered addi-

Below: Khorramshahr, Iran, scene of bitter fighting early in the bloody eight-year war between Iraq and Iran that began in 1980.
Right: A US patrol boat and the frigate USS *Taylor* escort re-flagged Kuwaiti tankers through the dangerous waters of the Persian Gulf during the Iran–Iraq War.

A view of the damage done to the frigate USS *Stark* after she was hit by an Exocet missile launched by an Iraqi Mirage in the Persian Gulf on 17 May 1987. Over 30 naval personnel were killed.

tional American naval vessels into the Persian Gulf. (A small US naval force had regularly sailed the Gulf since 1949 to demonstrate America's interest in the continued flow of oil to the markets of the Free World.) He also moved a carrier battle group near to the Strait in the waters of the North Arabian Sea. By 1985 the Navy's Middle East Force was stationing four frigates and destroyers in the Gulf on a regular basis, rotating these surface vessels in and out on a four-month basis.

By 1987 attacks on ships in the Gulf by both Iran and Iraq had escalated sharply – from five in 1981 to 179 in 1987 – the Iraqis mainly using aircraft and the Iranians mainly using mines, fast attack boats and land-based, Chinese-built, sea-skimming Silkworm missiles with 1100-pound warheads. Kuwait in particular was being hard hit by the tanker war, and President Reagan in May 1987 offered to have Kuwaiti vessels reflagged under the American ensign and stated that the United States Navy would protect these vessels in the Gulf.

By this time the Navy had more than 30 vessels in the Persian Gulf and North Arabian sea: a carrier, a battleship, their escorts, destroyers and frigates for escorting within the Gulf and minesweepers. In addition, a Marine amphibious force and the Navy's special forces Seals were also in the area and ready to move. Nor was the United States alone in sending naval vessels to protect the valuable exports of the Gulf nations: nine British destroyers and minesweepers and six French, six Italian, five Belgian and five Dutch naval vessels were also carrying out convoying and minesweeping duties in the strife-torn area.

That convoy duty during the tanker war could be dangerous was dramatically prove on the night of 17 May 1987 when the guided missile frigate *Stark* (FFG-31), on picket duty in international waters and outside the belligerents' declared war zones, was attacked by an Iraqi F-1 Mirage jet, which fired two Exocet missiles into the vessel, killing 37 men.

Subsequent investigation revealed that the missiles had apparently been fired in error by the Iraqi pilot. But though the *Stark* had been warned of the approach of the Iraqi jet by an AWACS plane, its chaff launchers were never fired, its Phalanx Gatling gun was only in standby mode, its fire control radar was not turned on, its 50 caliber machine guns were not loaded, its incoming missile audible signal had been turned off by its operator and the attacking plane had not been warned off until too late.

The ship was saved by the heroic damage control efforts of the crew, but the '*Stark* incident' demonstrated that the Persian Gulf was too dangerous a place for relaxed procedures. Thenceforth US Navy ships escorting convoys or on picket duty in the Gulf stood on high alert at all times.

Attacks on ships in the Gulf tapered off somewhat after the *Stark* incident, and in February 1988 the battleship *Iowa* and her escorts rotated out of the North Arabian Sea and were not replaced. Leaving the area, too, was the USS *Okinawa*, used as a platform for the Navy's Sea Stallion minesweeping helicopters. With the American presence being cut to 16 command and combat vessels in the Gulf, it appeared that the danger of further incidents might also be lessened.

But on 14 April 1988 the frigate *Samuel B. Roberts* (FFG-58) sailed into a minefield in the central Persian Gulf about 65 miles east of Bahrain. It hit an Iranian-built 385-pound mine which exploded on the port side of the keel. The detonation opened a hole 23 by 30 feet in the hull, destroyed 15 feet of the ship's keel and almost cut the frigate in two. The commanding officer reported that the force of the blast lifted the stern of the 445-foot vessel 10 to 12 feet. Ten sailors were injured in the explosion and resulting fire, but the ship was saved by the damage control efforts of the crew. The heavily damaged frigate was sent home in July aboard the chartered heavy lift ship *Mighty Servant II*.

Meanwhile, convinced that Iran was responsible for the damage to the *Roberts*, the

Captain Glen Brindel of the USS *Stark* was criticized by some after the Iraqi attack for not having readier air defenses.

military command authorities ordered a retaliatory attack on Iran. Operation PRAYING MANTIS was carried out four days later, on 18 April 1988. Nine Navy ships, plus contingents of Marines and Navy Seals, were assembled for the operation by the Joint Task Force Middle East commander. The sailors and Marines were ordered to sink the Iranian frigate *Sabalan* or any suitable substitute and to neutralize three Iranian gas-oil separation platforms being used as surveillance posts.

Two of the oil platforms were taken in textbook fashion, with naval gunfire forcing the Iranians on them to flee or surrender. Marine and Seal teams moved onto the platforms from helicopters to gather intelligence information and then demolish the structures. But on the third platform a stray shot hit a compressed gas tank, causing it to burn and incinerating its gun crew. After the assaults on the platforms, one of the naval groups (three vessels) sank an Iranian patrol boat after it had attacked the group with anti-ship missiles. Another group, with the aid of two A-6 Intruders, attacked and sank an Iranian frigate. One Intruder had left the frigate dead in the water from missile strikes, and then the other hit the frigate with Harpoon anti-ship missiles at the same moment one of the surface destroyers did the same.

Operation PRAYING MANTIS took place at the same time that Iraq was retaking the strategically valuable Fao Peninsula from Iran. It may be assumed that these virtually simultaneous defeats helped to convince the Iranians that they could not win the war and should negotiate a peace agreement with Iraq. This, in any case, is what they did, but before 1988 was over and the war had ended, the greatest tragedy of the Persian Gulf tanker war occurred, the downing of an Iranian airliner by missiles fired by the USS *Vincennes* on 3 July.

Certain facts about the incident are beyond dispute. There is no question that the *Vincennes* (CG-49), a guided missile cruiser of the *Ticonderoga* class fitted with the ultra-sophisticated Aegis antiaircraft weapons system, brought down the Iran Air Airbus, Flight 655, killing all 290 passengers and crew aboard. It is also clear that the airbus was in a commercial flying corridor when it was struck and that it was actually gaining altitude when it was identified and fired upon and was not descending, as interpreted by the inexperienced tactical information coordinator in the *Vincennes*'s combat information center.

In defense of the Navy and the ship's crew, however, other facts must be recalled in order to place the tragedy in its context of taking place in the 'fog of war.' First, the radar units on Aegis-equipped vessels track an airplane's course and speed, not its altitude; this has to be determined by continual monitoring in the vessel's combat information center. Second, the airliner was tagged as a 'target unknown' and was closing on the ship on a

Above: The frigate USS *Samuel B Roberts*, as she appeared in her 1986 sea trials.
Below: Severely damaged by an Iranian mine, the *Samuel B Roberts* is taken home for repairs on the deck of the chartered heavylift ship *Mighty Servant II* in July 1988.

CG-49
HOME OF
AIRAEGIS

constant bearing and on a classic attack path; furthermore, it was flying on the very edge of the commercial corridor (not in the center of the corridor as airliners usually did), and its altitude was lower than normal commercial flights. Third, the *Vincennes* was under attack by two Iranian gunboats at the time of the sighting, giving the impression that a coordinated attack might be underway (the Middle East Force had been alerted to a possible Iranian suicide attack over the 4 July weekend). Fourth, Iranian F-14 fighters had been flying out of Bandar Abbas airfield, from which the airliner had just taken off, in the days preceding 3 July. Fifth, an Iranian P-3 radar plane was on patrol in the area, a type of plane used to guide Iranian attack planes to their targets. Sixth, the *Vincennes* challenged the approaching plane to identify itself seven times, warning it that it was in danger. In addition, a nearby US frigate, the *Sides*, challenged it five times. Neither received a reply, nor did the plane change its course or take evasive maneuvers. Seventh, the two missiles fired by the *Vincennes* were launched after a full seven minutes had passed from first sighting, and then only when the plane was a mere seven nautical miles away from the cruiser. Finally, the ship's IFF (Identify Friend or Foe) radar incorrectly identified the Airbus as an F-14, and visual confirmation was impossible because of hazy weather and a ceiling of 200 feet. All in all, the *Vincennes* incident of 3 July 1988 must be marked down as a tragic mistake occurring in the heat of combat in a long-troubled war zone.

On 20 August the conflict between Iran and Iraq was halted under a United Nations cease-fire agreement, and by December US Navy convoying in the Persian Gulf had come to an end. It had been a long and troubling deployment for the Navy, but no one could then foresee that it was but a prelude to the much larger and potentially more dangerous deployment that would have to be made in the same waters in under two years time.

Background to the Gulf War

Matching Libya's Muammar Qaddafi in his hatred of the West and of Israel, and equally determined to be the leader who would bring the Arab world to new heights of power and glory, was Saddam Hussein of Iraq. Ruler of a nation of 18 million persons and composed one-half of Shiite Muslims, one-quarter of Sunni Muslims, and one-quarter of dissident Kurds with their own language and culture, Hussein had come to power in 1979 as head of the Sunni-dominated Baath Socialist party, and in the years that followed he had rapidly made himself into a full-fledged dictator, ruling through a combination of terror and propaganda and bloodily suppressing all potential opposition. He had also become one of the Arab world's most zealous advocates of playing 'oil politics' as a means of humbling the hated West.

Although more temperate Arab statesmen attempted to distance themselves from Hussein, realizing that the Western nations and Japan were their best customers for their oil, he became a popular figure among many Muslims in the Middle East, especially when he launched his invasion of Iran in 1980. The leaders of the Western nations, too, treated Hussein warily, but when his war with Iran bogged down and he toned down his anti-Western and anti-Israeli rhetoric, there seemed to be reason for optimism that he would moderate. Accordingly, his pleas for Western aid in his war with Iran were received favorably, and many nations began to sell him military equipment. Even the United States, still seeing the Ayatollah Khomeini as a greater danger to American interests, also moved closer to Hussein, removing Iraq from its list of 'terrorist-supporting' countries. By the late 1980s American agencies were actually sharing intelligence information with the Iraqi leader.

But when the Iran-Iraq War ended in 1988 Hussein soon made it clear that he had in no way moderated and was still dedicated to aggressive pan-Arabism, to gaining control of the area's oil supplies and to driving the Israelis out of the Middle East. He did not demobilize his million-man army, began to spend billions of dollars on new weapons (most bought from the Soviets) and placed renewed emphasis on developing chemical and nuclear weapons. (He had already displayed his willingness to use poison gas against dissident Kurdish villagers in 1987 and 1988, the number of victims running into the hundreds, and perhaps thousands.)

Further proof of Hussein's belligerent intentions came from his frequent speeches in which he displayed bitter anti-American and anti-Israeli animosity. These public pronouncements, while making the Iraqi leader increasingly popular to some Arabs, annoyed and alarmed such moderate Arab leaders as President Hosni Mubarak of Egypt and King Fahd of Saudi Arabia. Their concerns deepened when, in July 1990, Hussein turned his verbal fire on the heads of state of the United Arab Emirates and Kuwait, whom he accused of overproducing oil and thus driving the world price of crude down. He followed this by massing 30,000 of his troops on the border of neighboring Kuwait. Approached by the American ambassador to Iraq, April Glaspie, to ascertain his intentions, Hussein assured her that he would not invade Kuwait while his current talks with President Mubarak were still ongoing.

This promise was cynically broken when,

Iraqi dictator Saddam Hussein. During the Iran–Iraq War the US tended to support Iraq, a policy it would eventually regret.

Wreckage left by Iraqi bombers in Hamadan, Iran, in 1982. Soviet- and French-equipped, Iraq's air force was locally formidable.

Left: The cruiser *Vincennes*. On 3 July 1988, in a tragic case of war's confusion, the *Vincennes* downed an Iranian airliner that was mistaken for an attacking warplane.

on 2 August 1990, Hussein's tanks and infantry rolled into Kuwait, his soldiers looting, burning and raping as they went. The Emir of Kuwait, Sheik Jaber al-Ahmed al-Sabah, fled the country, and Hussein, after giving a number of excuses for the invasion, announced that Kuwait had been annexed as the 19th providence of Iraq.

Above: King Fahd of Saudi Arabia was one of the first to join the anti-Iraq coalition.
Top right: Chairman of the JCS US General Colin Powell greets crewmen on board the battleship USS *Wisconsin* in the Persian Gulf during the DESERT SHIELD buildup.
Right: CENTCOM commander General H Norman Schwarzkopf greets USAF reinforcements newly arrived in Saudi Arabia.

The Gulf War: DESERT SHIELD, 2 August 1990 – 14 January 1991

The United Nations Security Council demanded the immediate withdrawal of Iraqi troops from Kuwait, and US President George Bush froze all Iraqi and Kuwaiti assets in the United States. Bush also banned the importation of any Kuwaiti oil into the country, as did the Western European nations and Japan, but Hussein refused to back down. With the seizure of Kuwait he controlled 20 percent of the world's oil supply; if he also seized neighboring Saudi Arabia he would control 40 percent. Hussein undoubtedly believed that despite strong protests from the United Nations, the United States and other countries, no one would seriously oppose his *fait accompli*, but even if they did, he was convinced that his million-man army could defend Iraq and his new possession against any outside force.

The United Nations, with almost universal support (including the Soviet Union), placed a trade and financial embargo on Iraq. And the leaders of most other Arab states also refused to accept his seizure of Kuwait: this was, after all, not an ideological confrontation between East and West but simply an unprovoked attack made by one Arab nation on another. Using the overwhelming condemnation of Iraq by virtually all the nations of the world, and, most important, by the Arab nations, President Bush was thus able to organize a powerful coalition to demand the freedom of Kuwait.

US President George Bush responded to the August 1990 Iraqi invasion of Kuwait with speed and determination, swiftly building an international anti-Iraq coalition.

One of the first of the Arab leaders to step to the side of the United States and the United Nations was King Fahd of Saudi Arabia, who needed no further convincing after the American secretary of defense, Richard B Cheney, showed him satellite photographs proving that Hussein was massing troops on the Saudi border. Faud not only closed the Iraqi pipeline running across his country to the Red Sea but also agreed to allow American and coalition forces to use his territory as a military staging area to force Hussein out of Kuwait. Other Arab nations fell into line, as did Iraq's non-Arab neighbor to the north, Turkey, which agreed to cut off Iraq's other pipeline leading to the Mediterranean. Hussein was left with only Jordan's King Hussein, Libya's Muammar Qaddafi and the Palestine Liberation Organization's Yasir Arafat to support his actions.

Still he would not back down. He would, he was convinced, win as he had won his war with Iran. He had 5000 tanks (including over 1000 modern, Soviet-built T-72s), 6000 armored personnel carriers, 5000 artillery pieces, 600 aircraft (some of them late model Soviet Mig-25 and MiG-29 fighters and Su-24 and Su-25 bombers), French- and Soviet-made surface-to-air missiles, improved Scud surface-to-surface missiles capable of carrying a 1000-pound warhead far beyond their 300-mile designated range, chemical artillery shells and perhaps nuclear weapons (the Israelis had wiped out Iraq's French-built nuclear reactor at Osirak in a lightning air raid on 7 June 1981, but no one knew if another secret facility had been built).

As President Bush was working diplomatically to build up the coalition of nations arrayed against Iraq, the American military commanders, led by General Colin L Powell, chairman of the JCS, were working to build up their forces in the Middle East. Central Command, led by the Army's General H Norman Schwarzkopf, had been designed to forestall a Soviet push into the Middle East, but its plans were quickly modified to fit the new situation. Air Force combat units and Army airborne units (the 82nd Division and the 101st Division) were dispatched to Saudi Arabia, and three 15,000-man Marine brigades were flown in, soon to be followed by their equipment, which was brought to them by three flotillas of pre-positioned ships from Diego Garcia in the Indian Ocean. At the same time, Navy ships steamed into the area, both to enforce the UN embargo and to help move thousands of tanks, trucks and other heavy vehicles and tons of supplies into the area under the direction of the integrated Military Transportation Command.

Operation DESERT SHIELD (as it was officially designated on 7 August 1990) quickly expanded as thousands of troops and millions of tons of supplies and equipment began to move into Saudi Arabia. By December the greatest multinational military force assembled for warfare since World War II

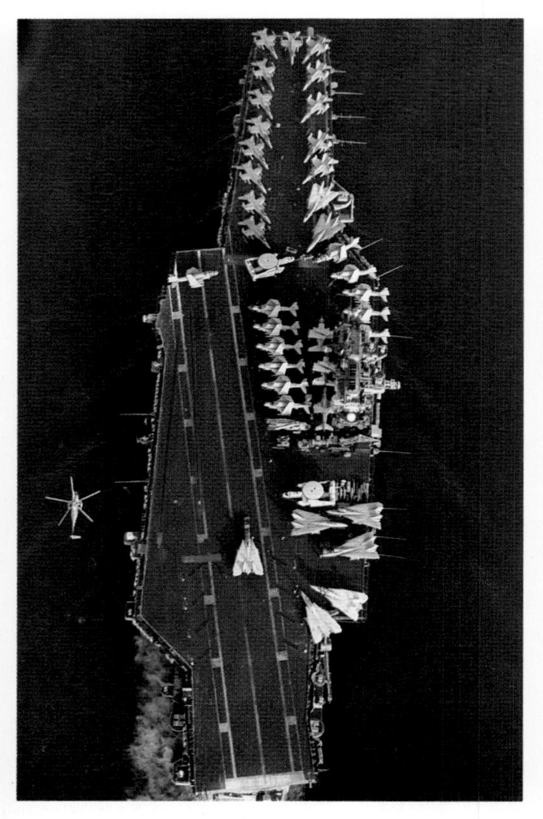

Left: Sixteen-inch shells in the barbette of the No 1 turret of the recommissioned battleship *Wisconsin* in the Persian Gulf.
Above: Tomcats, Intruders, Prowlers and two Hawkeyes crowd the flight deck of the USS *Independence* as she cruises in the Gulf of Oman in 1990 during the tense months of Operation DESERT SHIELD.
Below: A freighter rushes Navy small craft to the Persian Gulf in August 1990.

had been drawn together in the Middle East. The coalition forces included not only the half-million American men and women from the four services, along with their equipment, ordnance, and logistical backup, but also planes, ships, and the 1st Armoured Division (including the 'Desert Rats' of the 7th Armoured Brigade) from Great Britain; planes, ships and the armored Daguet Division from France; ships from Argentina, Australia, Poland and eight NATO countries; two armored divisions and a commando regiment from Egypt; an armored division from Syria; and men, planes, tanks, and ships from a number of other Middle Eastern countries which had joined the operation.

Above: USS *Saratoga* looms over a mosque in the Red Sea port of Suez as she hurries to the area of the Persian Gulf soon after the Iraqi invasion of Kuwait. Below: *Saratoga* launches an F-14 Tomcat of Fighter Squadron 74. In the foreground is an A-6 Intruder strike aircraft.

On 29 November the United Nations gave Iraq until 15 January to get out of Kuwait. Hussein was unimpressed. On 9 January a meeting between the American secretary of state, James A Baker, and Tariq Aziz, the foreign minister of Iraq, came to nothing. Even when, on 12 January, the US Congress gave President Bush explicit authority to use the American military to carry out UN Resolution 678 calling for Iraq to leave Kuwait, Hussein would not back down. Finally, a last-minute attempt at personal diplomacy by UN Secretary General Javier Perez de Cuellar just two days before the United Nations deadline also came to nothing.

Diplomacy, embargo and the threat of war had all failed to persuade Hussein to loosen his grip on the tiny, oil-rich nation. Now the 'Mother of All Battles,' as Baghdad Radio called it, was about to begin.

The Gulf War: DESERT STORM, 15 January – 27 February 1991

An aerial view of USS *Wisconsin*. At the start of DESERT STORM *Wisconsin* hit Iraq with scores of Tomahawk cruise missiles.

By the early morning of 15 January 1991, when operation DESERT STORM began, the Navy had six carrier battle groups in place or moving into position. In the Red Sea were the task forces built around the *John F Kennedy* (CV-67), the *Saratoga* (CV-60) and the *America* (CV-66). In the Persian Gulf were the *Midway* (CV-41) and the *Ranger* (CV-61), soon to be joined by the *Theodore Roosevelt* (CVN-71) and the *America*, which would be shifted to the Gulf from the Red Sea. Generally, aircraft flying from the Red Sea battle groups would concentrate on targets in western Iraq and the Baghdad area, while those in the Persian Gulf would hit targets in southeastern Iraq. Unlike Vietnam, in this war all air strikes would be theater-wide and under the joint coordinated command of the Joint Forces Air Component Commander, no aircraft flying on nationally-directed or service-specific missions or routes.

Also active in the battle area were a vast array of Navy and coalition ships. All ships (except those in the southern end of the Persian Gulf) were under the tactical control of Commander US Naval Forces Central Command, Vice Admiral Henry H Mauz, Jr, who was succeeded by Vice Admiral Stanley R Arthur. In all, some 120 American and 50 allied ships were on station when DESERT STORM began. The US vessels active in the war during the course of the operation, besides the six carrier battle groups, included two battleships, the *Wisconsin* (BB-64) and the *Missouri* (BB-63); numerous frigates, cruisers and destroyers; submarines; two hospital ships (*Comfort* and *Mercy*); 31 amphibious task force vessels; commercial vessels with assault logistical equipment; and two embarked MEBs (Marine Expeditionary Brigades).

From the earliest days of the air campaign, Navy aircraft flew often and with great effectiveness as part of the US-coalition air offensive. Navy Tomahawk land-attack cruise missiles (TLAMs) streaked into Iraq to land precisely 'on target' over 80 percent of the time; carrier-based Navy E-2C Hawkeye airborne early-warning surveillance planes helped direct the sorties carried out by Air Force, Marine, Navy and coalition attack planes; P-3 Orions flew long-range land and sea target-identification missions; and EA-6B Prowlers jammed enemy radar sets. A-6E Intruders and F/A-18 Hornets worked in tandem in attacking hardened aircraft shelters and bridges, the Intruders laser-targeting the shelters and bridges while the Hornets dropped laser-guided bombs on them. Swing-wing F-14 Tomcats, meanwhile, flew combat air patrols over surface combatants, made reconnaissance flights and attacked mobile Scud missile sites in western Iraq. A-6E Intruders and A-7E Corsairs fired SLAMs (stand-off land attack missiles) with great success.

Within two weeks, by 30 January, some 33,000 coalition sorties had been flown, Navy aircraft accounting for 4700 of them. Of the 31 designated strategic targets in Iraq, including chemical, biological and possibly nuclear sites, all had been hit and/or destroyed. Over half of Hussein's command and control centers had been put out of action. Some 29 air-defense installations had been hit, 38 of 44 airfields had been bombed, 70 hardened aircraft shelters had been destroyed and 33 of 36 key bridges had been bombed. Only 10 percent of Iraq's supplies were reaching its beleaguered troops in Kuwait (themselves under daily air attack), and 29 Iraqi aircraft had been shot out of the sky without the loss of a single coalition aircraft in aerial combat.

In addition, Navy A-6E Intruders had disabled an Iraqi mine-layer and an intelligence-gathering tanker, had destroyed Silkworm missile sites on the Kuwaiti coast, had attacked three Iraqi landing craft running for safety in Iran and had hit the Iraqi Al Kalia naval station. By the time the air campaign was over, coalition forces had rendered Iraqi naval forces 'combat ineffective' by sinking or destroying 14 Iraqi combatant ships, seven auxiliaries and four amphibious vessels.

In the meantime, the battleship *Missouri* had moved in and lobbed 16-inch shells with great accuracy into concrete bunkers on the Kuwaiti coast. The *Missouri* was relieved after three days by the *Wisconsin*, which continued the bombardment and then supported a Marine Corps probe of Iraqi defenses in southern Kuwait. The battleships' accurate gunnery was largely due to the use of RPVs (remotely piloted vehicles) which

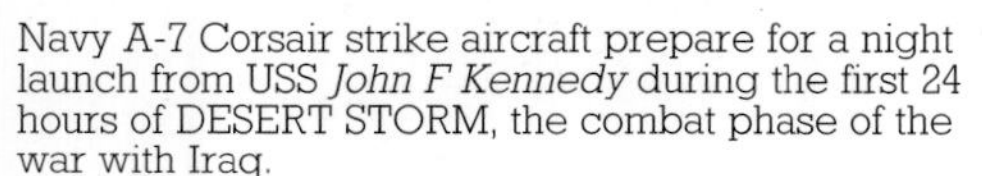

Navy A-7 Corsair strike aircraft prepare for a night launch from USS *John F Kennedy* during the first 24 hours of DESERT STORM, the combat phase of the war with Iraq.

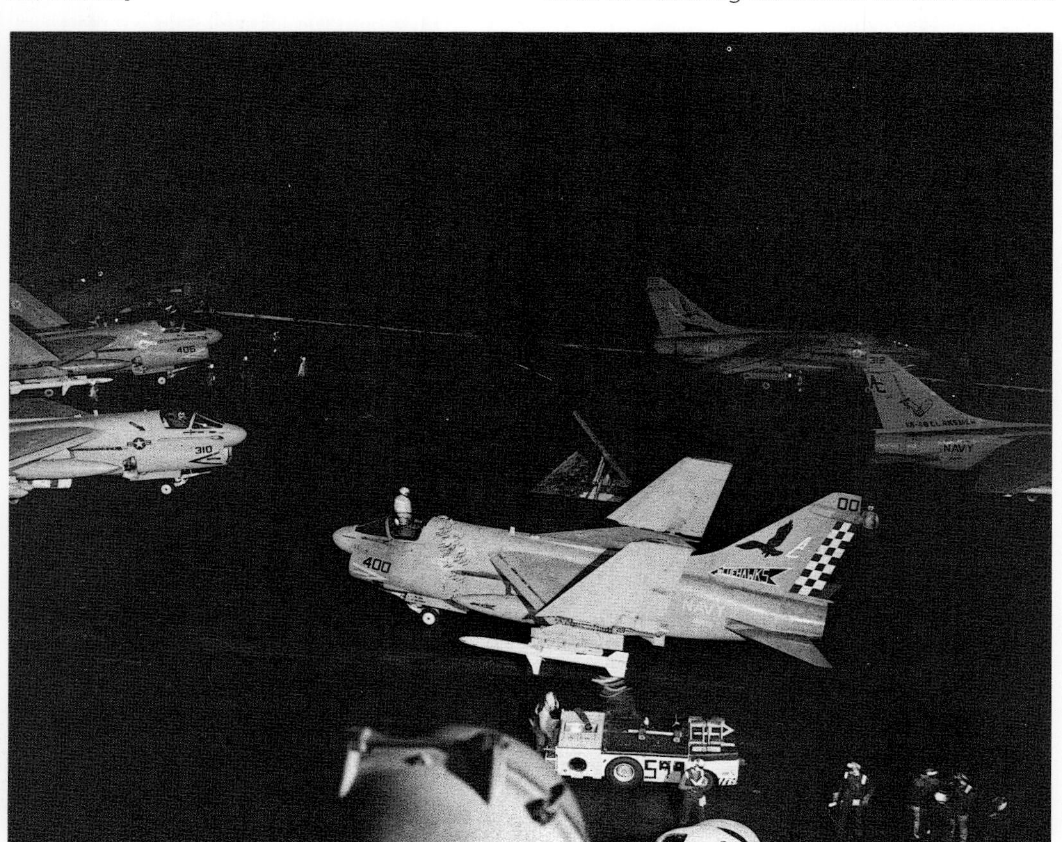

Above: General Schwarzkopf briefs the press on DESERT STORM naval engagements as of 30 January 1991.
Right: A pilot of a Marine AV-8B Harrier vertical/short take-off jet prepares to launch from the amphibious assault ship USS *Nassau* during the final days of Operation DESERT STORM.
Below: An A-6E Intruder strike aircraft is poised on USS *Saratoga*'s catapult before taking off for an operation over the Kuwaiti theater.

Above: Crewmen of the assault helicopter carrier USS *Guadalcanal* man 3-in/50-cal guns for air defense. Left: A helicopter of helicopter carrier USS *Tripoli* tows a minesweeping sled.

spotted their fall of shot. (At one point in the war, frightened Iraqi troops surrendered to a RPV, probably the first time in the history of warfare when humans capitulated to a robot.)

In the ground war of 24-27 February coalition land forces moved north directly into Kuwait from the Kuwaiti-Saudi Arabian border toward Kuwait City, while other coalition forces of the VII and XVIII Corps swept deep into Iraq in a grand left envelopment that forced Hussein to accept a cease fire in only three days. US naval forces also played vital roles in support of this ground offensive. These included moving toward the northern Persian Gulf to carry out a grand feint to convince the Iraqis that an amphibious landing on Kuwait's eastern shore was about to take place. As part of this feint, the *Missouri* moved up to its bombardment station while Amphibious Task Forces 2 and 3, with the 4th and 5th Marine Expeditionary Brigades on board, moved into position to effect a landing. Thanks to wide media coverage of earlier amphibious exercises on 24 January (the extensive media coverage deliberately assisted by Central Command), when the real offensive began a month later Hussein and his commanders were convinced that an amphibious landing on the Kuwaiti coast was imminent. As a result, on 24 February 50,000 Iraqi defenders badly needed elsewhere were left looking out to sea for a Marine landing that never came (although, as General Schwarzkopf later made clear, the Marines were combat ready and would have been landed on the Kuwait coast if they had been needed).

The Navy also supplied valuable aid to the coalition land forces in their movements into Kuwait and Iraq. A-6Es and F-18s provided close air support for the advancing troops, while other Intruders joined coalition aircraft in striking Iraqis fleeing north from Kuwait City toward Basra. And all the while the battleships continued to blast away at their designated targets in Kuwait and Iraq.

In sum, the Navy had held off any further advance by Hussein during the early weeks of DESERT SHIELD, had accounted for one-fourth of all sorties (26,000 of 103,000) flown during DESERT STORM, had expended 1100 16-inch shells, had fired nearly 300 Tomahawks from the Persian Gulf and Red Sea and had delivered and/or escorted some 95 percent of all matériel (18 billion pounds) arriving by sea for the support of DESERT STORM. Its losses amounted to one F-14 Tomcat, one F/A-18 Hornet and four A-6E Intruders downed by antiaircraft fire and one Intruder, two Hornets and four helicopters lost to non-combat causes. Two vessels, an amphibious assault ship, the *Tripoli* (LPH-10) and the Aegis missile cruiser *Princeton* (CG-59), hit mines while guiding the battleships into position in the northern Gulf, but both were saved through the damage control efforts of their crews. To the US Navy, as well as to the Army, the Air Force and the Marine Corps, the American people extended a heartfelt 'well done' for both DESERT SHIELD and DESERT STORM.

Rescue in Liberia: Operation SHARP EDGE

During August 1990, while the Navy and Marines were reacting to Iraq's invasion of Kuwait and building up for DESERT SHIELD, they were also called upon to effect a rescue mission in the West African nation of Liberia. Liberia has enjoyed a special relationship with the United States dating back to 1822, when it was established as a resettlement haven for freed American slaves. Liberia in the 20th century also assumed importance as the site of major American rubber plantations and of US telecommunications stations.

Headed by ex-army sergeant Samuel K Doe since his successful coup in 1980 (and subsequently as elected president since 1986), the Liberian government in 1989 faced a growing insurgency led by Charles Taylor and his National Patriotic Front of Liberia (NPFL). By 1990 the dissidents had begun to advance toward the capital city of Monrovia, and by early August the rebel NPFL and a splinter group, led by Prince Johnson and calling itself the INPFL were close to seizing the capital. Johnson was also threatening to

Firefighters of the assault helicopter carrier *Tripoli* prepare for damage control after the ship hit a mine in the Persian Gulf on 18 February 1991.

Navy divers plunge into the waters of the Persian Gulf to inspect damage done to the hull of USS *Tripoli* by an Iraqi mine.

take American hostages, a fearsome prospect, since the rebels had recently killed about 200 civilians at the Lutheran Church of Monrovia. Accordingly, on 4 August the US ambassador requested that the US government send troops to protect the embassy and to evacuate both US citizens and some other foreign nationals.

By the time the requisite orders went out, the 22nd Marine Expeditionary Unit (Special Operations Capable) and Amphibious Squadron Four (consisting of the amphibious vessels *Saipan* (LHA-2), *Ponce* (LPD-15) and *Sumter* (LST-1181) and the destroyer *Peterson* (DD-969) were already off the Liberian coast, well-briefed on their mission, and ready to effect their tasks. They had been dispatched from Toulon, France, on 27 May to be in position to react to events in Liberia if necessary.

Operation SHARP EDGE began on the evening of 4 August. Seven Ch-46 helicopters and one Ch-53D helicopter with Marine rifle platoons aboard landed at the US telecommunications office and swiftly evacuated 21 US citizens to the Navy vessels waiting six miles off shore. Simultaneously, more Ch-46s and Ch-53Ds landed 234 Marines at the US embassy. Here they set up heavy weapons and mortars to cover the building and grounds and evacuated 40 US and foreign nationals from the embassy compound. These operations were carried out under the watchful eyes of AH-1T attack helicopters and a command helicopter.

From 6 August through 21 August the helicopter crews, working with the ground Marines, continued to evacuate American citizens and foreign nationals from Monrovia. On 11 August Charles Taylor of the NPFL offered to turn over European diplomats and their families still in Monrovia to the Americans at the town of Buchanan just down the coast from the capital. The *Saipan* and *Peterson* were deployed to five miles off the coast of Buchanan, and a Seal force was sent in to carry out negotiations with the NPFL and agree on a landing zone for the helicopters. After four Ch-46s brought out 96 persons, Operation SHARP EDGE was for all major purposes an end.

During the operation more than 1600 American and foreign citizens had been evacuated without incident, and all US facilities in Liberia had been protected. In a situation that had all the earmarks of potential violence and international misunderstanding, the Navy and Marines had come through. SHARP EDGE may not have attracted much attention in the United States in the summer of 1990, considering the momentous events taking place in the Persian Gulf at that time, but it proved to the Navy and to its Marines that training, rehearsal and coordination were the keys to successful security and evacuation missions in foreign countries.

The Fall of the Soviet Union

While in the early months of 1991 the world's attention was riveted on the dramatic events unfolding in the Middle East, events of even greater historical magnitude were taking shape in the Soviet Union. *Perestroika*, Mikhail Gorbachev's attempt to restructure the collapsing Soviet economy along more market-oriented lines, was proving to be a therapy applied in doses that were both too little and too late. Again and again, when confronted with painful key decisions Gorbachev temporized. Price controls were *not* removed, the ruble was *not* made genuinely convertible, rules governing the right to acquire private property were hopelessly muddled and national production priorities remained fixed on heavy industry rather than being switched to badly-needed consumer goods. Meanwhile, the pace of economic collapse was accelerating: by 1990 the Soviet budget deficit had reached catastrophic proportions, nearly 20 percent of the reeling nation's total GNP.

But if *perestroika* was foundering, *glasnost* must, from Gorbachev's point of view, have seemed to be succeeding all too well. Not only had it opened the way for an alarming upsurge in the expression of strong national-

Evacuated by a Navy helicopter from civil-war-torn Liberia in August 1990, US and other foreign civilians are set safely down in neighboring Sierra leone.

USSR President Mikhail Gorbachev shakes hands with Russian President Boris Yeltsin in the aftermath of the abortive 1991 coup that almost undid them both.

ist sentiments in most of the USSR's constituent republics, it had also made possible the emergence of a nationwide liberal reform movement that was becoming increasingly critical of Gorbachev's many hesitations and inconsistencies.

As tensions between Gorbachev and the liberals mounted during the second half of 1990, the Soviet president made the critical error of turning to Communist Party conservatives for political support. The ideological gulf that separated Gorbachev from the conservatives was in reality much too wide to be bridged by any but the flimsiest and most emphemeral alliance of expediency, but the fact that Gorbachev had shown himself willing to make concessions to the right vastly increased both the size and the intensity of the liberal opposition to his regime and his own style of leadership.

The early months of 1991 witnessed a mounting series of confrontations between the liberals and the government, with the climax coming in March, when, along with a clumsy (and somehow rather halfhearted) threat of resort to armed force, the government attempted to bully the Russian parliament into ousting the republic's president, Boris Yeltsin, who had become the liberals' de facto leader. But the time when such tactics could easily succeed in the USSR had passed. The parliament resisted, 100,000 Muscovites took to the streets in protest and then all the nation's coal miners went on strike. Appalled, Gorbachev hastened to try to compose his differences with Yeltsin and to placate the liberals by proposing a new 'Union Treaty' that would considerably expand the powers of the republics at the expense of those of the central government. The liberals and the country in general reacted favorably. Now it was the turn of the conservatives to be appalled.

The conservatives' response took the form of an armed coup d'état. Launched in mid-August, just days before the Union Treaty was due to be signed and while Gorbachev was vacationing on the Crimea, it met with overwhelming popular resistance, and after 72 hours it collapsed. Far from restoring the authority of the Soviet government, the failed rightist coup had succeeded in destroying it completely.

In the months that followed, republic after republic declared its independence, and the question of what role the Gorbachev government had left to play in national life became ever more difficult to answer. By mid-December, Yeltsin had persuaded all the newly-sovereign republics save the three Baltic states and Georgia to join Russia in a loose-knit confederation to be called the Commonwealth of Independent States. This fragile entity came into being on 25 December 1991. Mikhail Gorbachev resigned as head of state, the red flag flying over the Kremlin was hauled down and the once-mighty Soviet Union, shaper of so much twentieth-century history, was no more, dead at the age of 74.

The Navy and the End of the Cold War

The Cold War had been fading away steadily ever since Mikhail Gorbachev came to power in 1985, but until the disintegration of the USSR in the autumn of 1991 Western military planners had always to take into account the possibility that some unpredictable set of circumstances might not only revive US-Soviet hostility but all too rapidly plunge the superpowers into dangerous confrontation. None of the Western armed services could therefore afford to let down its guard.

This was certainly true for the US Navy. Not only was the Soviet navy already formidable – larger in number of units (though not in

During the attempted right-wing coup in August 1991 an armed bodyguard protects Russia's President Boris Yeltsin.

An aerial view of the Soviet (now Russian) *Kiev* class carrier *Novorossiysk*. Visible on her flight deck are Yak-38 VTOL fighters and Ka-27 ASW helicopters. The future of the former Soviet navy remains problematical.

aggregate tonnage) than the US fleet, highly sophisticated and possessed of massive nuclear capabilities – but it had also continued to grow at an alarming rate all through the years when the Cold War was supposed to be waning. This was especially the case regarding submarines, which the Soviets considered the main arm of their navy. At the end of the 1980s five *Typhoon* ballistic missile submarines, each equipped with 20 SS-N-20 strategic missiles, and five *Delta IV* submarines, with 16 SS-N-23 strategic missiles on each, were launched. In addition, the Soviets were building three classes of attack submarines, *Akula, Sierra* and *Victor III*, all fully capable of opposing US submarines and defending their ballistic missile boats while also carrying SS-N-21 sea-launched cruise missiles. New *Oscar*-class nuclear powered guided-missile submarines with 24 submerged-launch, 550-kilometer-range SS-N-19 missiles were also being built and deployed.

For their surface fleet the Soviets were building two large-decked aircraft carriers of the *Tbilisi* class for Far Eastern and Mediterranean deployment and at least one *Ul'yanovsk*-class nuclear-powered large-deck carrier, these in addition to the four *Kiev*-class short-deck carriers already in service. The Soviet carriers had recently received over 650 previously-land-based combat aircraft from the Soviet air force, such as Su-27 Flankers and MiG-29 Fulcrums, and these planes were now performing navy missions, along with the Yak-38 Forger VSTOL fighter-bombers and Ka-27 Helix helicopters already on the carriers. Meanwhile, modern Tu-142 Bear-Fs were replacing the Tu-16 Badgers and Tu-95 Bears in the Soviet navy's long-range bomber fleet.

Also being built and deployed were a fourth nuclear-powered *Kirov*-class cruiser fitted with SS-N-19 ballistic missiles and a fourth *Slava*-class cruiser with SS-N-12 missiles. Undergoing sea trials was the 4000-ton *Neustrashimyy*, the initial vessel in a new class of guided-missile frigates. These were supported by at least 15 new *Sovremennyy*-class, 13 new *Bezboyazneunnyy*-class and 11 new *Udaloy*-class guided-missile destroyers. Overall, the raw number of Soviet naval combatants may have been diminishing as vessels that had exceeded their useful lives were being scrapped, but the lethality of this smaller-sized Soviet fleet was demonstrably growing. In 1990 alone the Soviets launched ten submarines and nine other major combatant vessels.

When the Soviet Union collapsed this powerful navy by no means disintegrated, even though its growth effectively stopped. On the contrary, the ex-Soviet navy's four major fleets – the Northern, the Baltic, the Pacific and the Black Sea Fleets – remained essentially intact, the first three passing under the control of Russia, while control of the fourth, the Black Sea Fleet, became a matter of dispute between Russia and Ukraine. (It may be worth noting here that possession of the Black Sea Fleet alone would overnight have made Ukraine the world's third largest naval power.)

The continued existence of this massive naval force still posed a difficult problem for US naval planners. With the passing of both the Cold War and the USSR, presumably the ex-Soviet navy represented a much reduced threat to US and Western security. But had the threat altogether vanished? That depended on the unpredictable future of the CIS and, especially, on that of the ex-Soviet navy's main new owner, Russia.

According to one scenario, all CIS member states would for the foreseeable future be so absorbed in their own grave internal economic and political problems that they would allocate no significant funds to their navy, leaving it simply to decay or selling off its assets to Third World buyers. But in another scenario the reform government of Russia's Boris Yeltsin would collapse under the impact of the nation's mounting economic distress, to be replaced by an aggressively nationalistic authoritarian regime that would again seek to use its still-powerful navy to challenge Western dominion at sea. Still another scenario postulated an intra-Commonwealth war, possibly between Ukranian- and Russian-led blocs, in which ex-Soviet naval focus would be called into play: such a war would necessarily pose a security threat to the West because of the danger that it, unlike most Third-World conflicts, could escalate to the level of nuclear exchange. The same would apply to any scenarios involving a Sino-CIS war.

There were many possibilities, some more likely than others. But none was wholly out of the question and several were potentially dangerous. For this reason alone, no US naval planner proposed – or responsibly could have proposed – a rapid, drastic reduction of American naval power as a consequence of the fall of the Soviet Union. Nor was there overwhelming political pressure in favor of such a course. Even in the presidential election year of 1992 most US voters and political leaders seemed sufficiently aware of the uncertainties surrounding the CIS's future to be willing to postpone reaping the 'peace dividend' that was supposed to result from reduced military spending in the post-Cold War period.

Nor was the continued existence of the mighty ex-Soviet fleet the only reason why many Americans were wary of making precipitate cuts in US naval strength. Ever since the end of World War II the US Navy and Marine Corps had repeatedly demonstrated an ability unique among the armed services to make fast, effective responses to unexpected challenges in far-flung places; and impressively often these challenges had been unrelated – or at most had been only tangentially related – to the Cold War. When the US response to such challenges resulted in armed clashes (as in Iraq, the Persian Gulf or the Gulf of Sidra) they made headlines, but less celebrated, though equally important, were the cases when *no* hostilities resulted, when the mere fact of a timely US naval presence in a potential trouble spot kept the trouble from materializing.

To many Americans there seemed no very good reason to suppose that either the frequency or the seriousness of such challenges would greatly diminish in the post-Cold War

Top right: The 24,000-ton ex-Soviet *Kirov* belongs to the world's only class of guided-missile battlecruisers and is one of the most powerful warships now afloat anywhere in the world.
Right: The old Soviet navy flag still flew beside this Black Sea Fleet *Kashin* class destroyer as late as February 1992.

092

period. The governments of Libya, Iran and Iraq were already overt enemies of the United States, the Assad regime of Syria was potentially hostile and militantly anti-Western Islamic fundamentalist movements in varying degrees threatened the stability of half a dozen other Middle Eastern governments, including that of Saudi Arabia.

The end of the Cold War, far from discouraging the flow of modern weaponry into the Middle East, seemed to have stimulated it. Since the end of the Gulf War both Syria and Iran had, according to mid-1992 US intelligence reports, bought hundreds of new T-72 tanks from Czechoslovakia, as well as sizeable numbers of Scud-C missiles from North Korea and MIG-29 fighters and SU-24 attack planes from Russia. In addition – and this was of special concern to US naval planners worried about possible future operations in the Persian Gulf – the Iranians had acquired two *Kilo*-class attack submarines from Russia and some 90 short-range CSS-8 anti-ship missiles from North Korea; and Iran was also reported to be negotiating for the purchase from Russia of powerful long-range AS-4 and AS-6 anti-ship missiles. Meanwhile, the North Koreans were preparing to demonstrate their new 620-mile No Dong-1 missile to interested officials from Libya, Iran and Syria, and the Chinese were energetically trying to increase their already significant sales of SAMs, F-7 fighters and artillery in the region. Even Iraq, despite the post-war international arms embargo, was slowly re-building its military strength.

As for North Korea and China, apart from their evident interest in being arms suppliers to the Third World, it was completely impossible to predict what the future policies of these still-defiantly communist states might be. China was already a nuclear power, and North Korea was probably close to becoming one. Between 1989 and 1992 China's military budget had shot up 52 percent, and in 1992 the Chinese were even negotiating to buy the aircraft carrier *Varyag*, then building in Ukraine. How these facts might bear on, for example, China's increasingly assertive claims to control the South China sea or on North Korea's relations with South Korea was unknowable.

What was more knowable was that the US Navy's main problem in the remainder of the 1990s would probably *not* be a want of potential challenges to face.

The Navy in the 1990s

How well would the Navy be able to accomplish the tasks it might be called on to perform during the rest of the century? Obviously the answer would in part depend simply on the number of ships, aircraft and men and women it had available at any given time.

When the decade of the 1990s began, the Navy had 14 fleet aircraft carriers, 179 other surface combatants, 33 ballistic missile submarines and 94 attack submarines, as well as a large array of tankers, pre-positioning ships and other types – in all, about 600 ships. It operated some 3600 aircraft, including 15 active carrier air wings and four Marine air wings. Its total personnel came to just under

US Navy Hawkeyes and Vikings make one of their final flights over the Cubi Point Air Station at soon-to-be-abandoned Subic Bay in the Philippines in March 1992.

582,000 men and women, and its share of the defense budget (about 35 percent) amounted to $99.6 billion. But the Navy also took for granted that, absent a major war, the numbers in every one of these categories would dwindle steadily throughout the rest of the decade.

Dwindle at what rate? Nobody knew precisely, but a rule of thumb favored by many analysts in the early 1990s spoke of a total of 450 ships, including no more than 12 carriers and 13 (11 active) air wings, by the end of 1995, *ie* a 20-25 percent reduction in five years. This did not, however, mean that the Navy's budget would necessarily decline in like degree, since the reduction in total number of ships would in part result from the natural process of block obselescence of vessels built in the early 1960s, a period of heavy naval construction. (A modern warship's service life averages about 30 years.) Nor, for the same reason, did it necessarily mean that the drawdown in ships would be as rapid in the second half of the 1990s.

Fleet size was not the only factor that could affect how well the Navy might be able to meet its obligations in the 1990s. Another had to do with America's changing relations with its allies. During the long years of the Cold War most of the world's anti-communist nations had considered the maintenance of US military power to be vital to their own security and had therefore been generally content – even relieved – to accept the presence of forward-positioned US forces in their territories. But this was not necessarily the case after the Cold War ended, as the Navy was painfully to discover in 1992 when the nationalist-minded legislature of the Philippines declined to renew the lease of Subic Bay to the United States.

Filipino protesters demand that Americans give up their Philippine bases. When the US finally bowed to such pressure in 1992, it lost some major military assets in Asia.

The giant Subic Bay naval facility had been an important US base since before World War II, and during the Cold War it had become – especially as the result of the gradual withdrawal of major US naval forces from Japan – not only the lynchpin of the Navy's defense line in the Far East but a crucial staging point for deployments into the Indian Ocean and Persian Gulf. Its loss was therefore a blow to the Navy, the more so because no very good alternatives were available. (Both the Senbawang Naval Basin in Singapore and a harbor on Guam were remote possibilities, but even if various political difficulties could be overcome, to develop either facility would probably cost more money than the budget-conscious Congress would be willing to spend.)

Japan, the other major anchor of the US Far Eastern defense system during the Cold War, was also a dwindling asset. Even though the US had gradually been reducing its military presence in Japan as the Japanese built up their own 'self-defense' force, at the beginning of the 1990s the US still maintained significant sea, land and air units in the home islands, on Okinawa and in the Ryukus. But as the Cold War faded away many Japanese began to question the propriety of these US contingents remaining in Japanese territory. Indeed, it was becoming increasingly obvious that, apart from mutual concerns about Soviet (or Soviet-sponsored) aggression in Asia, the US and Japan had never had very many security interests in common: Japanese support of the US-UN action against Iraq had, for example, been lukewarm, and Japan had always preferred not to link its policy toward Red China too closely to that of the US. To complicate matters, US-Japanese diplomatic relations – once so placidly harmonious – were increasingly being vexed by ill-natured disputes over one another's trade policies. In such circumstances the Navy had every reason to expect that its access to naval facilities in Japanese territory would decline over time (and thus the Navy had almost no reason to look to Japan for help in solving the problems caused by the loss of Subic Bay).

In Europe, the Navy's concerns centered less on the future availability of forward bases than on the larger question of what was to become of NATO in the aftermath of the Soviet Union's collapse. DESERT SHIELD and DESERT STORM had clearly demonstrated how the common security interest of the United States and Western Europe could still produce effective joint action, but the

AFT
PORT
AFT
STBD

Opposite top: A huge Navy floating drydock is towed away from Subic Bay during the US evacuation of the great naval base in 1992.
Opposite below: US servicemen and civilians board the carrier USS *Abraham Lincoln* in June 1992 as part of the US evacuation of the Subic Bay naval base.
Above: This state-of-the-art minesweeper of Japan's Self-Defense Force features a hull made of glass-reinforced plastic. In some quarters, both nationally and internationally, Japan's seeming desire to develop, modernize and expand its armed forces is viewed with disquiet.
Below: American servicemen pause in their efforts to evacuate Subic Bay to try to cope with the devastation caused when the volcano Mt Pinatubo erupted in July 1992.

Gulf War had *not* been a NATO operation. NATO had been created solely to defend Western Europe against attack by the USSR and its allies, a contingency that had no bearing on the situation that prompted the anti-Saddam Hussein coalition to be formed. Only some of the NATO states had actively participated in the coalition, other active participants were not NATO members, and Gorbachev's USSR, far from playing the role of adversary, had wholeheartedly supported the coalition's war aims.

52
52
JIM COLLE

Further evidence of the ambiguity of NATO's role in the post-Cold War era was provided in 1992, when the savage ethnic warfare that had erupted in disintegrating Yugoslavia began to reach comparatively large proportions. Many people in the United States and Western Europe – repelled both by the apparent senselessness of the fighting and by its increasingly atrocious character – began to call for a Western military intervention to stop the bloodshed. But though NATO was an obvious candidate to perform such a peacekeeping role, there was so little unanimity among the governments of the NATO states about how, or even whether, an intervention should be made that it was clear that if any action *were* taken, it would – as in the war against Iraq – almost certainly not be an all-NATO enterprise, as is the case in the action in Yugoslavia.

As long as the ex-Soviet Union remained militarily formidable and the West had any remaining doubts about what direction political developments in the CIS might take in the future, NATO would continue to serve its traditional, essential purpose. But realistic Western military planners had to take into account that that purpose might not outlast the 1990s and that no alternative function for NATO might be forthcoming.

For the US Navy, as for all Western armed services, a decline in the role played by NATO would doubtless have many consequences. Yet the exact nature of these consequences was hard to foresee because so much else was changing at the same time. The receding threat of global war might make NATO less necessary, but the potential threats posed by regional wars were steadily increasing. In a survey published in 1992, for example, US Under Secretary of Defense for Policy Paul D Wolfowitz estimated that by the year 2000 at least 15 countries would possess ballistic missiles, at least eight would have significant stocks of nuclear weapons, about 30 would be capable of conducting chemical warfare and 10 would be capable of waging biological warfare. As the survey noted: 'Paradoxically, while the United States can relax its warning-time assumptions for global war or conventional conflict in Europe, it may need to respond more rapidly than before to conflict in other theaters.' And what would all this mean for the Navy and Marines? Secretary Wolfowitz answered that question succinctly: 'Maritime forces will play a critical role in our ability to respond to crises in regions where we do not have forward land-based presence, a consideration that could become more important if global trends confront us with diminished access to bases and facilities ashore.'

In sum, the Navy of the 1990s could well be faced with challenges every bit as numerous, varied and sharp as those with which it actually had to contend all through the years of the Cold War. It would, however, be a leaner Navy than it was a decade before, drawn down in size by perhaps 25 percent and with less money to spend. Yet, if adequately equipped with formidable new weaponry such as Tomahawk cruise missiles, *Arleigh Burke* class aegis destroyers, *Seawolf* nuclear-powered attack submarines, improved Hornet fighter/attack aircraft and the like, it could still be just as tough and capable as ever. Certainly that is what the dedicated, superlatively trained men and women who served in the Navy would try to make it. But the rest, as always, would be up to the president, the Congress and the American people.

Left: A bow-view of the *Arleigh Burke* class aegis destroyer USS *John Barry*, one of the most potent ships of its kind ever built.
Below: An artist's impression of the new nuclear attack submarine USS *Seawolf*.
Overleaf: The *Nimitz* class supercarrier *Carl Vinson*.

70

INDEX

Page numbers in italics refer to illustrations

Acknowledgements

The publishers would like to thank David Eldred who designed this book and Ron Watson who compiled the index. The majority of the illustrations were supplied by the US Navy Public Affairs Department, the Naval Historical Center and the Navy Department in the National Archives. The publishers would like to thank these agencies and the following whose pictures appear on the pages noted.

The Bettmann Archive: 239 bottom right, 250
Anne S K Brown Military Collection, Brown University: 6-7
Bundesarchiv: 84 top, 142-143, 143 top right, 146-147, 147 top right
Library of Congress: 23 bottom, 44, 51 bottom right, 67 top
General Dynamics Corporation: 185 top, 198-199, 200-201
Imperial War Museum, UK: 119 bottom
National Army Museum, UK: 12
National Maritime Museum, UK: 10-11, 13, 21 top right, 22 bottom
Museum of the City of New York: 36-37 bottom left
New York Public Library: 8
Reuters/Bettmann: 223 top right, bottom, 226-227, 227 both, 228 top, 230 both, 231 bottom, 232, 233 top, 234 both, 235 bottom, 236 all, 237 both, 239 top and bottom left, 241 top, 242 bottom, 243 both, 244, 245 both, 246-247, 247 top, 248 both, 249 both, 252
UPI Bettmann: 222, 223 top left, 224 bottom, 225 both, 228 bottom, 229, 231 top, 233 bottom, 235 top, 240, 241 bottom, 242 top
US Air Force: 90 top left, 138 bottom
US Army: 163 top
US Coast Guard: 158 top
US Marine Corps: 41 top, 197 top